MAXIMILIAN I

(1459–1519)

By the same author

Society and Politics in Germany 1500–1750

MAXIMILIAN I

(1459–1519)

an analytical biography

Gerhard Benecke

Routledge & Kegan Paul

London, Boston, Melbourne and Henley

First published in 1982
by Routledge & Kegan Paul Ltd
39 Store Street, London WC1E 7DD,
9 Park Street, Boston, Mass. 02108, USA
296 Beaconsfield Parade, Middle Park,
Melbourne, 3206, Australia and
Broadway House, Newtown Road,
Henley-on-Thames, Oxon RG9 1EN
Printed in Great Britain by
Redwood Burn Ltd
Trowbridge, Wiltshire

Library of Congress Cataloging in Publication Data

Benecke, Gerhard.
Maximilian I (1459–1519)

Includes bibliographical references and index.
1. Maximilian I, Emperor of Germany, 1459–1519.
2. Holy Roman Empire – Kings and rulers – Biography.
3. Germany – History – Maximilian I. 1493–1519.
I. Title.
DD174.B46   943'.029'0924 [B]   82–608

ISBN 0–7100–9023–4   AACR2

Contents

Illustrations

vii

Maps

Table

Preface

Maximilian lived for nearly sixty years. He established the fortunes of the House of Austria once and for all as those of a first-class European dynastic power. He married two of the richest women in the Europe of his day. He tried to establish hegemony in his capacity as Holy Roman Emperor Elect, even using culture and technology to help his cause. He controlled large parts of Austria, Germany and the Low Countries but never seemed to have a penny to his name. He mounted crusades, fought Turks on paper, and fought Swiss, Hungarian, French, Italian, Netherlands' and German princes and burghers in reality. By turns he tried to ally himself with nearly every major and minor power in European diplomacy. At the age of eighteen he married the heiress of Burgundy, from the richest court in Europe; he was a widower at twenty-three, king in Germany as elected *Römischer König* at twenty-seven, and German Emperor Elect at thirty-four. He subsequently set up the dynastic base of his grandsons, Charles V and Ferdinand I, through skilful marriage alliances with Aragon-Castille and Bohemia-Hungary.

Three biographies of Maximilian have appeared in English. The first, in 1902, was a brief essay; the second, a popular account of the 'kings, queens and battles' variety, appeared in 1913. The third came in 1941 and dealt with its subject in terms of literary criticism. At school and university few late-medieval and early modern European history courses can avoid assessing the importance of the Holy Roman Empire under Maximilian I in the era of Renaissance humanism on the eve of the Lutheran Reformation. Yet only those who read German are able to piece together a substantial picture of

Maximilian. It means reading a variety of works often only available in the really large national libraries. My aim is to help to fill this gap by presenting a biographical sketch based on analysis of some interesting themes, and not narrative, which may begin to show Maximilian's place in the dynastic territorial Austrian, federal Reich German, and European dynastic, republican and ecclesiastical society of his day. I have concentrated less on dynastic-diplomatic narratives of Maximilian's high politics, such as his French and Italian wars and policies. Instead, I have tried to give some insights into Maximilian's style of home affairs and German-Austrian leadership, making use of the extant literature, supplemented by archive research of my own.

It is my aim once more to test against the evidence the prevailing view of Maximilian's success as leader of Renaissance German society on the eve of the Reformation on the one hand, and failure as a European politician on the other. This Janus-headed ruler was neither medieval nor ultra-modern, but a shrewd operator in his own time and place: Machiavelli's Prince and Castiglione's Courtier all rolled into one, residing north of the Alps and date-stamped '*circa* 1500'. I have reconstructed the fiscal and social as well as personal impact of Maximilian's style of government upon his territorial and federal subjects in Austria and Germany. It has involved a regional and case-study, local approach, centred, above all, on Innsbruck, Tirol and East Swabia, in order to pinpoint the underlying factors that in large measure determined the personal flavour of decisions taken to influence the broader issues of politics and control during the reign. Here we see a powerful ruler caught between feudal and commercial interests, satisfying both to a considerable extent by offering more standardised, bureaucratised, prerogative and proto-absolutist types of government. This applies especially to the nature of Maximilian's personal administration; to the way in which he treated his own tenants and servants, so indicative of his wider political actions, preoccupations and attitudes as a Habsburg. The reader may hope to base his own evaluation upon the following analyses of a very vigorous style of governance, reconstructed from archives recording the decisions, writings and thoughts of Maximilian I himself, and of those close to him in holding the reins of power. In that task I have tried, however inadequately, to follow historians like Lacey Baldwin Smith, whose book, *Henry VIII. The Mask of Royalty*, published in London 1971, tells us that:

> Henry . . . was for ever of the happy conviction that every problem must have a direct and immediate solution. . . . There is a singular lack of proportion to Henry's intellectual and emotional approach to life which might have been acceptable in an adolescent or understandable in an undergraduate but terrifying in royalty. (Panther paper edition, p. 102).

Maximilian also had that volatile royal something about him. The Habsburg in his quest for Eurodynastic grandeur was after all really hardly less *nouvel arriviste* than was the Tudor in consolidating his position on the English throne. Both were the sons of new men: Maximilian I of Frederick III; Henry VIII of Henry VII.

Here, then, is the first attempt at an analytical biography of Maximilian I in the English language: an attempt to analyse him in terms of his own society, of his own making, from some of the published and unpublished sources and secondary works; to make this information available in as brief, uncomplicated and readable a manner as I feel able; to regard over-simplification as a worse sin than that of omission; to begin to fill a gap in our understanding of central European history around the year 1500. I seek, ideally, to provide socio-biography for general readers as well as for students of history, who may all know something about the period already. Without more appreciation of Maximilian's role and career no overall view of European society and politics at the traditional dawning of modern times can be really feasible.

Whom did Maximilian rule as territorial and federal overlord? How are his loyal subjects to be identified and understood? What can we then say about Maximilian in particular, in person, and about his handling of the putative Habsburg myth of early modern Europolitics in general? From my studies of internal administrative records covering day-by-day drafts and copies of letters and memoranda, called the *Maximiliana*; instructions and records of government information and action, called the *Verfügungen*; and a variety of *Kopial- und Gedenkbücher* and records of estate management, it emerges that Maximilian was an alternately enthusiastic and hard-headed, hard-working bureaucrat, as well as an extrovert, careful to cultivate an image of popularity – as well with his contemporaries, as with us in posterity.

This book is a prelude to the essential task of integrating biography and fact with structural and social analysis, to make us more conscious of the individual within his group at the time that he lived. Is it really all that different from the Rankean, archival-positivistic notion – *Wie es eigentlich gewesen*? Or the Marxist notion of class-consciousness? The reader is to be let into the sources, there to think for himself. May the uncompromising approach thus chosen preserve a sense of period, document and person in a way in which Wilhelm Dilthey outlined before the First World War, when he wrote that 'everyday life can be described, the insignificant as well as powerful, the ordinary as well as exceptional.'

For encouragement I would like to thank Professor Francis Carsten, the colleagues and students at his research seminars in the University of London; Philip Broadhead, Richard Eales and Bernard Fraser for valuable advice; Mrs Sue Macdonald for her typing also of many drafts; the British Academy for two grants contributing to the Archive routine; and Karin and Brigitta Benecke for continuous, unselfish support, alternating inspiration with common sense. To Andrew Wheatcroft's friendship, suggestions for improvements to the text, and patience at my ultimate waywardness, I pay tribute. The work is dedicated to an older, and wiser generation – above all to Wilfriede Butchard, Britta Nilzén, Åke Nilzén, Catharina Nilzén, and Peter Butchard.

G.B.
Canterbury

Acknowledgments

Publication has been substantially aided by a grant from the Twenty-seven Foundation, to whose Awards Committee I am deeply grateful. We like to thank the following for permission to reproduce the illustrations: Österreichisches Staatsarchiv (Haus-, Hof- und Staatsarchiv), Vienna, for plates 1 and 14; Archiv des Stiftes Melk, for plate 2; Germanisches National-museum, Nuremberg, for plate 3; Galleria degli Uffizi, Florence, for plate 4; Katholisches Pfarramt St. Georg, Wildpoldsried, for plate 5; Staatliche Münzsammlung, Munich, for plate 6; Musée Clos-Lucé, Collection Saint-Bris, Amboise, for plate 7; Staatliche Museen Preussischer Kultur-besitz, West Berlin, for plate 8; Alte Gallerie am Land-esmuseum Joanneum, Graz, for plate 9; Stiftspfarramt Neu-kloster zur allerheiligsten Dreifaltigkeit, Wiener Neustadt, for plate 10; Musée Nationale du Château de Versailles, for plate 12; Österreichische Galerie, Vienna, for plate 13; the curator of the St. Barbarkapelle, Gossensass bei Sterzing, for plate 15; Albertina Graphische Sammlung, Vienna, for plate 16; Kunsthistorisches Museum, Vienna, for plate 17; Museum der Stadt Villach, for plate 18; Bischöfliches Dom- und Diözesanmuseum, Mainz, for plate 19. Every effort has been made to contact the copyright holders and obtain permission, but unfortunately in some cases this has proved impossible.

1

Introduction

Habsburg Maximilian I was the leading central European politician of the Renaissance era. Yet what do we really know of his style of government? What was it like to be one of his subjects? In the 1490s a very conservative burgher lawyer, publicist and civic politician in the Upper Rhenish part of the German empire parodied all novelties in society and shipped his fops by the flotilla in veritable armadas on to the dangerous sands and rocky cliffs of morality and common sense.[1] His fools included those court historians who fawningly praised their prince and got everyone into trouble:[2]

> I wish I had a covered ship
> Wherein all courtiers I would slip
> And those who eat at nobles' board
> And hobnob with a mighty lord
> So that they may be undisturbed
> And by the rabble never curbed.

When, a few years later, Maximilian began work on his autobiography, it grew to provide employment for an ever-widening circle of poets, illustrators and latinists. The result was the *Weisskunig*, *Theuerdank* and *Freydal* which glorified young Maximilian as a knight in shining armour, the man who battled with as much adversity as Jesus Christ, in his time and place, had ever faced, to save Burgundy and Italy from the French, and Christendom from the Turk.[3] The near-contemporary biographies of Habsburg servants Grünpeck and Fugger added weight to these gallant exploits.[4] The whole enterprise was a stroke of brilliant state propaganda for the Habsburg dynastic complex that Emperor Frederick III

1

and his son Maximilian I bequeathed to their heirs, Charles V and Ferdinand I. Notwithstanding anti-Habsburg sentiments during the era of the Thirty Years War, culminating in 1642 with the accusation of the future Swedish court historiographer, Buguslav von Chemnitz, that the Habsburgs were imperial tyrants,[5] Maximilian's posthumous reputation continued to grow throughout the subsequent centuries.

In the middle of the nineteenth century the systematic archive studies of Leopold von Ranke produced a reaction: Maximilian was no longer an idol.[6] Influenced by Ranke's interpretation, Heinrich Ulmann of Greifswald University in the 1880s and 1890s produced the still standard biography of Maximilian. In two substantial volumes Ulmann examined Maximilian's politics in the German empire. He admitted leaving out Maximilian's youth, Burgundian marriage and wars, and the details of his territorial politics in his family patrimony, the Austrian lands. Even so, no student of the period can ignore Ulmann's widely researched work.[7] To historians like Ranke and Ulmann, Maximilian was a restless war lord, out for personal and dynastic gain with all the considerable charm and brutality that he could muster. Against Maximilian in federal German affairs stood the dry administrator, Count Berthold of Henneberg, Archbishop Elector of Mainz and active Archchancellor of the German empire. Berthold led the party of federal reform that demanded an efficient home administration, based on co-operation of a majority of the territorial rulers within the regions and circles of the German empire as a priority over any foreign affairs. He tried to revitalise the traditional oligarchy of Electors as the German king's natural and permanent counsellors in federal politics in the 1490s. Berthold was prepared to support Maximilian against the French in Burgundy and Italy only if the king redressed grievances at home first. He and Maximilian headed the two chief 'parties' in the empire, 1495–1504. Berthold stood for home affairs; Maximilian for foreign warfare. The two sides co-operated sufficiently to plan a new set of reforms in law, order and taxation in 1495 at the Imperial Assembly at Worms. A federal system of government appeared on paper, but then no lasting agreement was reached over its practical implementation. Maximilian especially was not prepared to set an example in his Austrian lands by subordinating his powers as a territorial ruler there to a federal parliament, chancellery, judicature and treasury that would cover the whole German empire. None of the powerful Electors or ruling princes could, therefore, be expected to lead the way.

Thus the federal executive of 1495 was thought to have remained far too weak, and territorial rulers retained a free hand over their local affairs. Berthold continued to distrust Maximilian's endless demands for crusading money against the Turks, which was then only spent ostensibly in curbing the expansionist policies of neighbouring Christian rulers and governments, notably France, Venice and Hungary. Maximilian feared a loss of his prerogative powers to a federal government, law court and treasury over which he had no real control, as indeed happened with the Nuremberg imperial government of Electoral, ruling princely and imperial burgher representatives, which was appointed to rule alongside him in 1500–2. Of course, this brief survey drastically simplifies the relations between Maximilian and Berthold, and the debate continues to this day with vigour among German and Austrian historians.[8]

A very engaging personal view of Maximilian was emerging at the same time as Ulmann was researching in the 1870s. In a publication of Maximilian's early private letters dating from his Burgundian years after 1477, Victor von Kraus revealed an articulate, self-conscious and humorous person.[9] A recent brief study has given us a first picture of Maximilian's childhood and upbringing under his father, Emperor Frederick III, in the family castle and courtyard of Wiener-Neustadt on the Hungarian frontier in the 1460s and early 1470s.[10] The catalogue of an exhibition on Frederick III adds courtly culture to the period.[11] In the 1950s a brief outline biography appeared as an introduction to a reprint of the autobiographical *Weisskunig*, by Rudolf Buchner of Würzburg University. As a separate paperback it has become the standard short life of Maximilian.[12] A Buchner student has recently produced a well-researched biography of Berthold.[13] Publications on the culture of Maximilian's court have always been numerous, and two of recent impression provide a good introduction to this field. They are the Innsbruck exhibition catalogue of 1969, and a cheap, well–produced reprint of engravings and woodcuts, called *Maximilian's Triumph*.[14] Maximilian also patronised court and church music, combining the talents of the Burgundian Netherlands and of Renaissance Italy in his Innsbruck *Hofkapelle* under Heinrich Isaak and Ludwig Senfl. Their music is now generally available on stereo-record and tape, which allows us to hear once again, for example, popular songs of the time, like Isaak's 'Innsbruck, I must leave you'.[15] The first three of five planned volumes have appeared to retell the story of Maximilian's life in great narrative length and breadth. It is the work of Hermann Wiesflecker of Graz University. It provides as yet no new interpretation of Maximilian, but it does give a number of insights into the man and his diplomatic-dynastic surroundings for which all students of the period must inevitably be grateful.[16]

The conventional history of court, culture and diplomacy has been extremely well researched for the period of Maximilian I, and it would seem to be a considerable waste of time to go back to the sources and cover the same ground yet again. What has not been dealt with, despite German and Austrian historians' traditional enthusiasm for formal administrative, constitutional and legal history, is the problem of Maximilian's economics and home affairs. Work on the Fuggers has, of course, helped, but it has concentrated on the banking family rather than on Maximilian's economic policies and finances as a whole.[17] So our study will make considerable use of the economic documents in the *Hofkammerarchiv*, Vienna, as well as of a number of boxes containing documents about court finances and miscellaneous draft letters from the court chancellery officials, which are in the *Haus-, Hof- und Staatsarchiv*, Vienna.[18] To this must be added the *Maximiliana* and the *Kopialbücher* in the Innsbruck archive. The affairs of the German empire that centred especially on military grants, Turk taxes and federal judicial reforms from the great reforming Imperial Assemblies of the period, although usually so well-covered by Ulmann, will eventually also have to be re-examined from the Mainz archchancellery archive, now at the *Haus-, Hof- und Staatsarchiv* as elsewhere.[19] After more than a century of planning, the first collection of the *Reichstagsakten* (*Mittlere Reihe*) from the time of Maximilian I has been published.[20] It is of crucial importance to the detailed understanding of federal German politics in the era of *Reichsreform* which culminated in the great Imperial Assembly at Worms in 1495. Linked to the examination of Maximilian's finances is the search for information about the groups of ordinary people who worked and lived under King Maximilian. The manuscript collection of the *Haus-, Hof- und Staatsarchiv* with its tax and estate records of the Lower Austrian lands, and the fiscal records of the *Hofkammerarchiv* provides a mass of original material.[21] Of published works in this field, studies on prices and wages, and an estimate of the population of the Austrian lands have begun to provide a statistical background to assessments of the standards of living of the various groups, ranks and orders of society under Maximilian, as well as tentative estimates of the patterns of economic growth and recession around 1500.[22] It is all too true that the society and economy of the Habsburg lands under Maximilian I is largely still an unexplored subject even to Austrian and German historians in the field.

A start has been made to glean information about ordinary people from the Vienna and Innsbruck archives in local and regional studies, in order to reconstruct a first impression of life under Maximilian from the view of the day-labourer, artisan and mine-worker, through to the peasant, burgher, court official and servant, their families and households in the Austrian lands. What is said here will have to be tested against the evidence from other archives and sources, especially those in the south German towns and territories. The reader may bear the following questions in mind. What was it like to live under Maximilian's style of politics and taxation, law and local administration? Did Maximilian keep his coronation promises? Did he protect his more economically vulnerable subjects, or did he allow them to be increasingly exploited, and if so, with what results? How did his reign influence the standard and quality of life of his direct territorial subjects in the Austrian lands? It is because we need to know more about the mentality and impact of Maximilian's style of political leadership and government on all his subjects in the German empire and Austrian lands of the Renaissance, and to combine it with the diplomacy and war leadership of the few who used up the resources provided by the mass of the common people, that we may attempt to call this approach a contribution to the task of social biography.[23]

2

Man and Image

Maximilian grew up tough and fit. He liked physical exercises and indulged in outdoor activities all the year round. He delighted in being seen to be active: he was always on the move. In the autobiographical work that was ghosted by the dilettante humanist, Joseph Grünpeck, forty-year-old Maximilian looked back on the exploits of his youth. Through coloured pen-strokes Maximilian relived his childhood exploits from the castle at Wiener-Neustadt through to the Burgundian marriage and the seemingly endless warfare with France first in the Netherlands and Burgundy, and then in North Italy. Grünpeck was in service during the crucial years when Maximilian became middle-aged, 1497–1501. In 1497 the king had had a noticeable attack of syphilis (*morbus gallicus*) in the form of mouth-sores whilst sipping wine with the monks at Füssen, as recorded in their monastic chronicle. One may doubt whether he was miraculously cured as the monks implied. Six years later the monks recorded a happier event. Whilst Maximilian was once again enjoying their hospitality the townsfolk reported that wonderful small stars had fallen out of heaven into their clothes.[1] He suffered leg damage in a serious riding accident near Augsburg in 1501. The result was diagnosed as the onset of melancholia, that luxury disease of brooding introspection and suspicion so fashionable in European court and town circles during the Renaissance. Maximilian pulled himself out of his depression by reliving the exploits of his years of health and strength not only for his own safety's sake but also for the greater glory of his Habsburg-Burgundian house and dynasty. A major personal exercise in Habsburg self-glorification was the result,

7

entitled *The Histories of Frederick and Maximilian*, created around 1500 and completed for public release after 1514.[2]

We will follow Grünpeck to see how Maximilian himself wanted his younger years to be seen by posterity. The images are in a stream of consciousness and not strictly chronological. He first appears outside Neuss in 1475 as Frederick III and Charles the Bold negotiated a truce, and for the first time discussed a marriage alliance between their children and heirs, Maximilian and Mary. The background scene was a damaged fort in woodland, flanked by shielded cannon. The middle ground depicted a Hussite-style *Wagenburg*, enclosing the imperial and ducal tents. In the foreground, sumptuously robed and suitably crowned, Frederick and Charles were introducing Maximilian and Mary to each other.[3] There is no firm evidence that this meeting ever took place outside the fertile imagination of Maximilian some twenty-five years later.

Maximilian's next appearance presents a flash-back to infancy. As the birth-blood was being washed away, the new-born stood up in his wooden bath-tub: a sign that here indeed was no ordinary mortal. The illustration depicts a plain room full of people with the main action under a large window next to a well-blanketed crib, carved with insignia suspiciously like those of a fifteenth-century baby Jesus. Maximilian is naked up to his archducal hat and gold necklace.[4] The boy was living in the unpretentious and healthy surroundings of Frederick's household at Wiener-Neustadt: eating plain, wholesome food; learning counting, reading, writing and dog-Latin; talking a mixture of German and south-alpine Slav dialect; and playing hard with his peer-group of courtiers' and servants' children in order to develop his motor-skills in riding, weaponry, hunting and mock war-games. His early favourites were sword-play, archery and jousting, preferably with a barrel-end for a target with variations provided in such exploits as chasing kitchen-garden ducks from horseback, armed with spear, dogs and a pack of playmates, the latter following more discreetly on foot beyond the castle moat (Plate 1).[5]

How healthy was Maximilian? Our evidence is a mixture of official, Greek classical medicine, based on the four body fluids of blood, slime, yellow and black bile to be regulated by

bleeding and the examination of urine; the alchemical
tradition of dietary and bowel control as developed by the
Ulm school of herbalists since the 1460s; and finally a
mish-mash of gnostic, astrological and occult Platonic natur-
alism as typified by men as learned as Ficino and as
pseudo-scientific as Abbot Trithemius, a forerunner of Para-
celsus. Maximilian tried all the medical fashions from
excessive attention to bowel-movement, to humours and
bleedings, from zodiacs to horoscopes. The medical section in
his library, however, contained only a few remarkably archaic
and popular handbooks. They were the herbals and pharma-
copœia of the late thirteenth and fourteenth centuries, mainly
in newly printed versions as incunables, plus occasional, more
recent middle-brow tracts such as Surgeon Hieronymus
Brunschwig's *Liber de arte distillandi simplicia et composita*
(Strasbourg, 1508). Although he kept as many as twenty-three
physicians on his payroll at one time or another, it is perhaps
more useful to adapt Machiavelli's adage about Maximilian's
politics to the ruler's views on keeping healthy and fit, namely
that Maximilian listened to the advice of all and heeded none.
Maximilian consulted many famous doctors but usually went
in for self-curing via the patent remedies of the traditional
peasant wisdom of healing by spells, herbs and homoeopathy.
This did not prevent him from poaching doctors with high
reputations whenever and wherever he could find them
among the servants of his friends, relatives, rivals and urban
hosts, whom he met during years of endless travel. He used
the personal physician of his brother-in-law, Albrecht of
Munich; of his second wife, Bianca; of his father, Frederick
III; of the Bishop of Brixen; no less than three in the service of
Archduke Sigismund; of the city council at Zürich; the
Portuguese doctor of Charles the Bold; and those of the Dukes
of Mecklenburg who came to the Reichstag at Augsburg in
1518; of the city of Basle; and of Milan; plus three academic
necromancers used for diplomacy, astrology and pharmacy
(Plate 2).[6] They included the famous humanist Cuspinian.
They have helped to document about fifteen major crises in
Maximilian's life.[7]

As an infant Maximilian was spoilt by his Portuguese
mother and given unsuitable sweetmeats instead of milkslops.
He was a late developer who may have had a slight speech

defect until he was about nine years of age. He was then robustly healthy until his late thirties. In 1497 he suffered from mouth-sores, diagnosed as *morbus gallicus*, and the onset of the then rampant disease of syphilis. In 1501 he fell off his horse near Augsburg and damaged a leg, which always thereafter gave him pain. In 1507 came chronic catarrh which he tried to shake off with violent physical exercise. After 1514 Maximilian always travelled with his coffin, and he now seldom mentioned his ailments in any great detail, rather they were usually disguised as indisposition due to melancholia. The high spirits of youth had turned into the choleric moodiness of old age. In 1515 he had to travel in a cart to Vienna, since his bad leg prevented riding. Was this also due to the onset of gout from which his father had suffered so terribly in his last years? Podagra was certainly worth a popular sermon or two, cheering a congregation of peasants or artisan-labourers, since it was a disease which they could not catch, on account of their more basic diet. Podagra was seen as the Scourge of God meted out only to the rich. After 1514–15 Maximilian was using ill-health as his excuse to stay away from the battlefields, above all of north Italy. Travel on horseback was now almost impossible, although he tended to visit even more places than he had done when personally more agile and mobile.

Serious illness beset him in 1517 whilst visiting the Netherlands. It was ascribed to the damp air. Had he become arthritic as well as bronchial? In that year the papal court circulated a rumour that Maximilian had suffered a stroke. In Germany there was now much talk of his *Blödigkeit*, old age, weakness, even touches of senility. He went to take the waters at Baden Spa in 1517, possibly hoping that mud baths would cure his leg. Was this bad leg really a cover for other illnesses of an even more debilitating nature, including hardening arteries, gout, bronchitis or asthma, gallstones or even stomach cancer? Already in 1512 Dr Tannstetter had warned him that the next eclipse of the sun would be an omen of impending fatality, and since he had been brought up to believe that his guiding planet, Saturn, was moody and melancholic, he organised his funeral, made an almost endless succession of wills and prepared for the unexpected but inevitable. On 8 June 1518 he saw an eclipse of the sun, and began to appreciate the self-fulfilling nature of Tannstetter's horoscope. After returning to Innsbruck from the Reichstag at Augsburg, the local innkeepers and purveyors refused his entourage further credit. Maximilian's resulting fit of rage possibly brought on a stroke in October. He left Tirol and at Wels on 15 December 1518 he was feverish and bed-ridden. Along with several physicians, Dr Baptista, who was the late Empress Bianca's *Leibmedicus*, was sent for in all haste from north Italy. Maximilian complained of heart pain and discussed religion and death with Georg Reisch, his Carthusian monk. The emperor died between three and four o'clock on the night of 12 January 1519.

epared a report of ary 1519. Cause of bowel failure. He rrhoea and fever, two days later. His ed with diarrhoea have had cancer of

pared a report of er. The cult of his nd metal; it was repeated in charcoal, tempera and oil paints, in miniature right up to larger than life, from two- to three-dimensional, low and high relief as well as free-standing, wearing hats and crowns, robes, tunics, jerkins and armour. From the jousting and cavalry suits of mail that remain and from the lack of specific mention as regards the subject, we may surmise that he was of medium height, powerful, athletic, short-necked, and bull-chested. He was the practical warrior and outdoor type much admired in the Renaissance era.[9]

Undoubtedly the most well-known portrait of Maximilian is by Albrecht Dürer who did a sketch in charcoal of the emperor as an old man, just some months before his death, as he appeared at the Reichstag at Augsburg in 1518. A highly stylised version, much approved by Habsburg officialdom, is in Vienna, along with the original drawing. In Nuremberg there is a less flattering and more fleeting watercolour made

from the same sketch (Plate 3). Against a blue-wash background and under a large black felt cap, a ravaged face is
stiffly set. The long hair is reddish blond and flecked with
white. It is still quite thick and hangs naturally to the nape of
the neck. The head is held high and the posture is erect, as
befits an old warrior. The eyes stare out in a somewhat glazed
manner. They are turned inward. Dürer has caught Maximilian in a mechanically public pose, lost in thought with his
mind on other things. The mood is by no means unflattering
for a tired old man who had been wielding political power
non-stop for forty years. A tremendously prominent hooked
nose helps to draw attention away from the deep lines on the
cheeks and neck, and to offset the protruding lower jaw which
was to be the hall-mark of Habsburg family inbreeding in
subsequent generations culminating in the extreme physical
distortion of Charles II of Spain in the later seventeenth
century. In Maximilian that trait was there: a large nose,
prone to colds, with a jutting chin and distorted jaw that made
efficient mastication difficult and slobbering easy. Dürer has
beautified the mouth and only hinted at its clumsy build
whilst also lessening the lines of anger, pain and frustration
which had built up around the mouth over the years. The
portrait was probably offered to Maximilian's daughter,
Margaret, Viceroy of the Netherlands at Brussels, to which
Dürer cryptically refers in his diary: 'but since she so violently
disliked it, I took it away with me again.'[10]

Maximilian took after his father in posture, looks and build.
Both held themselves very upright; both had a fair complexion
with blond or reddish-tinged hair worn to neck length, large
noses and prominent chins. Both were thick-set and of athletic
build. A very slight tendency towards obesity may be seen in
the formation of double chins, especially in the son. One can
compare an Italian portrait of 1452, done when Frederick III
was thirty-seven, with a carved bust of Maximilian, aged 56,
attached to an antler candelabra, produced in about
1516 (Plates 4 and 5). The striking similarity between father
and son is captured in the determined features on a double
portrait medallion (Plate 6). Maximilian was a vigorously ugly
man with thick features whom great artists like Dürer tended
to beautify and flatter in their commissioned work. Portraits

from the Netherlands were often less flattering than those from south Germany and Austria, as shown in the bulbous, thick-necked and almost sneering, sly and cunning features of a side-view done in about 1510 (Plate 7).

There are enough remaining portraits of Maximilian for us to be able to balance ideal with reality in the plastic image, and to compare it with the literary output, whereby political, military, recreational and cultural exploits are very evenly divided between myth and reality, fantasy and hard-core fact. Between these sides yawns a deep credibility gap, although the ruthless romance of the White King and of Theuerdank may be seen to share the charm of the painterly realism in Holbein the Elder's sketch, done in about 1510, of a tired traveller on horseback – Maximilian, well-wrapped against wind and weather in dusty overalls entering Augsburg, encaptioned 'der gross kaiser maximilian'. To it one may aptly supply Maximilian's words about himself, 'my true home is in the stirrup, the overnight rest and the saddle' (Plate 8).

The final truth lay in the mask of death, portrayed in the sunken face and eyes, still absently peeping through their half-closed lids; the bared mouth, enormous hooked nose and prominent chin upon which the stubble still grew (Plate 9).[11] Maximilian, like his father before him, had always insisted on shaving, for why hide the nobility of a jutting jaw behind a beard? Here we leave the last word to Ernst Bock, the historian of Maximilian's Reichstags and of his greatest exercise in federal Reich policing, the Swabian League.[12]

His rosy optimism and utilitarianism, his totally naïve amorality in matters political, both unscrupulous and machiavellian; his sensuous and earthy naturalness, his exceptional receptiveness towards anything beautiful especially in the visual arts, but also towards the various fashions of his time whether the nationalism in politics, the humanism in literature and philosophy or in matters of economics and capitalism; further his surprising yearning for personal fame combined with a striving for popularity, above all the clear consciousness of a developed individuality: these properties Maximilian displayed again and again.

13

Frederick's hopes for his son to continue to enlarge the fortunes of the Habsburg dynasty in line with his insanely ambitious gnostic formula of AEIOV from 1437, whereby all the vowels of the alphabet spelled the message that the whole world was at Austria's feet, were confirmed when a wise Jew detected that pre-teenage Maximilian's fiery eyes portended his growing up to scare even the bravest of men.[13] A real little dragon-slayer for the dynasty, who was now given St George as a patron saint, was a matter of pride to father and son alike. By contrast, Maximilian was being brought up as immodestly as his circumstances were modest. Ruthlessly pragmatic Maximilian indeed turned out to be, challenging his father's methods whilst totally conforming to his ends. Maximilian may be seen as an individualist and opportunist who had merely to uphold the self-satisfied principle in politics: that that which was naturally good for Austria, Germany and Europe was the mere existence of himself and his Habsburg dynasty as its leader and ordained policy-maker. If he stated this divine mission often, loudly and visually enough, then it would begin to be believed. On this basis responsibility and blame could always be shifted away from the ruler by seemingly open government whereby real decisions taken in secret should never be revealed in such a way as to harm Maximilian's popularity with the German public.[14] This method was aptly characterised in his own words: 'In order to have sound reason for applying the law, and not fall into ill-repute.'[15] It must be clearly distinguished from Frederick III's style of politics, which is now seen as having been inflexibly traditionalist, contrasting a fear of losing any formal prerogative powers in theory with an understanding that these had long disappeared in practice. It must also be seen separately from Charles V's subsequent lethargy, although it had much in common with Ferdinand I's practical, political realism. Maximilian is placed in the middle, between father and grandsons, as a vigorously charming extrovert, diplomat and reforming conservative.[16]

After sketching in his Styrian childhood, Grünpeck's *Historia* divides Maximilian's life into two more stages. The stage of his earlier wars, fought, above all, in the Netherlands, skilfully avoids mentioning the disastrous campaign against the Engadin Swiss of 1499. Instead, his skill in handling mercenary foot-soldiers, lance-toting Landsknechts from south-west and alpine Germany, is given full coverage.[17] In a forest of colourful tents, Maximilian is handing out his silver and gold table-ware to pay off eager mercenary captains, only in the following picture he receives similar objects back again as gifts from the hands of the envoys of foreign heads of state. When taken together these two illustrations provide shrewd comment on Maximilian's mediating role within the high economy of European palace and parade-ground, as the wealth of the one is squandered in the activities of the other, linked as the families of the surviving warriors of yesterday became those of the courtiers of tomorrow. Not without conscious irony was the dead sheep in the linked necklace of Habsburg-Burgundian dynastic dress, which Maximilian always wore when he received ambassadors along with their presents, referred to in the curiously hang-dog-like sheep at their feet in the illustration. The biblical image of the good shepherd was in practice the head of state who fleeced his subjects, close to Machiavelli and Reynard the Fox.[18] However, Maximilian's court was visible and his actions were public: he was seen and heard; he was approachable. He went hunting whenever he could; he jousted until forced to desist by his bad leg; and he boasted that in the years of his brief Burgundian marriage he had happily been able to spend 10,000 fl. on a masked ball.[19]

The second stage was seen to have just begun at the time of the first draft of Grünpeck's *Historia* around 1500. The forty-year-old had taken part in his last joust and was now becoming an elder statesman. He would turn to the arts and sciences not only as a patron, but more personally in the fashionable Renaissance guise of an *uomo universale*. He would still need to go to war in Italy, above all against the French, and increasingly against the Venetians, but his days of strenuous riding and hunting would be tempered by more sedentary hobbies. As a present from his territorial Estates in Tirol, courtier Degen Fuchs provided him with a wood-work bench, which was set up in 1503 at the castle housing the Innsbruck Court in 'a small attic room for our personal amusement'. Its ornate carvings, almost hiding the vices and

15

clamps that it sported, stare at us today as a wonderful toy for a wealthy grown-up.[20] The popular image of the 'artisan' ruler was naturally buttressed by the notion of the academic, clever and intellectual ruler: the know-all. In Grünpeck's *Historia* Maximilian is being handed a globe by a courtier wearing the small crown, representing the erroneous Renaissance view of Ptolemy, whilst a Landsknecht gapes at it over the king's shoulder. The picture contains a rare comment in Maximilian's own hand, asking for a fourth person to be included in the action to help this illusive allusion to himself encompassing the world with geographical science and warfare.[21]

Grünpeck's *Historia* may thus be seen as the real beginning of Maximilian's self-glorification which came to full fruition in the last seven years of his life after 1512. What was to be expected from a very extrovert and active, yet moody and easily distracted military ruler in his mid-fifties, now experiencing the aches and pains of too much travelling, stress and good living, suffering from catarrh, probably gout and syphilis, high blood-pressure and perhaps even the first indications of some form of stomach cancer?[22] An indication of his need to romanticise the exploits of youth as the central act of a consciously new policy of Habsburg Euro-dynasticism may be observed in the more mundane and petty bric-à-brac of everyday court life. Maximilian's tableware included a very broad serving-knife, probably a fish-slice, which was incised at the base of its blade with the imperial double-eagle and a figure enthroned under a baldachin with long robes, imperial crown, sceptre and orb. The slice was one of a set made in 1496 in memory of many a successful royal hunt, shoot and fish with elder cousin Sigismund of Tirol, who had just died.[23]

Maximilian could not afford the expense of self-glorification by massive feats of architecture and sculpture. The closest he came to the Michelangelesque was his tomb at Innsbruck, finished only in the decades well after his death. Instead, he closeted himself with his favourite secretary, Marx Treitzsaurwein, and worked out a publishing plan in 1512. His books would include woodcuts and engravings from South Germany's leading artists, set to the rhetoric of her humanists, orators and poets in the mode of Dürer, Celtis and Peutinger. The original list of 21 was first cut to 14 and then expanded to 37 titles. The venture was crowned with preliminary success in the publication of the *Theuerdank* in 1517, rated as Germany's earliest and possibly greatest piece of bibliophilia.

Theuerdank and its sequel *Weisskunig* gave a highly favourable version of Maximilian's Burgundian marriage and subsequent wars. Despite this self-glorification, it truly represents the fact that Maximilian did take massive military gambles which he won, time and again. That is not to say that he invariably won his individual sieges and battles, nor that his campaigns were always successful; far from it. He barely held his own against the French in the Netherlands, 1479–93; he lost to the Swiss in 1499; never succeeded in curbing the rebellious Gelderlanders; and his north Italian campaigns against the French after 1496 and from 1514 were an expense which he could ill afford. When he took on Venice after 1509 it proved to be the graveyard of his international reputation, leading furthermore to the virtual bankruptcy of South Tirol and Inner Austria, as well as the cessation of the crucial, long-distance trade at Vienna and Augsburg. Maximilian's wars tended to end in pyrrhic victories with the notable exception of the defence of Burgundy after 1479, which ended in the successful conquest of Franche Comté in 1493. He was also successful in his intervention in the war over the Bavarian succession to Duke George the Rich of Lower Bavaria who died in 1503, ending in the Habsburg seizure of Kufstein in 1504. To achieve this, Maximilian had come very close to death in battle outside Regensburg earlier in that year, as the Czech mercenaries of the Elector Palatine withstood Maximilian's personally led cavalry charge by retreating behind their *Wagenburg* of baggage wagons. From the vantage point thus gained, they pulled him off his charger with their long, hooked halberds. He was rescued just in time from a butchering by a cavalry rally under his general, Duke Eric of Brunswick, which won the day. Within weeks of the occurrence, this battle was being enacted with words composed by the Habsburg imperial poet laureate, Conrad Celtis, in Vienna. A printed text embellished with a hasty woodcut by Hans Burgkmair appeared for distribution at Augsburg.[24]

17

The 1517 printed version of *Theuerdank* contains 118 woodcuts to the same number of verses, each recounting a separate episode on the journey of Maximilian from Styria in Austria to Mary of Burgundy in the Netherlands during 1477. The artists were Leonard Beck, Hans Schäufelein, Hans Burgkmair, Laschitzer, and five blocks are by unknown hands. The type-face is a magnificent copy of a beautiful German gothic handwriting, exquisitely joined. Here is the story.

At the beginning of time, 6444 years ago, there lived an old King, called *Romreich* [famed-rich], who had a daughter and heiress, called *Ernreich* [honoured rich]. His kingdom was in the west. As Romreich grew old, Ernreich grew nubile. Romreich's advisers suggested a suitable marriage for Ernreich but he postponed the matter until after his peaceful death in a beautiful garden, whereafter his choice was revealed in a last will and testament. It was to be Prince *Theuerdank* [precious thanks]. Ernreich thereupon sent a messenger to Theuerdank since she was a dutiful daughter, willing to obey the fourth commandment.

However, at Ernreich's court there were three politicians who each wanted to marry her, and they made a secret pact to destroy Theuerdank, planning to hold him up on his journey to Ernreich and to arrange for his 'accidental' death. They are *Fürwittig* [too-clever-by-half], *Unfalo* [accident-prone] and *Neidelhart* [envy-harbourer], who each occupy a pass on the road between Theuerdank's and Ernreich's.

In the meantime, at the court of Theuerdank's parents Ernreich's message is received. Theuerdank prepares to act on it but will only accept the hand of Ernreich if on the way to her he can have adventures that will prove him to be worthy of her. His father sends him off with the admonition to remain true to God's teaching and to commonsense [*die Vernunft und die göttlichler*] Yet the Devil in the guise of a wise old intellectual and politician tempts Theuerdank THREE times with worldly wealth, power and pleasure. Theuerdank refuses these offers. Instead, he calls upon *Ernhold* [steadfastly-honoured], a knight about court who

18

liked to observe the honest deeds of men, retell them to posterity, and revile, as a way of punishment by revelation of the truth to posterity, those men who commit dastardly deeds from base motives. Ernhold then appears on almost all the woodcuts as the historian, messenger and chronicler of the story. He sports a wheel of fortune on his military tunic, and that wheel at times reveals a human being clinging to its rim as it rises and falls endlessly worshipping its goddess, Fortuna.

Next day Ernhold and Theuerdank arrive at the first pass and Fürwittig takes them to stay in his town. He persuades Theuerdank to await further news of Queen Ernreich from the comfort of his residence. They go hunting. In various settings Theuerdank has shooting 'accidents', slips on mountain paths, falls from horses, is attacked by bears, stags, avalanches and rock-falls. Theuerdank shows his amazingly quick reflexes. At one point he is even induced to put his hand into a lion's mouth. Nothing awkward happens. Theuerdank even survives an episode on thin ice. Eventually he realises that Fürwittig is at best a *faux bonhomme*, and he rides on, longing for his Queen Ernreich.

Fürwittig sends word ahead to Unfalo, saying that he has failed. Unfalo meets Theuerdank at the second pass and invites him home. 'Home' includes a craggy castle which they mount in order to admire the view. Once inside, the door is locked and Theuerdank is asked to descend an outside stair of rotted steps. However, his sense of balance is so good that he does not fall. He then survives another round of hunting, shooting and fishing adventures. Theuerdank is even invited to inspect the muzzle of a loaded cannon with a naked light. As a shot is fired, Theuerdank ducks. He is led into a room where two lions attack him: he slays them with a shovel left conveniently in the room. Then he is enticed onto the sea in a leaky boat showing too much canvas with a storm brewing. He cuts the canvas and uses it to stop leaks. On shore again Theuerdank praises God for a safe delivery. Unfalo now arranges for Theuerdank to be struck by lightning, but it just misses. He has 'accidents' with crossbows and hand-guns. On a mountain a peasant throws rocks at him but Theuerdank sees them coming, throws himself flat and they bounce free. He falls ill and Unfalo's doctor gives him diluted medicine. Theuerdank diagnoses himself and arranges to have his own mixture at full strength, which could kill or cure him. It cures him. Then he catches a high fever and Unfalo's physician suggests hot and heavy food, making him worse. Theuerdank fasts on cold water and cures himself. Unfalo shoots a mountain goat above Theuerdank's head but it bounces once too often and merely falls at his feet. When Theuerdank is invited to put to sea with a drunken crew he begins to realise that Unfalo is not his best friend. This feeling is confirmed when Unfalo burns down the house in which Theuerdank is sleeping. He moves on, but not before Unfalo has alerted the third [and last] accomplice, Neidelhart.

Theuerdank is now being tested in war. At the third pass Neidelhart excuses the failure of his friends, Fürwittig and Unfalo, since they had only tested to see if Theuerdank was indeed the right and worthy person to marry their mistress, Queen Ernreich. Neidelhart houses, wines and dines Theuerdank and Ernhold in the grand manner and then invites them to go to war with him against a mighty King [Louis the Spider] who is being beastly to Queen Ernreich. Neidelhart sets 'suicide' traps for Theuerdank in siege-war, open battle, and encounters on the open sea and in the rivers. Theuerdank carries out his military and naval tasks with courage and with quick reflexes. He is even able to capture an armed band of a hundred foes with only THIRTEEN cavalry of his own by tricking the enemy into believing that reinforcements, although still invisible are just behind him. There were no reinforcements. Neidelhart stirs up citizens of a town [Ghent, Bruges] to rebel against Theuerdank, who is persuaded to pacify the mob. He retreats to a castle just in time to escape being lynched.

Queen Ernreich becomes impatient. She orders Neidelhart to bring Theuerdank straight to her court. Neidelhart poisons his food and drink. A porter tells Ernhold of this and just as Theuerdank is about to start eating, Ernhold warns him. This is Ernhold's only intervention during the whole epic, which he so faithfully

witnesses. As Neidelhart enters the dining hall, Theuerdank
lunges his sword at him but he escapes.

Theuerdank finally arrives and meets Ernreich. They
attend mass next morning but Fürwittig, Unfalo and
Neidelhart have also arrived. They are still plotting. They
organise a tournament at court. Ernreich says 'no', but
Theuerdank accepts since he must prove himself to his
bride and demonstrate his prowess to her courtiers. He
wins. The same evening he does battle with the two best
native foot-soldiers. He wins again. In the tournament held
in the foreign manner, Theuerdank wins by shattering the
most lances. It is a three day event. Ernreich has watched it
all. She dines with Theuerdank and tells him that she has
had enough of the anxiety but he still does single battle with
an old knight who cannot reconcile himself to the fact that
the Queen will be married by a foreigner. Theuerdank wins.
That evening there is dancing and merry-making, whilst
Ernreich crowns her man with laurels. Fürwittig, Unfalo
and Neidelhart are put on trial. Ernhold is the witness for
the prosecution and the three evil counsellors confess.
Fürwittig is beheaded, Unfalo hanged, and Neidelhart
thrown off the castle wall to his death.

Queen Ernreich assembles her council of state and
Ernhold declaims the adventure of Theuerdank's deeds,
ending by making the point that he has deserved peace
now. Yet a real Christian ruler must crusade against the
infidel who now threaten Ernreich's realm. Will
Theuerdank go crusading? He retreats to his private
chamber and prays to God. Whilst at his devotions, an
angelic spirit warns him to follow the Commandments and
resist the hypocrisy of this world. He must now avoid
reaching above his station and resist over-ambitiousness
and arrogance [*Hofart, Hochfart*]. He must always remain
sincere and loyal in his dealings with his fellow human
beings. Then the angel suggests he accept the Queen's offer
and go on crusade, since it is God's wish, too. Before
Theuerdank embarks on crusade he begs for the Queen's
hand, but the marriage will be consummated only when he
has cleaned the realm of all its enemies.

The story breaks here. The planned parts of Theuerdank's crusade were never produced. Maximilian was hoping all his life to go on crusade and he died in January 1519 with that unfulfilled yearning uppermost in his mind. The nearest he had come to seeking out and destroying Muslim and Turk mercenaries had been in 1493 when he campaigned with Tirolean levies in Inner Austria, after having first used them to put down the Gossensass miners' strike on the Brenner. Instead of the crusading story, scenes of Maximilian's wars with France were subsequently added by Burkard Waldis (died 1556). An *ad hoc* and swift ending was inserted on Maximilian's orders. Ernhold, now acting as the scribe, wonders at Theuerdank's good fortune, concluding that it could only have occurred with God's help. The hero is left standing in a ring of swords.[25]

Within a generation of Maximilian's death twelve of his planned titles either had been published or at least in part they had been made public as sumptuously illustrated manuscripts. This 1512 plan comprised works on The Funerary Triumphal Arch, Weisskunig (white King), Theuerdank, Freydal, Triumphal Procession, Genealogical Chronicle, Genealogical Tree, Artillery, The Seven Circles of Pleasure, The Book of Heraldry, Book of Steel, Book of Armoury, Hunting, Falconry, Cooking, Fishing, Gardening, Building, Morality, Devotion, St George. The last three titles were added in Maximilian's own hand. They were soon dropped along with The Genealogical Tree, Armoury, Gardening and Building. To the remaining fourteen were then added eighteen new proposals, entitled Testament, King Wundrer, Cellar-Book, Book of Dalliance (*Puelerpuech*), Book of House-Keeping, Music-Book, New Prayer-Book, The Book of Twenty-Four Faiths, Book of Pulleys and Levers (*Haspelpuech*), Book of the Black Art, Book of Magic, The Emperor's Book, The Book of Austria, The Holy Calendar, Book of Jousting, The Book of Ruling Princes, Mirror of Colours, The Book of New Inventions.

Other ideas included a book about the Viennese Brotherhood of St George founded by Otto the Cheerful; a book as to 'how a ruling prince should best govern the Netherlands' (one cannot help wondering that this might have done Charles V and his son Philip II some good, had it ever materialised); a similar work on governing the Austrian Habsburg lands (though it seems that Ferdinand I had little to learn in this respect); a book describing the territorial authorities or *Reichsstände*; a book of honour; and a study on reform of the Gulden coinage. The twelve works that actually appeared in print, manuscript or at least as fragments were the Triumphal Procession, Tournaments and Masked Balls, the Triumphal Arch, the Holy Relatives of Emperor Maximilian, the Genealogy, the fragmentary Latin Autobiography, Theuerdank, Artillery Books, Hunting Book, White King, the Historia Friderici et Maximiliani, and the Tirolean Book of Fishing.[26]

Treitzsaurwein and Maximilian planned to cover the faculties of magical, mechanical and liberal arts but in fact their genre was the currently fashionable semi-autobiographical adventure story of courtly romance. Its driving force was dynasty-worship. Maximilian can thus be seen as the real creator of the Habsburg ancestor myth of early modern European absolutism. What he never carried out was his planned patronage of Celtis's scheme to provide a cosmography, or early encyclopaedia, of the German-speaking lands, with a comprehensive survey of its rulers, geography and artefacts including medallions, coins, triumphs and commemorations. To a large extent the market for this was not to be satisfied finally until Sebastian Münster's *Cosmographia* produced in the 1530s and 1540s.[27] Yet the achievement remained in early modern folk memory. Maximilian had built up a dynastic-patriotic myth for the Old Reich in general and for Austria and its Habsburg patrimony in particular. He combined the following elements of Habsburg public relations above all in print, woodcut and engraving: the political, diplomatic, personal, ancestral and imperial. It was the work of an old man in his late fifties, who had been very active in his younger years – in war, women and allied courtly pursuits. By pomp, circumstances and mystification he manufactured his own myth by trying so hard that he finally seemed to convince even himself that it was true. Maximilian may thereby be said to have been his own public relations manager. His charm hid a ruthlessly ambitious and mercenary nature. He typified the successful prototype in modern business and diplomatic, institutionalised life. He had the man of action's conventionally superficial interest in knowledge, science and art combined with excellent health in his youth: hall-marks of a successful head of state or government leader. But his success also lay in the way in which he created his own dynastic image.

After 1512 Maximilian planned his own definitive official genealogy using the finest skills of Nuremberg's artists, craftsmen and schoolmen. Two hundred sets of his 'Triumphal Arch' were printed and distributed as Habsburg dynastic state propaganda in 1518. The woodcut draftsmen included Dürer and Holbein. The ancestors in the 'central portal of honour and might' included most of the famous medieval monarchs of Europe. Then followed scenes of his battles from Guinegate near Thérouanne, 1479, Gelderland, Utrecht and Flanders, Liège, Netherlands, Franche Comté, Hungary, Switzerland, Italy, Bavaria-Palatinate, Gelderland, against Venice, and Guinegate, 1513. His personal prowess was glorified as founder of a lay brotherhood of knights of St George, 1494; planner of crusades against the infidel; as a specialist in artillery warfare; great linguist and diplomat; devout discoverer of relics; fearless hunter, good jouster and dancer, patron, architect and genealogist. A greater self-advertiser could hardly have been found.[28] Real life, out of which the mythology was forged personally, had been led within the confines of Europe's most successful high noble, royal, dynastic diplomatic marriage market. Like his father before him, Maximilian was no passive onlooker in this greatest game of all for late feudal Europe, which was dynasticism as a necessary precursor to the authority needed for effective early modern state-building. Here are the vital details of Maximilian's personal place within his own Habsburg tribe, given in the form in which they survive in a contemporary manuscript in the Vienna archives,[29] supplemented by equally contemporary portraiture.

Parents

Frederick III b. 1415 21/9 d. Linz 1493 19/8

married 1452 Eleonora, daughter of King Edward of Portugal, b.1437

    d. 1467 3/9 (Plate 10)[30]

Maximilian and his siblings

1   Christoph b. 1455 16/11 d. 1456 21/3

2   Maximilian b. Wiener-Neustadt 1459 22/3
Elected Holy Roman King 1486 26/2, crowned 9/4
Took title of Elected Emperor 1508 10/2
d. Wels 1519 12/1
married 1477 20/8 Mary, heiress of Burgundy, b. 1458 12/2
d. Bruges 1482 28/3
married 1494 16/3 Bianca Maria, daughter of Galeazzo of
Milan, b. 1472 d. 1511 1/1

3   Helena (Eleonor) b. 1460 3/11 d. 1461 28/2

4   Kunigunde b. Wiener-Neustadt 1465 16/3 d. Munich 1520
    6/8 (Plate 11)[31]
married 1487 1/1 Duke Albert IV of Bavaria
Children (Maximilian's Wittelsbach nephews)
William IV of Bavaria b. 1493 d. 1550
Ludwig von Landshut
Ernst d. 1560
and four nieces

5   Johann b. 1466 9/8 d. 1467

Maximilian's Burgundian parents-in-law

Charles the Bold b. 1433 d. 1477 5/1

second wife, married 1454 Isabella, daughter of Duke Charles of Bourbon. Mother of Mary d. 1465

third wife, married 1468 Margaret of York, Mary's step-mother
d. 1503

Maximilian's children

(a) legitimate (all with Mary of Burgundy, none with Bianca Maria)

1 Philip the Fair b. Bruges 1478 21/6 d. Bruges 1506 25/9 married 1496 21/8 Infanta Johanna (the Mad) of Spain b. 1479 6/11
 d. 1555 11/4

In 1489, when Johanna was ten and Philip eleven years old, Maximilian started negotiations for their marriage, leading to betrothal six years later (1495) and subsequent union in the Netherlands when the groom was eighteen and the bride seventeen, thus mirroring the romantic match of Philip's parents, Maximilian and Mary, two decades before.

2 Margaret b. Brussels 1480 10/6 d. Mâlines 1530 1/12

3 Franz b. 1481 2/9 d. 1481 26/9

(b) natural children (mothers not identified)

1 George of Austria d. 1557 5/5, Bishop of Brixen 1525, Archbishop of Valencia 1539, Bishop of Liège 1544. Had a natural son, Georg ab Austria, d. 1619 as Chancellor of Louvain University.

2 Friedrich von Amberg b. 1511 d. 1553 21/4

3 Maximilian von Amberg married Elizabeth of Oettingen widow of the Count of Pohlheim

4 Leopold, Bishop of Cordoba. Had a natural son, Maximilian,
 Archbishop of Compostella, d. 1614.

5 Anna, wife of Franz von Melun, Duke of Espinoy

6 Elizabeth Anna, wife of Ludwig von der Mark

7 Dorothea, wife of Johann Enno, Count of Friesland, 1589

8 Cornelius

9 Margaret, wife of Franz von Hitlery

10 Martha, wife of Count Louis of Helfenstein

11 An unnamed son

12 Barbara ab Austria.

Maximilian's grandchildren

1   Elenora b. Louvain 1498 24/11 d. Bruges 1558 17/2

2   Charles V b. Ghent 1500 25/2 d. Estramadura 1558 21/9 married 1526, Isabella, daughter of King Emmanuel of Portugal, b. 1503 4/10 d. 1539

3   Isabella b. Brussels 1501 18/7 d. near Ghent 1526

4   Ferdinand I b. Medina del Campo 1503 10/3 d. Vienna 1564 25/7

5   Maria b. Brussels 1505 17/9 d. 1558 18/10

6   Catharina b. Torquemada 1507 14/1 d. 1557

The following two lives illustrate the workings of Maximilian's marriage politics. The first is that of his daughter, Margaret (1480–1530), and the second, the Hungarian dual betrothal of his grandchildren in 1515, centred on the future Ferdinand I.

After two betrothals in Aragon and Savoy, unsuccessful because the men died too soon, Margaret eventually made a fine career as an effective regent of the Netherlands, holding the reins of government for her nephew, Charles. Maximilian entered the marriage market early with her. In 1482, at the age of two Margaret was betrothed to Dauphin Charles Valois and sent to France as part of a temporary peace made at Arras in the following year, when Charles became king (Plate 12). In 1491 Charles married Anne of Brittany, the heiress Maximilian had hoped to wed. In 1493 Charles sent Margaret, then aged thirteen, back to the Netherlands. Her next bridegroom was John of Asturia and she was sent to him at Burgos in April 1497. By October he was dead. In 1501 Margaret was married to Duke Philip of Savoy, who died three years later. By 1505 Margaret was an unsuccessful pawn in the marriage market around Henry VIII of England. Then came the death of her brother, Philip the Fair, in 1506 as well as the increasing onset of madness in her sister-in-law, Johanna, the first signs of which were reported in 1503 when she had demanded to walk to Flanders from Spain to join her husband. Maximilian supported Margaret's elevation to the regency of the Netherlands in May 1507. At the age of twenty-seven a career in politics replaced the waiting game of diplomatic marriage. She now had charge of the fortunes of her seven-year-old nephew, the future Charles V, and liaised between Maximilian and the Burgundian Netherlands Estates. The latter had never really liked Maximilian, but needed his children and grandchildren for unity and continuity especially against the dynastic claims of France. In 1508 Margaret was instrumental as arbitrator between Maximilian and France, and as alliance-builder between Maximilian, England, Spain and the papacy in 1513. The young Charles wisely kept his Aunt Margaret on as regent upon reaching his majority in 1517.

From 1507 Maximilian was using his grandchildren, Ferdinand, then aged four and living in Spain, and Maria, aged three and in the Netherlands, in marriage negotiations involving a similar exchange of young people with the Bohemian-Hungarian royal dynasty. His plans were successful in 1515 and came to effective marriages in 1521. This negotiation determined that, after a childhood in Spain, Ferdinand should grow up to be the leading central European Habsburg politician, based on Vienna, Prague and Germany. As such he was the real successor to Maximilian I and Federick III. Compared with Ferdinand, his elder brother Charles V always remained a stranger to Austro-German and Balkan-Danubian home affairs, first as a Burgundian Netherlander and then increasingly as a Mediterranean Spaniard.

What made Maximilian different from the normally active politician was the frantic exploitation of his own limited resources in such a way as to link his modest ancestry and progeny with Jesus, Caesar Augustus and Charlemagne as the naturally most glorious event in Christendom. This applied above all to his wars, as exemplified in a cycle of drawings from the Augsburg School of Hans Burgkmair, to which an elderly Maximilian paid particular attention in that grand year of self-glorification 1512. Vigorous battle scenes in front of towns, across bridges, fields, meadows, storming walls, accepting surrenders, sieges with cannon behind palisades, on foot, on horseback, in woodland, along alpine valleys, and along river-banks and sea-coasts complete the picture of his most memorable campaigns between 1478 and the Venetian

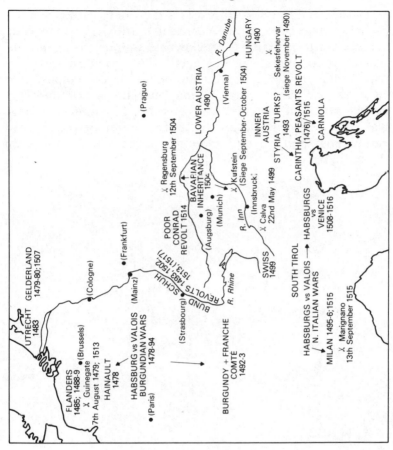

Map 2.1 Maximilian's wars,
1478–1516

wars (not ended until 1516 – and then only rather ignomi-niously). The energy and success of youth were conjured up graphically to revitalise the hollowness and increasing 'melan-cholia' (crankiness?) of old age.[32] The grandest image of Maximilian, as seen by himself to be his bequest to posterity, can best be summarised by mapping his major dynastic, foreign and civil wars (see Map 2.1). For Maximilian's image was truly forged in warfare, his ability to initiate war, to lead campaigns, and, always more problematically, to sustain them financially.

3

The Politics of Land-Hunger

In the fifteenth century human beings even of the upper classes died relatively young by the standards of the later twentieth century in Europe. Maximilian was faced with an exception. His father, Frederick III, lived into his seventies, ruling as German king and emperor for fifty-three years (1440–93), and breaking the record of Emperor Augustus himself, as the humanist orators at Frederick's funeral in Vienna in December 1493 were pleased to point out.[1] Maximilian had to wait until he was thirty-four years old before becoming sole ruler in the Austrian lands, and in the federal German empire. By the standards of his time, he was already middle-aged and elderly. But Maximilian had not spent his days waiting in powerless intriguing as a crown prince. By contracting the Burgundian marriage at the age of eighteen, he had entered the centre of European power politics, a position which he thereafter never relinquished for even a day, however much he may have needed rest, holiday and retirement.[2] At an early age, therefore, Maximilian had learned the first golden rule of success in European dynastic politics, that self-help through marriage and kinship was the surest road to power. Young Duke Maximilian had to defend his marriage success in Burgundy against the territorial claims and military strength of the French monarchy for fifteen years (1478–93). Maximilian learned his politics, diplomacy and warfare in the hardest school of pragmatism, self-help, deception and intrigue that Europe had seen, dominated by the Valois rulers of France, King Louis XI (the Spider), and his children, Regent Anne de Beaujeu, and King Charles VIII, the most economically powerful rulers of their day.

31

In which lands, at what times, and in which capacity did Maximilian exercise political power? The list is long and varied, determined by Maximilian's own restlessness, economic needs and military campaigns. For he never stayed more than a few days, weeks or rarely some months in one place. At one point in his career when he was greatly in need of money to pay mercenaries in his war for the Hungarian succession to Mathias Corvinus, which he was losing, and when he was only receiving opposition from his father, Frederick III, Maximilian wrote, 'God knows, I am heartily tired of traipsing around [*vmbzotln*] from place to place, and I only do it because of my poverty.'[3] An honest confession, for Maximilian during the whole of his political career never settled down. The economic demands that he made on any city, castle or monastic establishment at any one time were insufficient to provide for his needs and military plans for more than a few days, weeks or months. To remain free of bankruptcy Maximilian kept on the move.

His first political brief in 1477 was to act as co-regent of the Netherlands with his wife Maria, the only legitimate child and heir of Duke Charles the Bold of Burgundy. Maximilian kept large parts of the Burgundian dynastic state from disintegration, independent even of some of the justified territorial claims of the French king. But as ruler in the Netherlands Maximilian was personally unfortunate. His marriage ended after less than five years when Maria, who was pregnant for a third time, rode out to hunt with her falcons and her horse stumbled, throwing her into the bole of a tree. She died of internal injuries in the spring of 1482.[4] At eighteen, Maximilian had by reason of marriage become ruling Duke of Burgundy, at nineteen, a father, at twenty-three, a widower.

In the internal affairs of the Netherlands Maximilian had to contend with the hostility of Flanders, Zealand and Holland. His embargo on trade with France above all damaged the manufacturing industries of the leading towns of Flanders; Bruges-Sluis, Ghent and Ypres, where artisans and burghers rebelled at his war policy against the French king because it threatened their own standard of living. Even worse, Maximilian encouraged economic rivalry between Brabant and Flanders. In an economic policy of divide and rule, he supported the rise of Antwerp at the expense of Ghent and Bruges-Sluis. Thus it was, above all, Brabant with its towns of Antwerp, Mâlines, Louvain and eventually also Brussels that guaranteed loyalty to the Habsburg succession in the Burgundian Netherlands of the later fifteenth century.

Maximilian was only able to survive in the Netherlands after 1478 because of his own military skill. As he received no substantial aid from the territorial rulers of the German empire or even from his father in the Austrian lands, Maximilian had to defend himself with the income of his Burgundian subjects, buying mercenaries and war equipment with money grants from the Netherlands Estates. This entailed endless bargaining at territorial assemblies and with Estates' finance committees, which he conducted with considerable skill. Up to 1485 his military successes were considerable. At his first pitched battle, at Guinegate in the Pas de Calais in 1479, against the troops of King Louis XI, nineteen-year-old Duke Maximilian dismounted and fought among his German and Flemish footmen, who formed a solid bloc or *Wagenburg*, which slowly pushed the French centre off the field.[5] The use of traditional, central European, Hussite War tactics, using fraternisation with foot-soldiers, were the actions that saved young Maximilian from a similar death in a ditch to that of his Burgundian father-in-law, Duke Charles the Bold, two years previously in 1477. But the glorious exploits of war as propagandised by the ruling classes of the day were not sufficient to win Maximilian the loyalty of the Netherlands, where the States General wished to set up their own regency government over Maximilian's infant son, Philip, after Maria's death in 1482, and seek a permanent peace and trading link with France. Maximilian had sired an heir and now that his native wife was dead, the Netherlands Estates had no more use for him. Even if Maximilian had agreed with them, where could he have gone? He was now used to having his own political power, and outside the Netherlands he controlled nothing, for his father refused to give up any vestige of his imperial and territorial status in Germany or Austria. It was unlikely, therefore, that Maximilian would relinquish without a struggle his claims as co-ruler and regent of the Netherlands for his son, Philip.

The presence of Maximilian in the Netherlands meant continued war with France and therefore economic sanctions, unemployment and recession in Flanders' trade, industry and communications. Maximilian spent most of the 1480s campaigning against France and fighting civil wars on land, river and sea against rebellious Netherlands provinces and towns. In 1488 the rebellious townsmen of Bruges held him prisoner in a house on their main square threatening him with extradition to Ghent, where the townsmen talked of executing him, although he was by now a crowned king of Germany. In a letter which was smuggled out of prison in the sole of a shoe, Maximilian urged his father, Frederick III, and the German Electors, especially his friend the Archbishop Elector of Cologne to rescue him. But too much zeal with a full-scale invasion of the Netherlands, for which the German Imperial Assembly had in fact granted six thousand troops in 1487, whilst Maximilian was still held by the townsmen of Bruges in 1488, could well have endangered his life even further. He wrote:[6]

> I will explain my predicament succinctly and briefly as follows
> First, the reason why I have not written for so long is that I have wished to determine clearly the truth of my position, in which I have been comforted up to a point, but I am still imprisoned.
> Second, I estimate that without money to run my own administration and protect the life of my son, I must surrender him and swallow my anger, for otherwise they will give me poison to eat and kill me.
> Third, these two estimates I consider my comfort and true way out, otherwise I shall surely perish.
> Fourth, if God should help me out of here, then from that very moment onward I will be prepared to serve His Imperial Majesty or the German Empire. My captor will give me money enough if they are fair enough to let me go, but if they have me executed as they are threatening all the time, then I am indeed paid. They are taking all my servants from me.[7] This is my last letter, once and for all.
> Fifth, it is not my fault that I was imprisoned so pitifully,

but I feel that everyone has wished me evil whether friend or foe.

Sixth, most gracious lord, I beg you for the sake of God and justice for advice and help. I would like to have written more but can not for this is the last, and I write in great anxiety.

> Your Imperial Majesty's humble son Maximilian.

Although he had been elected and crowned King of Germany by his father, Emperor Frederick III, and the six German Electors of Mainz, Cologne, Trier, Palatinate, Saxony and Brandenburg at Frankfurt-am-Main in 1486, Maximilian still owned nothing in Germany. The Netherlands provided his infant son with a state, but Maximilian was still empty-handed. The Flanders rebellion of 1488 demonstrated that Maximilian was now left as a monarch without land, waiting for his father to die before he could inherit leadership over the German empire and in the Habsburg patrimony. But was that patrimony worth having? In 1489 King Mathias Corvinus of Hungary ruled in Vienna, and Emperor Frederick III was an exile in south Germany. Lower and Inner Austria were in Hungarian hands. Upper Austria, comprising the County of Tirol, parts of the Upper Rhine, East Swabia, Alsace and the *Vorlande* at the east end of Lake Constance were ruled by a Habsburg cousin, Archduke Sigismund, who was negotiating to sell most of his lands to the Bavarian Wittelsbach dukes, and they had already lent him more money than he could afford to repay out of his domain revenues. Of all the Habsburgs, it now looked as if only the ten-year-old Philip of Burgundy would retain any territory, and even his inheritance was divided between the claims of the territorial Estates, Maximilian, and the King of France. Despite the fact that Frederick III was still alive to claim all family property, Maximilian returned to the German empire and to the Austrian lands to regain lost territory for his dynasty. Two problems faced King Maximilian in 1490. He had to prevent the Tirol from going Bavarian, and he had to drive the Hungarians out of Lower and Inner Austria. Both aims were achieved. He had learned to live with heavy debts and still retain some freedom of action. He had become an expert military enterpriser and an effective general of foot-soldiers and artillery. These were at one and the same time his greatest and his sole assets after twelve years of governing the Netherlands.

With the help of the Tirol territorial assembly Maximilian forced his elderly cousin Sigismund, who had no legitimate children, to retire from governing Upper Austria in return for a pension equivalent in size to the regular revenues of the whole County of Tirol (Plate 13). Bavarian claims to debt repayments from Sigismund were frustrated by exploiting internal inheritance feuds within the Wittelsbach family, by their conflict with the Swabian League, with Frederick III over their capture of the imperial town of Regensburg, and by the elopement of Duke Albrecht of Bavaria with Maximilian's only sister, Kunigunde. The brothers-in-law understood each other well, although the old emperor was furious and wanted his daughter back. Kunigunde, it seems, was very much in love with her Bavarian Albrecht.

With the regency in Tirol, Maximilian had thus found an alternative to the Netherlands, and another power base of his own. In terms of his political career, he had exchanged the Burgundian Netherlands for the Tirol. Then Mathias Corvinus conveniently died without legitimate heir in April 1490, and from Innsbruck and the south German imperial towns Maximilian raised enough money, arms and troops to campaign through Lower and Inner Austria into Hungary itself. Before the campaign gathered momentum, Maximilian had time to scribble a short note expressing his last-minute doubts to his old kinsman, Archduke Sigismund, whom he had just replaced as ruler of the County of Tirol (Plate 14).[8]

> High-born ruling prince, friendly dear cousin. We would like to keep you informed of the latest news. Our cavalry are rushing about hither and thither [*grasser vreiterey*], so no-one can be certain what is the sensible and wise thing to do with them. But your dear Mr Stadion[9] will soon give you a full account. Graz, Sunday after Annunciation, 1490. *per manu propria* [signed] Maximilian, Roman King.

Maximilian's mercenary cavalry and Landsknechts committed the atrocity of totally sacking the ancient religious capital of Szekesferhervar (Stuhlweissenburg) in November 1490. The troops refused to continue the war, because of the frost on the ground. They wanted double pay, otherwise they threatened to disperse and take their booty with them.[10] Maximilian could also no longer afford their pay for his Tirolean resources were far too slender and he was totally dependent on the goodwill of the territorial Estates and his father, Frederick III. Maximilian soon reconquered Lower and Inner Austria for his father, although the Hungarian crown that Maximilian had with some justification demanded for himself fell instead to King Ladislas of Bohemia, the brother of King Sigismund of Poland. The real gain went to Frederick III who returned to Austria and settled at Linz, refusing to let his son have any financial support whatsoever. In this way Frederick helped to force Maximilian to make peace in Hungary (November 1491) and with France (May 1493), however, not before Habsburg mercenaries had regained Franche Comté from the Valois.

Emperor Frederick III, perhaps quite rightly, regarded his only legitimate son, Maximilian, as a military adventurer, a spendthrift and shiftless soldier, going from place to place and using up resources to fight wars whilst still recovering from the debts of previous campaigns, and only succeeding in getting into worse penury.[11] The best thing was to starve such a power politician into observing peace for lack of money, men and equipment. Yet the finances of Frederick III were probably just as bad as those of his son during these last quiet years at Linz in Lower Austria above the Enns, 1490–3. Frederick only survived by borrowing from rapacious courtiers like the brothers Sigismund and Heinrich Prüschenk, who were owed not much short of half a million gulden at the end of long careers in the treasury and at court as councillors first for Frederick and then for Maximilian.[12] Yet Frederick recognised his penury and sat quietly at peace with most of the world around him if at all possible, ignoring all in that frantic era of double-dealing and warfare, which he himself recognised and despised in his great old age.[13]

As ruler of Upper Austria Maximilian was far richer than his father in Lower and Inner Austria. The revenues and resources of the Tirolean silver-mines alone spoke for considerable actual and potential wealth.[14] Yet Maximilian's hasty style of politics which he backed with regular threats of military action, recruitment of troops and a full artillery-park seemed to place him in a far worse economic position than his father. The subject of Maximilian's finances is the key to any real understanding of his reign. Was he really hopeless at economics, as biographers have usually claimed without, however, looking at his finances in detail?[15] The economic evidence in the Vienna and Innsbruck archives would seem to speak against this traditional assumption. But it is clear that Maximilian used up far more money than the system of credit to rulers at that time generally allowed. That he achieved this without total bankruptcy shows his considerable skill as a financier in his own right. If the Fuggers grew rich on assets which Maximilian had to alienate to them, then it is equally true that the Habsburg dynasty grew powerful because of the political bribes that the Fuggers dispensed in the name of the future Charles V in 1519, shortly after Maximilian's death. This was indeed the first great age of monopolistic finance capital and Maximilian was one of its largest operators, albeit on the debit side. He played the traditionally weaker hand of the debtor, and he survived. But at whose expense? To begin to answer that we turn to a survey of Maximilian's lands and subjects, which he at last inherited on the death of Emperor Frederick III in August 1493.

4

Austria – the Land

In 1493 King Maximilian became sole ruler of the Austrian Habsburg patrimony. To his existing holdings in Upper Austria were added the lands of Lower Austria and Inner Austria.[1] Upper Austria comprised the County of Tirol which extended into the North Italian plain with capitals at Innsbruck and Bozen (Bolzano). Within its sphere of influence were the Bishoprics of Brixen (Bressanone) and Trient (Trento), which, although technically autonomous within the federal system of the German empire, were client states under the Habsburgs. To this complex, Tirol – Brixen – Trient, Maximilian later added the County of Görz (Gorizia). At Rovereto (in Trient) and Ampezzo (Görz) Maximilian's political entity of Greater Tirol cut into the Italian plain and involved him in frontier rivalry with mainland Venice. To the west, Maximilian's Tirol bordered on, and came into painful conflict with, the Swiss Confederation especially in the Engadin Valley and along Lake Constance. Three further regions were also part of Upper Austria, and these regions were affiliated to the County of Tirol and its administration at Innsbruck.

The first of these regions was the *Vorlande* between Tirol and Lake Constance, centred on Bregenz, Feldkirch and Bludenz, and run with the co-operation of surrounding high noble dynasties friendly to the Habsburgs, such as those of Montfort and Fürstenberg. The second region comprised a number of landed estates, which included high and low jurisdictions, and areas of hunting and forest rights in East Swabia near Augsburg, all centred on the Margraviate of Burgau.[2] East Swabia was Maximilian's favourite territory. It was here that

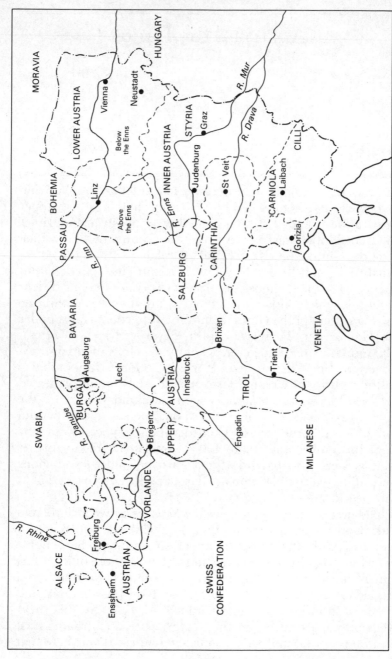

Map 4.1 Maximilian's lands in 1500

he indulged his craze for hunting, and the region ranked equal
to the Inn Valley in Tirol as the place that the restless king
learned to value highest as approximating most closely to his
concept of home as a place of security and recreation. To this
Maximilian could add his love of Augsburg town with its
contado adjoining the autonomous Bishopric of Augsburg. The
area as a whole acted as a buffer between Habsburg and
Wittelsbach spheres of dynastic power, and its rivalries were
duplicated along the middle Inn valley to the south. The lands
that provided lines of communication between Augsburg in
East Swabia and Innsbruck in Tirol were thus the heart of
Maximilian's empire. The third region included in Upper
Austria was the residual and scattered Habsburg holding in
Alsace and along the Upper Rhine, a pale reflection of earlier
attempts to uphold a strong post-Hohenstaufen royal and
imperial presence on the borders with the Swiss, Burgundians
and French in the Vosges and Black Forest, and between the
Rhine and Upper Danube. Ensisheim acted as administrative
centre of Habsburg high jurisdiction here. The town of
Freiburg in the Breisgau served the area as the effective centre
of its trade and communications. Just as Augsburg was
essential to the Habsburg presence in East Swabia, so
Freiburg served a similar purpose for the Habsburg regions of
Upper Rhine.

Upper Austria was thus a convenient geographical express-
ion for disparate dynastic property that Maximilian held
between the Upper Rhine, the Upper Danube and along the
Inn Valley in the north, cascading over the Alps on to the
Italian plain in the south. The only solid bloc of territory with
real traditions of continuity in internal affairs was, however,
the County of Tirol with its Estates of nobles, towns and free
peasants. The *Vorlande*, especially Habsburg East Swabia,
Alsace and Upper Rhineland, were too fragmented to develop
their own politically significant territorial assemblies. They
were no match against Habsburg governors, nor could they
emulate effectively the privileges of the Estates of Tirol. In
practice they followed the dictates of the Habsburg government at Innsbruck, which Maximilian ran with the support of
the territorial Estates of Tirol on generally amicable terms.

Geographical expressions for the Habsburg lands of Austria

have changed over the centuries, as the frontiers have been readjusted to new dynastic and political situations. It is therefore essential to describe Lower and Inner Austria in terms of what was generally understood by these regions at the time of Maximilian I.[3] Lower Austria comprised the two provinces above and below the River Enns, which flows into the Danube to the east of Linz. Linz, Wels and Gmunden were the principal towns of the province above the Enns (*Ob der Enns*), where Maximilian liked to spend part of the winter, especially around Christmas. He died at Wels in January 1519 *en route* from Innsbruck to Vienna where he wished to organise a crusade against the Turks. The province above the Enns shared borders with the Archbishopric of Salzburg and the Bishopric of Passau. Both ecclesiastical principalities were clients of Maximilian and members of his group of political friends at the Imperial Assembly. Both were of strategic importance. Salzburg offered easy communications between Innsbruck, Linz and Vienna, acting as a buffer between Wittelsbach Bavaria and Habsburg Austria. Passau controlled the junction of the rivers Inn and Danube, pushing well into Wittelsbach Bavarian and Upper Palatine lands, which later helped to make Regensburg accessible to the Habsburgs as their favoured town for the holding of Imperial Assemblies.

The province of Lower Austria above the Enns, with its capital at Linz, provided residence for Frederick III during the last three years of his life. Its territorial Estates of clergy, higher nobles, knights and town councillors were active in assembly and committee, and they were less predictably loyal to Habsburg policies than the Tiroleans. In 1493 on the death of Frederick III, the Estates at Linz wrote to Maximilian to reject the candidacy of his childhood friend, Sigismund Prüschenk, for the top post of Lord Lieutenant (*Landeshauptmann*). They refused to put into writing why they objected to him, but Maximilian avoided confrontation by employing Prüschenk in a neighbouring province. The matter shows the independence of mind of the territorial Estates above the Enns.[4]

The province of Lower Austria below the Enns (*Unter der Enns*) was the economic centre of Habsburg Austria. With its capital and by far most populous town of Vienna, and with excellent communications along the Danube and into the rolling plains of Hungary, it was the first German-speaking *entrepôt* for goods moving between south-eastern Europe and the German and Bohemian-Moravian hinterlands. The burghers of Vienna looked back on a century of political factiousness, of which Maximilian had gained experience as a very young child in the 1460s, when his family were very nearly starved in the besieged town castle, as a result of civil wars in the Habsburg family. These wars had ruined the economic power of the Viennese monetary system over the Danube basin.[5] Maximilian never forgot his early experiences, and, like his father, he never resided in Vienna thereafter. He used the town for planning and provisioning some of his campaigns and for holding important conferences, and he had his father buried in its *Stephansdom*.

The territorial Estates of this province below the Enns were carefully wooed by Maximilian, for they provided him with continued control over his richest revenues from agriculture in wine, fruits and cereals, as well as the customs dues from trade. But the province was also the most strategically vulnerable of his lands, with its open frontiers to Bohemia-Moravia and Hungary, so that Maximilian had a necessary interest to avoid internal conflict with his own territorial subjects there. An important regional government functioned from the *Hubhaus* in Vienna. It employed prominent members of the territorial Estates and it was never in practice subordinated to Maximilian's government at Innsbruck, nor to the officials of his travelling household, except in a very personal and *ad hoc* manner. The Vienna administration was as often as not held together by great territorial subjects like the Counts of Hardegg, marcher lords with lands stretching from the Czech frontier to the north in a great arc to the south-east, protecting Vienna from the Hungarian plains and the river-ways into Inner Austria. Count Henry of Hardegg was the younger brother of the very Sigismund Prüschenk who had been Maximilian's close friend in his youth and against whom the territorial Estates at Linz had banded themselves in 1493. The Prüschenks were employed to protect the Lower Austrian eastern border. Maximilian allowed them to create a state within a state. They were his most powerful subjects and his most substantial native creditors.[6]

Inner Austria comprised Styria, Carinthia, Carniola, the client Bishopric of Gurk and the escheated marcher lordship of Cilli. A substantial number of enclaves in Inner Austria belonging to the distant Bishoprics of Freising and Bamberg in the Bavarian and Franconian spheres of influence also guaranteed a certain degree of loyalty from these ecclesiastical states to Habsburg policies in the German empire. The largest single province, Styria had considerable mining wealth comparable with that of the Tirol, at least once the relatively advanced metallurgic manufacturing industries of Styria were taken into account. Styrian finished iron and alloy goods, such as blades, were used in farming as well as in war, and were exported all over Europe, as being of the best quality and finish of tempered metals made anywhere in Renaissance Europe.[7] Maximilian grew up at Wiener-Neustadt, at that time a Habsburg refuge from rebellious Vienna, on the borders of Lower Austria and Hungary, just inside the province of Styria. Many of the men who made careers in the service of Frederick III and Maximilian I were of Styrian or Tirolean noble origin, as was the case with the Prüschenks and Liechtensteins.

The main problem facing the inhabitants of later fifteenth-century Inner Austria was how to defend themselves against Turkish raids.[8] Most of the territorial assemblies of Styria, Carniola and Carinthia were called with this problem in mind. The level of taxation was consequently very high, and the need for military support from Maximilian meant that the Inner Austrian Estates were in no position to adopt strong policies in opposition to Habsburg officials at Graz, Judenburg, Laibach and St Veit. Under Maximilian, the south-eastern borders of Inner Austria continued to be the main area of incursion by the Turks. Maximilian personally organised and actually led one campaign against the Turkish raiders, an undertaking which was grandly termed a crusade at the time in 1493. Significantly, this campaign took place in Inner Austria, but it failed miserably in its efforts to seek and destroy any Turkish mercenaries. A fortified border with the Turks had still to wait for another generation and Maximilian, in effect, did nothing to protect his Inner Austrian subjects against the endemic slave-raids that the Turks operated from the Balkans. It was in Inner Austria that Maximilian was to face his most serious peasant revolts towards the end of his reign especially in 1515.[9]

5

Austria – the Population

Population figures for the reign of Maximilian I do not exist. The 1490s were, however, a time of experimentation with imperial poll-taxes. Detailed records listing subjects who paid poll-taxes at territorial state level, such as those of the Archbishopric of Salzburg, were partly examined before some of these archives were destroyed by bombing at Frankfurt-am-Main during the Second World War.[1] But not enough systematic work has been done, although many documents still survive. Thus we still have to resort to guesswork, and make inferences from information of neighbouring regions in order to substitute for Austrian estate and tax records which have either not survived, or were often not kept more systematically until the substantial growth of administration in the reign of Ferdinand I, Maximilian's successor in Austria. Whether by accident or design, the 1520s form a great divide in Austrian history perhaps for no other reason than that the records prior to this time are often far too haphazard for any serious quantification. As well as being inevitably crude, our demographical survey thus has to make use of some information from after the reign of Maximilian. It begs the question as to how rapid was change within pre-industrial early modern Austrian society, a problem to which we must return once more evidence has become available in order to modify the way in which materials have been used here.[2]

There were probably a million and a half inhabitants in the Habsburg Austrian lands ruled by Maximilian I. Lower Austria below the Enns (including Vienna) may have accounted for half a million and this made it the most populous of all the Habsburg provinces with one-third of the whole Austrian population. Next came Lower Austria above the Enns and Styria in Inner Austria with about 300,000 people each. Tirol and Carinthia had something over 100,000 each, with the Vorarlberg region on the Swiss border comprising only about 32,000 inhabitants. The neighbouring client state of Salzburg may have contained about 75,000 people. These figures presume errors of up to 20 per cent at the earliest point of calculation, 1527.[3]

With a population of one and a half million, Maximilian's Austria compared roughly with the combined populations of Scotland and Ireland. Habsburg Austria contained about one-ninth of the estimated total population of the German empire around the year 1500 and it was nearly twice as populous as the Swiss Confederation. Austria had perhaps one half the population of Tudor England and Wales. Valois France probably contained a population that was twelve times as large as that of the Austrian lands. The Italian peninsula was about seven times more populous than Austria.[4]

A recent estimate has been made of the number of taxable buildings in the Austrian lands around the year 1527. These could be more readily ascertained than actual population figures from estate and tax registers. There is no agreement about household sizes, although average multipliers fluctuate from four to seven souls for this period. Lower Austria below the Enns, including Vienna, had a probable housing stock of 80,000. Next came the province above the Enns with 56,000 dwellings, Styria with 41,000, Carinthia with 22,000, Tirol with 18,000, neighbouring Salzburg with 12,500 and Vorarlberg with a mere 7,000. According to late sixteenth-century urban evidence there were still only about twelve towns in Habsburg Austria that had more than three thousand inhabitants. Of these, Vienna may have had up to 50,000, with Steyr, Schwaz, Graz, Innsbruck and Wels at 5,000–9,000. Krems, Klagenfurt, Wiener-Neustadt, Linz, St Pölten and Klosterneuburg were estimated to have had between 3,000 and 5,000 people each.[5]

A recent study of the distribution of housing in Vienna for the mid-sixteenth century has to serve also as an indication for the other, more modest towns in Habsburg Austria some fifty years earlier. In 1563 just under 1,000 households of artisans and craftsmen were traced in the Vienna records. Forty per cent of these artisans and craftsmen owned the accommodation in which they lived. The rest rented their houses, flats or rooms. This social group was the backbone of the Viennese population, making up about a third of the static population, and occupying one-third of the traceable, owned and rented housing stock in the town.[6] Household sizes, including domestics and apprentices, as well as children and relatives, varied from two to twelve, averaging six souls for the higher social groups, and four per household for the rest.[7] About 10 per cent of the urban population, including officials and those calling themselves by the title of 'burgher', represented the upper social group. About 30 per cent of the population made up the middle group of small traders and craftsmen, and 60 per cent the lower group of domestics, labourers, lodgers and migrants. Six times as many people lived in the suburbs than lived inside the walls of the old town, although this changed during the time of the first Turkish siege of Vienna in 1529, as more of the well-to-do began to seek security behind the town wall.[8]

Naturally, Vienna was something of an exception as an urban centre as it was anything up to five times as populous as its next Austrian rivals. In the mid-fifteenth century, when Vienna was still the residence of the Habsburg court, it is estimated that court and nobility, clergy and university totalled more than one-quarter of the whole population, roughly equal in size to all those who called themselves 'burghers'. The 'burghers' comprised town council families, merchants, guildsmen and even craftsmen. Almost half the population made up the lower stratum, including labourers, domestics, Jews, carters and persons in the transport trade, poor folk in recognised institutions, licensed beggars and women, generally self-employed or more specifically earning a living as prostitutes.[9]

6

Standards of Life

What do the records tell us about the living standards of Maximilian's subjects? Can we focus on any detailed evidence, despite the unsuitability of the sources when we try to seek from them answers to questions of a social nature, more applicable to evidence deposited by advanced, modern societies like our own? What was life like for the ordinary person in Austria around 1500? The question is easy to ask and the answers can perhaps only be vague. However, question and attempted answers may be considered to be essential, for if the matter is not raised as one goes to the archives, then one wipes off the face of history about nine-tenths of all human beings who have ever lived. Yet can one really produce social history from records that were not created or kept for any ideological or humanitarian purposes? The student of early modern societies is bound by unsuitable, fragmented and pragmatic documents, which he interprets with little hope of any ultimate accuracy. This factor goes some way towards explaining why many writers have tended to avoid the simplifications and guesswork that sometimes lie behind social history, and here German and Austrian historians have not usually shown any lack of caution.[1] Undoubtedly any plan to follow up questions that are strictly unsuitable to the archives that survive is dangerous. A start has to be made, however, and we will look at the urban situation, then examine conditions in the countryside and in the mines, looking further at pre-industrial labour, and include a full survey of life at the court of Maximilian and his second wife, Bianca Maria Sforza. This court was probably the largest single enterprise within the tertiary sector of the pre-industrial Austrian economy, and it gives a significant insight into the ruling attitudes towards handling domestics, old-age pensioners and the deserving poor – above all, as seen through the eyes of Maximilian himself.

Our method is to let archive materials speak for themselves. Considering the lack of evidence that we have so far from the period, it becomes essential to provide the reader with case studies, and to shun theoretical interpretations until we know more social-historical facts of life and labour in this transitional period from Renaissance to Reformation and Counter-Reformation. This chapter, then, raises general issues which should be kept in mind to orientate the reader for the immediately following detailed chapters.

For the cities, good communications were vital. Due to the unhealthy conditions of urban overcrowding, towns were net consumers of immigrants, above all from surrounding farms, villages and smaller towns and markets. Although towns did not encourage social mobility, they certainly facilitated a great deal of geographical mobility. Their markets, shopping, manufactures and professional services also occupied those labouring families who were able to satisfy the standards set by traditional craft, guild and mercantilist authorities, headed by the oligarchic town councils themselves. When an urban community was prosperous, it tended to foster long-distance trade. In the case of the Augsburg textile industry, raw materials were imported, and finished goods were sent out. In the case of Viennese *entrepôt* activity, textiles, cattle and wine converged on the city, were shuttled, exchanged and then sent on their way again. After 1509 in particular the Venetian War disrupted Vienna's prosperity. Leading merchants petitioned Maximilian accordingly in 1512.[2] Where a town had more modest horizons, it tended to specialise in the local victualling trades and in the smaller local crafts. Thus Wels had few merchants, but many inn-keepers, butchers, cobblers, tailors and the like for local needs, whilst its leading burghers were these very same small craftsmen and retailers. Even a town like Innsbruck, acting as a capital for Maximilian's government, had a real problem controlling its own middlemen in the food and drink trades, as shown with legislation against bakers in chapter 12. Ultimately, there was little room for growth and perhaps even less for innovation in Maximilian's cities, towns and urban markets due to the very success of the severely unimaginative, deflationary and restrictive economic policies of master-guilds and councils. The opportunities of a Dick Whittington remained largely a myth in the towns of Austria around the year 1500, as shown from an analysis of ordinary urban life in chapter 7, taken from the records of the Viennese burghers' hospital.

If life was by no means secure in town, then it was even more capricious in the open country. Especially in Inner Austria, Maximilian's officials faced two inherited problems. Firstly, there were the continued invasions of the Turks, marauding from Bosnia, which had led already to serious peasant unrest against the rule of Frederick III in 1476 for his government's failure, despite the levying of heavy direct arbitrary taxation, to protect them. Secondly, most of the Habsburg high jurisdictions had been alienated to nobles and clergy in Styria, Carniola and Carinthia, many of them to courtiers and therefore to absentee landlords. It affected the peasants' quality of life in that they came under a particularly capricious patrimonial jurisdiction which restricted their rights of appeal and made the imposition upon them of harsher land and excise taxes, in the interests of an inefficient provincial anti-Turk defence system, all the easier for the provincial territorial assemblies of their landlords. Maximilian, to be fair, tried to circumvent trouble, especially in his travels in Inner Austria in 1514 – the year *before* the great peasant uprisings there – by paying more personal attention to ordinary estate management over his serf tenant farmers on his own domains, which is shown with the land-tax register analysed in chapter 8. But he did not keep up the personal pressure. Maximilian's finances were too overburdened by more weighty dynastic and foreign diplomatic and military policies for him to provide directly effective paternalist rule over his Inner Austrian peasants. Their interests were bargained away to rapacious courtiers – burgher, noble and ecclesiastical – in return for services rendered to the Crown elsewhere.

The true test of Maximilian's propagandistic popularity came with very brutal peasant revolts in Inner Austria

51

between March and August 1515. They formed part of a regional central and south-east European crisis, stretching from the Upper Rhinelands and Swabia through to Hungary. It was created by the harsher exploitation of feudal rents and services, as landlords and overlords rivalled each other by moving out of mere estate management and into territorial state-building. Towns and markets had had more financial power to accommodate themselves to this drive for newly centralised authority by supplying trained lawyers, fiscal and educational officials at court, *Landtag*, committee and commission levels of executive control. Peasants retaliated by forming secret societies to combat the pull of this new, urban-centred prerogative authoritarianism. Peasant conspiracies were thus a hall-mark of Maximilian's reign. As shown on Map 2.1, secret societies like the peasants' 'Laced Boot', with its own flags, signs, insignia, rituals and oaths, spread across the regions of Habsburg territorial and diplomatic influence from Alsace in 1493 down the Rhine to Speier in 1502; from the traditionally anti-Habsburg lands of the Swiss in 1513, back into the Upper Rhineland around Freiburg-im-Breisgau, and on to Baden and Württemberg. In these regions the secret societies of the *Bundschuh*, 'Laced Boot', and *Arme Conrad* – a 'Poor Conrad' *jacquerie* – took on the anarchic moral self-justification of the countryman against constituted authority, because of the unplanned and unreliable exercise of power by Maximilian and his fellow territorial rulers, officials and landlords both ecclesiastical and lay. In their yearning for custom, for the good old law, the peasants wanted more swift and efficient government – but in *their* interests of tenancy, profit and property. What an ideal! The governed wanted altruistic governors, and were accordingly rewarded with brutal oppression.

In Alsace, especially at Schlettstadt, Maximilian lent all his prerogative power as territorial and royal overlord to the urban city councils to put down peasant and artisan unrest, above all by closer supervision of inns, strict closing hours, swift curfew, suppression of public meetings and more effective mobilisation of mercenary Landsknechts, garrisoned at the expense of town councils.[3] That the problem was endemic is shown with the need to rehabilitate the rank and file of peasants after each conspiracy, provided that sufficient ring-leaders had been made an example of and executed. It encouraged the people to obedience, as happened with the royal pardon to former members of the 'Laced Boot' on 13 August 1496.[4] The appointment of an executioner, as shown in chapter 12, was thus an important event, something well worth publicising. Peasant truculence was the reply. They made slow payment of taxes in kind, and quibbled over customary duties in respect of payments like carnival chickens and rabbits in February, lambs at Easter, through to the more bountiful stooks of corn in tithe during August, and best animals in blood-tithe at butchering time in November. It all meant that peasant riots could flare up, as indeed they frequently did, at any time of the year. There was a low threshold of violence, understood by peasant and official alike, which is a theme running through chapter 8 on rural life.

Maximilian was not the only ruler, in his time, to face this problem. His overburdening direct taxation to pay for ambitious wars and alliances was emulated by all the territorial rulers of his day. So, too, was peasant unrest in return, and it is worth repeating the point that a very high level of crime with violence was the normal state of affairs. In its turn, this made swift, arbitrary, royal prerogative justice very desirable to all who had any property to protect. That applied to the serf peasants themselves, caught in the unhappy and contradictory trap of wishing to keep a low level of customary taxation whilst demanding more efficient – and therefore more tax-expensive – exercise of justice from their madly centralising rulers. Here Maximilian stands out because of his formal power as head of the Holy Roman Empire, especially at Reichstag level, and because of his dynamic, hard-working personality and nature as an extrovert in politics and administration. When the neighbouring ruler, Ulrich of Württemberg, failed to cope with his rebellious peasants as a consequence of the lingering 'Poor Conrad' conspiracy of 1514, Maximilian set into motion, via his client regional police force, the Swabian League, a Habsburg counsel of advice which was to develop into a caretaker government until 1534 under Charles V and Ferdinand.[5]

Just as an assessment of religious development in the era of

Maximilian is overshadowed by the events of Luther and Charles V at Wittenberg and Worms, 1517 and 1521, so too are the peasant revolts of this earlier period dwarfed by the events of 1525, which themselves were so inextricably linked with matters of religious action and justification.[6] Our problem is to let the peasants of the Maximilian era speak to us in their own right, for they surely did not see themselves, when they formed their secret societies once again in the 1490s, as forerunners of something much grander thirty years later when church and state briefly began to fall apart. Big events have a way of blighting periods immediately preceding them. The years 1517, 1521, 1525 have done just that, and no worse example can be found than that of the 'Laced Boot' and 'Poor Conrad' in relationship to the Peasant War of 1525.

To this one may add the Inner Austrian rebellion of 1515, for by the time of that explosion Maximilian had raised the taxes in such a way that extraordinary territorial assembly grants, paid almost exclusively by the peasants and urban markets, had become an annual, monthly and even, at times, weekly burden. He had alienated his powers to rapacious creditors, mostly his prelate and noble courtiers. He had failed to protect the open countryside from Turkish raids. He had destroyed trade by closing the frontiers with Italy due to his unnecessary wars with Venice, the leading commercial centre of south-east Europe. It had driven interest rates to impossible heights, overburdening peasants with heavy mortgages not offset by new market outlets for their produce. One could almost say that a very 'Chinese' style of rural, market, secret society activity was the natural outcome, here in the heart of Renaissance Europe.[7] The Habsburg peasant truculence, examples of which are dealt with in chapter 8, was the more widespread result.

If Maximilian could, therefore, hardly expect to increase his revenues from town and country because of the very inflexibility of guild mercantilism and feudal agriculture, where was he to turn for desperately needed cash and supplies? His future lay in exploiting the mining wealth of his alpine lands, made buoyant by sheer good fortune at that very time, in order to create the bullion and creditworthiness needed to finance his expanding courts, governments and armies. Chapter 9 shows the opportunities and difficulties which he experienced in this task. Firstly, as Maximilian himself admitted in his personal correspondence to Cousin Sigismund of Tirol in the early 1490s, he was immensely fortunate in finding so much new mineral wealth in Styria, Carinthia and Tirol, from both old and new seams and workings of silver, copper, iron, lead and salt. The Inn Valley and its tributaries were his treasure chest, and with the real help of the Fuggers, by whom he was by no means so easily outmanoeuvred, as has often been suggested by writers who have not studied Pölnitz carefully enough, Maximilian was able to establish himself as a great power in Innsbruck and Augsburg. The remarkably modern methods of division of labour in the mines of Maximilian's client archiepiscopal state of Salzburg, combined with the awkward labour relations at Gossensass in Tirol during 1493, as examined in chapter 9, show us that the industry was the true career of opportunity, of capitalistic exploitation and self-help in a very nineteenth-century sense (as only we could say it), in these Austrian Renaissance years around 1500. Here, standards of life could break the bounds of traditional inflexibility, lack of growth and endemic insecurity as experienced in town, market and countryside still based upon existing techniques of medieval farming and manufacture. Like any modern businessman, Maximilian exploited up to the hilt his mining, bullion and fiscal opportunities, and in chapter 9 the verbatim documentation of the 1493 strike against lower wages and increased productivity shows that there was nothing 'backward' about his mining industry.[8]

Naturally, the main court household, centred on the refurbished fifteenth-century *Hofburg*, which perched on the rim of Innsbruck town between the citizens' houses and the fast-flowing River Inn, benefited from the mining boom along that very river valley. However, Maximilian had greater ambitions than merely to run a provincial court in a solvent manner. True, he spent much on his hunting castles, as at Spaur and Fragenstein, often staffed by his bastard children and, in due course of time, by their progeny.[9] Yet his extremely ungenerous financial arrangements for his second wife, Bianca Maria Sforza, who had brought him a massive dowry from Milan, show that wherever possible Maximilian would cut corners once he was assured of the loyalty and dependence of his own employees and subjects, high and low alike. Life at his court was indeed more secure for the ordinary male and female worker, as the dinner registers show, than it was in a craft, at a mine or on a farm; but it was dragooned, communal and no doubt at times institutionally petty and humiliating. In the regular few weeks of the year that Maximilian spent at Innsbruck, he probably spent most of his energy in adjudicating in ludicrous squabbles between his domestic and secretarial staff, and between them, the inn-keepers and journeymen of the town itself.[10] An unseemly episode was the brawling that took place among court servants and townsmen over a homosexual affair involving Michael Schuster, Michael am Galian and a less attractive character with the name of Newly Noble, *Neulich Edl*, which came up for adjudication in front of Innsbruck court officials in 1492.[11] Such material, scattered through the archives, shows that thresholds of violence may have been just as low at court and in town, as they were, certainly at times of tax-collection, troop movement, bad weather, bad health and bad harvest, in the open countryside.

Yet the surplus revenues from mining wealth did give servants at court an added degree of security. The salt rents that Maximilian authorised for payment to old-age pensioners at court,[12] above all, as reconstructed through the prosopography of Margreth Wuestin in chapter 11, demonstrate that service at court, despite lack of regular pay and clothing, offered a safe haven by the standards generally pertaining in the job-world of 1500.

This leads us to an examination of psychological factors which always determined the amount of confidence that a population had in its beliefs and in its government and leadership stemming from those ever-volatile relationships between secure economy, secure status and secure belief. We try to uncover elements of that by providing insights into the everyday regulating of economy and society in the practical politics of chapter 12, inextricably entwined with the necessities of nature and subjectivism of mentality experimentally provided in chapter 13.

The uncertainties of the growth-cycle naturally led to the unimaginativeness of organised agriculture, craft manufacture, transport and retail trade, balanced against the sudden and fleeting opportunities of mining, which allowed sporadic conspicuous consumption, warfare and endless travelling ('traipsing around' or *vmbzotln*, as Maximilian called it). Maximilian did not keep perpetually on the move because he was an old-fashioned, medieval ruler, any more than Henry Kissinger and Jimmy Carter jetted between America and the Middle East in the 1970s because they did not trust the postal system. The herculean tasks of bureaucracy which Maximilian carried out every working day of his adult life, were linked inevitably to his Habsburg dynastic cosmology of astrology and Bible, gnosticism, miracles and faith, which seemed to make it all very well worth while to Maximilian himself, and probably also to the majority of his Austrian and German subjects. For Maximilian was the stereotype bureaucrat, who did not lack the conventional attributes of faith. He was always depicted in church up at the front, and then larger than life. His hunting castles, where inventories survive, all include a writing stand or desk in his personal rooms, along with a bed, bedding, weaponry and precious little else. He was conventionally half-learned and superstitious, as only the typically extrovert man-of-action can be: an open-faced gnostic who loved red tape, rules and regulations, plus a bit of fun for himself. Aspects of this are given above all in chapter 11 with his unrealistic last will and testament, where he sought to provide charity to the *menu-peuple* in the eleventh hour before his own death, if only to glorify his name here below in posterity, then all the more securely to enter the gates of heaven up above in eternity. The overriding uncertainties of the age are encompassed at chapter 13, seeking in a new way for a biography of the life and times sort to bridge the gap between nature and astrology, science and belief, as the courtiers and rulers of Tirol sought to predict the immediate future for themselves with elaborate prognostication.

7

The City

A recent study argues that the relationship between real prices and wages for the unspecified labourer in the German regions, as well as the amount of regular work available to such a person, was so favourable in the fifteenth century that he achieved a level of well-being that was not reached again by his descendants until well into our own century. During the course of the sixteenth century, crucially selective price increases began to cut the value of wages and this trend continued inexorably until the era of industrialisation towards the end of the nineteenth century. In other words, common standards of living reached a high point in the reign of Maximilian I and from there they continued to fall for nearly four hundred years, before picking up and reaching all-time record levels in our own century.[1] The decline of wages in terms of purchasing power is calculated for the course of the sixteenth century, and it seems that the main cause of this decline in common living standards was the continued increase in population, on which so much more research has yet to be done.[2] As there were relatively more people than there were jobs, those in work had to be grateful increasingly for any economic conditions that they were offered. For example, in 1548 the Estates of County Lippe, acting as employers and sitting in their local parliament in Westphalia, north-west Germany, discussed this problem as recorded in their minutes:[3]

> Since the serious damage of poverty has created a great
> mass of day-labourers and servants, that neither the
> landlords nor anyone can pay necessary day-wages or

servants' keep, let alone provide enough food, we
recommend that our gracious lord [i.e. the government]
provide us for the good of everyone with a decreed policy
[*Ordnung*] outlining to what extent the landlord is liable for
providing food, and what each and everyone should earn in
day-rates or other wages.

Using evidence already collected in the 1930s as part of a
history of wages and prices in early modern Germany and
Austria, statistics have been produced for towns like Nuremberg, Augsburg, Cologne, Frankfurt-am-Main and Vienna. In
Hamburg, for example, the official wages of carpenters and
weavers rose by 40 per cent during the sixteenth century,
whilst the price of their basic foodstuff, ryemeal for black
bread, rose by 380 per cent. Similar trends were traced for
England, France, the Low Countries and Poland.[4] What had
happened, one wonders, to the favourable wage situation
recorded at the end of the fifteenth century? Can we believe
that Nuremberg, for example, which was recently optimistically described for the period of 1470 to 1500 as having few
families crowded close to one another and as providing
acceptable conditions of work, sufficient pay at least for a
daily meat dish, except on fast days when there was ample
fresh and salted fish, was by no means exceptional with two
meat courses per day? And this study was not centred
exclusively on the richer town burghers and town council
families.[5]

In graphs produced for the sixteenth century, wages have
been calculated as the cost of a man's labour, and, therefore,
as an aspect of prices in general. This wage-as-price line dips,
becomes horizontal, or at best rises gently in a way similar to
the price lines of manufactured goods. The line for cereals, as
essential, high-calorie foods, climbs steeply off the page as the
century wears on. In sixteenth-century Austria it is estimated
that wages remained constant, that manufactured goods rose
by one quarter at most, whilst cereal prices increased by an
average of two and a half times. Even so, a building worker at
the end of the sixteenth century could still earn, in a full day's
work, the equivalent of 23,000 calories of rye, pease or beans.
If he used his wages to buy meat and dairy products, then he

only earned enough to purchase 7,000 calories.[6] The conclusion from this is that, although meat prices did not rise, they remained beyond the reach of ordinary family budgets. However much cereal prices rose, flour products were still the best buy in calorific terms. The more that cereal prices rose, the less the labourer and his dependants could afford to buy anything else. Perhaps the problem is not so much to trace the depressing decline of real wages in early modern times, as to question how this decline came about, and indeed whether the working family was really quite well off *before* this economic decline was firmly under way.[7]

As the transition is put around the year 1500, the records of the reign of Maximilian I become of crucial importance. We will examine some of them, with these two questions, above all, in mind. Firstly, is the gloomy picture of wage decline from the fifteenth to the twentieth century exaggerated? Secondly, is the picture of work and plenty that was given for later fifteenth-century Nuremberg, if extended to the towns of the empire as a whole, perhaps not an overoptimistic view of common standards of living at the end of the medieval era?

An overall analysis of the price and wage lists in Pribram's study of fifteenth- and sixteenth-century Austrian evidence, covering Vienna and the two provinces of Lower Austria, gives the following trend. The ratio of high wages to prices was probably at its most advantageous to the worker in the mid-fifteenth century. There was a dip in this prosperity in the 1470s, recovery up to the 1510s and a decline once more in the 1520s to a position worse than that of the 1470s. In the 1530s the situation steadily deteriorated for the wage-earner as one depressing decade was followed by another. Looking back over the early modern centuries of 'hard times' for labouring families, the 1520s provide a watershed. These years seem to have been the last time for centuries that Viennese labourers could earn enough to live well. How tenable is this view?

The Vienna *Bürgerspital*, or town charity hospital, has left careful records of its housekeeping.[8] Its commissioners paid six to eight kreuzers a day, plus keep, to journeymen builders and carpenters between 1440 and 1540 in the summer time. The kreuzer was worth four pfennigs. The 'without-food' wage rate was between one-twelfth and two-thirds higher than the net rate of pay with meals included. Winter rates were a standard one kreuzer below summer rates, and summertime operated for two-thirds of the year for all labouring jobs that the *Bürgerspital* provided. Apprentices received one-half to one whole kreuzer a day less than journeymen. A master craftsman was paid only one kreuzer a day more than the journeyman. The tilers (*Ziegeldecker*) were the best paid among the Vienna *Bürgerspital*'s work force. A journeyman tiler netted ten kreuzers a day between 1440 and 1540, an indication, no doubt, of the hazards of his trade. The navvy only earned four to five kreuzers a day.

Agricultural labour in the *Bürgerspital*'s fields outside the city was on the whole less rewarding, although harvesters usually received their keep as well as pay. This, of course, made economic sense in that it ensured that labourers were not impaired by hunger from working to full capacity in the day. The state of their dependants who had to exist on their take-home pay did not seem to have concerned the employer. The skilled vineyard worker received two and a half to six kreuzers a day, but at harvest-time this could go down to one and a quarter kreuzers a day, as seasonal labour and the generally favourable weather and time of year presented vineyard overseers with a superabundance of labour.

Other harvesting rates were according to piece-work (*Accordlohn*) – still standard practice today. One and a half kreuzers were paid for chopping one *Fuder* of fire-wood, about thirty-two heavy baskets full. In contrast to this slave-rate, scything and stooking, as perhaps the most physically exhausting of all jobs, were suitably well-rewarded at fifteen kreuzers a day. The scyther had to stay on a first-class diet, and as the economy ultimately depended on the speed and thoroughness of his work in the corn fields, he commanded a good wage for a job that had to be well done. This equally applied to the thresher who could earn between ten and twelve kreuzers for every thirty *Metzen* (1350 litres dry measure) of ready grain that he flailed on the granary floor. In 1470 threshers were briefly asked to provide their own keep and the *Bürgerspital* paid them an unusually high rate of twenty-two kreuzers a day.

Yet these high rates were only paid to the skilled and

healthy labourer at harvest time. High earnings for brief periods of the year had to tide labouring families over the weeks and months of relatively low employment with the inevitably serious petty debts that this entailed for their family economy. At the *Bürgerspital* only the carpenters and builders had regular, full-time employment. A number of navvies were hired according to need for periods of time fluctuating between several days to several hundred days a year. Although there was a certain degree of job security for the workers hired by the *Bürgerspital*, in that they knew that they would be hired every year, yet they never knew with certainty for how long any one period of employment would last or when exactly they would next be called upon.

The relatively highly paid tilers were employed for between twenty and a hundred days every year by the *Bürgerspital* in the period between 1452 and 1778. This left room for a great deal of economic uncertainty, as a tiler needed more than one employer, but enough idle time to be on call to do jobs for regular customers, like the commissioners of the Vienna *Bürgerspital*. A vineyard worker, on the other hand, was more sure of the time and duration of his work. In accordance with the fairly predictable growth-cycle of the crop, his services were usually only called upon in March and April. Whereas the scyther and thresher picked up most of their year's pay in the autumn, the skilled vine-pruner and tier earned most of his in springtime. No doubt also the tiler found that he had most work in the gusty late autumns, notorious in the region.

Full employment, regular pay and job security meant greatly different things in practice to each early modern employer and to each of his labourers. How did the best day-wages of full summertime employment compare with the prices of high-calorie foods? Once again we are fortunate in that the Vienna *Bürgerspital* left detailed accounts. However, this institution could buy in bulk and therefore more cheaply than the labourer, craftsman or their wives buying tiny amounts at retail cost daily in the markets and small shops. Assuming, for lack of shopkeepers' actual price records, that the day labourer could buy flour at the same favourable rates as could the commissioners for the *Bürgerspital*, and assuming full summertime employment, then the journeyman builder with his maximum eight kreuzers a day without keep earned on average the equivalent of twenty-four pounds of rye flour per day. Naturally this equivalent does not take into account the cost of clothing and heating, let alone loss of earnings through illness, underemployment and unemployment. The navvy at that time would have had a maximum earning power of eighteen pounds of rye flour a day. This is reckoned from the recorded cost of rye flour to the *Bürgerspital*, which ran at between one-third and one-half a kreuzer per pound in the later 1520s and earlier 1530s.

Fernand Braudel has estimated that a Mediterranean labourer needed one and a quarter pounds of cereals daily to keep fit for work around the year 1600.[9] This condition was certainly met, indeed with plenty to spare, by the Viennese workmen of the 1520s, at least judging from the *Bürgerspital*'s records.[10] Always providing that the employee was in full employment, he could still earn enough in the Vienna of the late and immediately post Maximilian era to feed a family of ten if need be. This picture loses its theoretical cosiness, however, if we consider not only price increases, but also price fluctuations. For example, within the period 1520–40, wheat flour ranged in price from one third of a kreuzer to two and two-thirds kreuzers per pound, which represented an eight-fold fluctuation within a mere two decades. Looking at the generation of 1520–40 in retrospect, what use is it to estimate an average of two-thirds of a kreuzer per pound for this commodity when even one month of unusually high cereal prices could lead to hunger and perhaps to a weakened labour force, whose resistance to disease would be seriously eroded.

Although day wage rates remained fairly constant between 1440 and 1540, or rose only slightly, high-calorie commodity prices rose far more rapidly. In 1440 wheat stood at five kreuzers per *Metzen* (that is, per forty-five litres dry measure). By the 1530s its price was between thirteen and thirty-six kreuzers per *Metzen*, entailing a near three- to seven-fold price increase, on top of a large price fluctuation of up to eight times. In terms of price rise over almost one century this looks puny indeed to us today, but then our price inflation has up to now at least always been accompanied by an even greater wage inflation. This was, however, not the case in fifteenth-

and sixteenth-century Vienna, where the workman had to suffer price inflation without accompanying wage increases. Uncertain climate and harvest were natural causes of price fluctuation, but to these factors had to be added demographic, political and military uncertainties and upheavals. Vienna and its fertile plain were under threat and then under siege from the Turks in the 1520s, and prices consequently fluctuated drastically.

At such times, as the price of flour shot up to seventy-eight kreuzers per *Metzen*, the Viennese housewife turned to alternative foods. Oatmeal was one resort at a cattle-fodder price of under three kreuzers per *Metzen*. This soon reached seven kreuzers and when it became too expensive in its turn, there were always cabbages as a last resort, costing one pfennig (one-quarter kreuzer) each in the early 1530s, or sweet turnips at three kreuzers per *Metzen* in 1463, rising to eleven kreuzers in 1530. For the price rise tended to hit the poorer and cheaper foodstuffs even harder than the better quality goods, as demand for, say, cabbages and turnips rose and demand for flour products fell, proving that times of dearth display a peculiar economic logic of their own. In more normal times the better paid and more secure worker sent his wife to market to buy high-grade flour which increased *three-fold* in price in Vienna between 1469 and 1536. The poorer and less job-secure worker made do with commodities like sweet turnips, the price of which increased *four-fold* over the same period of time.

Bürgerspital price lists are by no means exhausted by this brief survey. We have concentrated on the more popular high-calorie commodities, as they determine the balance between health and sickness, life and death to the labourer and his family. It was less important for the labouring family to know the price of a sheep or the cost of prunes by the hundredweight, for they could not afford either. The employers, on the other hand, were more interested, for they could afford them. Meat prices, for example, hardly rose at all during the whole period, and this indicates that the social rift between the haves and the have-nots was deepening. In the 1520s in Vienna one pound of beef was the same price as three pounds of rye flour and, given the wage rates, the common family could afford the one or the other, not both. In calorie terms, beef was, of course, a foolhardy buy for a family who budgeted just above the hunger line.

Naturally the common housewife had to go for the bargain in the market place, and the chance of survival that her family had was probably quite frequently dependent on her skill in switching to alternative cereals when high grade flour and rye products, for example, became too expensive. As her family economy was dependent on day wages, it seems unlikely that she could buy in bulk when food was cheap or put anything by for a rainy day. The common family was thus subject to the full impact of day-to-day market forces. To relieve his insecurity, the labourer was given the dubious blessing of cheap, fixed-price beer by the town council, an arrangement which, one may feel sure, only caused his family further hardship. Institutions like the *Bürgerspital* manufactured and offered for sale in their tap-rooms a fixed-price brew to the working man. The constant price no doubt entailed fluctuations and deterioration in quality, but the town's politicians must have regarded this as a lesser evil than the one that they would face at the hands of the crowd if they increased the price of beer.

The evidence from the *Bürgerspital* for the period 1440–1540 strongly indicates that a price rise occurred which was indeed more steep than any wage increase. The fact is, however, that in those one hundred years it was still possible for the labourer to earn enough to feed his nuclear family, regardless of its size, provided, of course, that he remained in full employment and in good health. Price increases had thus not seriously begun to pauperise commoners in Vienna during the earlier part of the sixteenth century. As time went on, wives certainly had to be more careful with their buying, and if the daily meat course that has been surmised for Nuremberg had ever been a reality, then it would have disappeared long before 1540, even among a relatively prosperous work-force like the Viennese. However, as we shall see in chapter 11, the *menu-peuple* were offered some minimal security, as in the case of old-age pensioner Margreth Wuestin, but it all depended on the conventional Christian conscience of her employer – in this case the grand figure of King Maximilian himself. Chapter 9 also shows that in the more dynamic mining industries employees could and did go on strike for more pay and better conditions of work. A combination of volatile labour relations, insecurities of weather, harvest, health, production and employment naturally led to very low thresholds of violence, as skinners of Scheibbs probably pointed out to the Carthusian employer-monks in rural Austria. This is a speculation from an episode in the next chapter.

8

Rural Life: Thresholds of Violence

The Vintschgau is a high mountain valley in South Tirol where in 1499 on the Calva Maximilian experienced his most humiliating defeat at the hands of neighbouring Swiss peasants and mercenaries, whom he had attempted to oppress with illegal taxes and with pettifogging. Vintschgau agriculture was organised from the church towers of fortified townships that spread down to Meran. From the fifteenth century peasant life was regimented as parishes kept strict hours of work and rest during the day by ringing bells which echoed down the valley and up to the high pastures. At weekends no work was permitted between 3 p.m. on Saturday and 3 p.m. on Sunday, with an extension of one hour in summer-time at the lower end of the valley, and a two-hour earlier start and finish in higher settlements. Summertime was longest at altitudes well below one thousand metres, where it ran from St George's Day (23 April) to Martinmas (11 November). At around the thousand-metre mark, summer was shortened from St Veit's (15 June) until Michaelmas (29 September). On the highest pastures summer ran merely from St Jacob's (25 July) to St Bartholomew's (24 August), the month in which cattle grazed close to the mountain tops, beyond the tree line. Fines were levied for unnecessarily ignoring the church bells' call to rest. In Maximilian's reign the minimum fine was a day's labouring wage – anything up to twelve kreuzers.[1] Work at night or during holy-days was forbidden unless prior permission was purchased from the authorities. Bakers had their ovens inspected at least once a month in spot-checks which could imply more than just a sensible fire-precaution. Any house with a hearth could be visited at any time by ruler's and landlord's bailiffs.

By minute control of time and place of work, the authorities knew who was producing what, when and where, and at what price, quantity and quality. Everyone was regulated in his work-shop, fields and meadows at parish level. In the interests of fire-precaution there was also no inviolable privacy at the hearth. How then could peasants riot or rebel? It did not happen without connivance at least from some local headmen, elders or *Schöffen*, bailiffs and parish clergy, themselves disenchanted at times of high crisis, caused by local shifts in weather, health, harvest and warfare. At such times the leaders of a community could become as demoralised as their charges, feeling that their overlords in the towns and fortified castles, whether ruling prince, prelate, noble and patrician, had overtaxed and underprotected them and their charges.

What were the living standards of country folk? The Austrian archives are full of estate records (*Urbare*) and from the 1490s alone several thousand survive, yet their analysis for social history as a whole has hardly begun. However, we do have some details from the period around 1500, and it is worth looking at examples to indicate the value of these sources. The *Urbar* or estate record of Ortenburg from 1499 gives evidence of conflict between Habsburg bailiffs and peasants over rents and tenancies. The bailiffs were interested in increasing the duties of the peasants and began to record services which were claimed to have been carried out in the past and which the current generation of tenant farmers would need to be coerced to do again. For example, 'Note, near Woltspuhl is a meadow that the Maltzpulhers and all those who live nearby *should* mow, harvest and deliver to my Lord.'[2] The *Urbar's* purpose was to increase the landlord's income at the tenant's expense.[3]

Like many estate records of the time, the 1499 *Urbar* of Ortenburg in Inner Austria lists the duties of tenant farmers – in this case 124 of them – but it is especially interesting in that it brings to light a conflict between tenants and bailiffs, leading to the removal of at least one recalcitrant tenant which must have been a common occurrence at the time. Surprisingly, Maximilian I is also named as having taken an interest in the case. Here emperor and peasant come face to face.[4] It is worth examining the document that wound up the original charge of tenant disobedience some ten years later.[5]

Item, Lienhart Zott used to pay annual rent of five pounds
of pennies for his tenant-farm in the Liser, and for this our
most gracious Lord the Roman Emperor and King has
given him another farm in exchange, called the farm at
Oberaich near Väschendorf which Christian Räss rents at
the annual rates [there follows the list of rents in kind] . . .
Concluded by Imperial and Royal fiat, will and wish,
recorded by this letter.

Elsewhere in the same *Urbar*, peasants are reported to have
refused to pay the increase in their rents. We know from the
fate of Lienhart Zott that the least they could expect was a
summary termination of their farming contract. Zott was
fortunate to receive another farm. This *Urbar* reflects the kind
of peasant truculence that must be seen as the most common
start to more politically serious protest, depending on whether
the local authorities would be forced by the extent of their
debts to the treasury to make an issue of the matter. The
following are reported to have been perhaps typical peasant
replies in the bailiffs' *Urbar* entries: 'but he is not prepared to
pay so much rent', 'he gives no chickens or hares', 'now he is
not prepared to pay so much'.[6]
It is clear that in the Ortenburg region in 1499, 124 tenant
farmers were being assessed for more rent. Equally, Maximilian, as the direct landlord, informed himself of the affair. His
involvement in the machinations of Europolitics thus did not
exclude an interest in common estate management. In
Ortenburg those peasants who refused to pay what the
officials considered full rents were also prepared to speak their
minds. Having done so, they could expect (as did Zott) to be
moved out of their holdings. Whether they would then obtain
a new farm was up to the labour market and the whim of
official and landlord. In Zott's case Maximilian intervened in
his favour, a great moment indeed for the humble serf-peasant
family, as the myth came true and they received judgment
seemingly handed down from the emperor himself.
An *Urbar* entry like the one from Ortenburg concerning
Lienhart Zott can help to throw light upon the human beings
whose labour and produce was the basis of the whole
economy, which was essential to the workings of government

and society. It was the peasant producer-manager who made possible what the records of state tell us about the politics and diplomacy of the period. Let us be clear that without the peasant-manager, without the serf-tenant farmer, there would be no records at all. Of course, no one really disputes the idea that the economic basis of early modern society lies in its peasants and labourers, their work, produce and taxes. What is perhaps still in dispute is the claim that the records of early modern labour relations and living standards are sufficient to allow a reconstruction of the history of the common man which would be neither banal nor misleading. The economic and fiscal archives still lie fallow. However, in order to strengthen this claim and show what rich finds are yet to be uncovered in the documents, we turn to an example of a mundane early modern labour dispute.

In 1510 the Carthusians at Gaming in Lower Austria were in conflict with their employees, butchers and skinners. Scribbled between the boards of his price-guide for the buying and selling of commodities, the Carthusian master of purchases left record of his plan of action. He would ask what neighbouring skinners were receiving, before deciding whether or not his own employees' demands for better pay and sustenance were unfair. He wrote:[7]

> The skinners notify that from skinning they hardly earn more than ten pfennigs a day [i.e. their take-home pay is two and a half kreuzers]. Instead they want one pfennig for each skin. We must ask the other skinners at Scheibbs, namely Master Paul and Master Ruprecht about this. Whilst they are at work they insist on having lots of wine to drink.

Underlying such a dispute are the general problems, firstly, of what living standards were like, and secondly, how did they accord with the aspirations of employer and employee, landlord and tenant. The general view is that if conditions were worsening in towns and markets with all their trading and financial resources, then village and farm communities could be even worse off. The organisation of credit never favoured the villager and tenant-farmer, let alone the agricultural labourer. For example, the peasants of Styria were paying interest at four pennies per week on each pound of pennies they borrowed during the later fifteenth century. It represented an interest charge of 80 per cent per annum, and led to sporadic pogroms against local Jewish communities, accused of harbouring usurious, ungodly money-lenders. These rural and open-market pogroms were a vicious amortisation of peasant bankruptcy, whereby Jewish small creditors paid, often with their lives, for debts which common people had contracted with them. Rulers, landlords and their ecclesiastical, legal and financial officials sometimes welcomed a pogrom since it diverted popular anger, outrage and riot away from themselves, their own policies and property. Frederick III granted a pogrom in Styria in 1478 after which the territorial Estates set up registers in all lordships and towns to record debt transactions between peasants and their money-lenders. Significantly, these registers were called Jews' books, and such a *Judenpuech* survived for Kloster Rain. Yet one may wonder how effective these measures were, quite apart from their pragmatic cruelty and inhumanity. Decrees forbidding peasants to contract debts without prior consent of their landlords go back to at least 1444 in Inner Austria, and the demand for Jews' books as debt registers was repeated by decree of Emperor Frederick III in 1492. At that time the authorities were hoping to get interest rates down to two pennies per 300 per week – that is, to about 30 per cent per annum.[8] The official church ideology of course was a dead letter when it continued to condemn anything over 5 or 6 per cent. Yet credit control through pogroms immensely reduced thresholds of violence, as the majority were stirred up to stamp out heterodoxy by psychotic means. Pogroms or witch-hunts could not satisfy peasant common sense when frustration with heavy taxation and a bad harvest forecast an intolerable level of insecurity for the coming season. At such times the authorities themselves, and not their Jewish scapegoats, had to take responsibility for unjust and unrealistic fiscal policies.

The ruling authorities could handle individual cases of peasant hardship on their own merits, but they had not learned to cope amicably and equitably with larger, more regional crises. Matters were to become much worse before territorial governments began to consider local consultations at community or *Landschaft* level in order to defuse well in advance any conflicts likely to occur because of fiscal mismanagement. It was not to happen effectively until the Reichstag at Speier in 1526 after the great peasant uprisings of the previous year. Styrian estate records of the 1490s show peasants as serfs and tenant-farmers complaining vigorously about unfair treatment; of losing tenancy unjustly; over-taxation and arbitrary fines when they had been prevented from paying rents that were in any case often new, uncustom-ary and illegal because of the physical constraints of the weather, combined with the material disruption of Turkish marauding. The battle for produce was an endless wrangle between peasant and tithe-lord writ large. That was the true basis for the natural state of the countryside as a secretive and violent place. An artist's landscape Romanticism was as misplaced in the 1490s as a glossy colour-supplement of downtown Calcutta in 1980.

How much peasant complaining was genuine? How much was opportunistic tax-evasion? Although we may never know, it is probably fair to assume that the answer was six of one and half-a-dozen of the other. We know, as yet, practically nothing of peasants' and bailiffs' rival crop-watching associa-tions in central Europe. No doubt the rôle of the aged, infirm and under-age was vital in this respect. But serf tenant or *Grundholde* Jörg Kreuzer at least saw the justice of his case, and appealed directly to the aged Emperor Frederick III at Linz against dispossession by the landlord, Herr Conrad Freber. Sensibly paternalistic landlords also existed, as with Herr Hans Stubenberg, who in 1499 advised his heir, 'Dear son, make sure your poor people are well managed. Take from them what they owe, but store enough of it for tax payment purposes, and *never* take the best head of cattle from them as death duty.'[9] As regards this warning, one wonders how much of it was merely the voice of landlordly common sense in husbanding limited resources, and how much a response to the real threat of peasant violence and insolent intimidation, accumulated as experience from everyday farm management. Landlord Stubenberg was legally entitled to the cattle death-duty, but he was not foolish enough to attempt to enforce his right. Other landlords, especially the courtiers and absentees like Cardinal Matthias Lang, were less squeamish in this regard, and if the peasants wanted a fight, then so be it. It was precisely the rise of this more unscrupulous type of landlord that was to upset the balance between paternalist local nobles and obedient tenant-farmers. High interest rates and even higher indebtedness due to unnecessary foreign wars with the Venetians especially, plus renewed Turkish raids with hints of some fifth-column activity among the poorer nobles of Inner Austria led to a massive showdown between Maximilian's government and his peasants between March and August 1515.

Serf tenant farmers, under the jurisdiction of prelate, noble, domain official and patrician, went on strike against the level of tithe, land-tax and customs duty that they were expected to stomach. They used their priests and parish organisations, with which some of them, as headmen, were thoroughly familiar, to create secret societies. These accumulated to become a league or *Bund*. Then they went on the rampage, destroying landlords and their property. In Carniola it took from March until mid-May for the rebellion to reach its head. On 17 May, the Brothers Mynndorffer, who as Maximilian's castellans had received the landed estate of Castle Meichau in lieu of the emperor's unpaid debts to them, were attacked by the serfs and executed. They were small fry and therefore accessible to the peasants in their fury. The Mynndorffer wives were forced to wear peasant garb. It was rebel policy to teach the high and mighty just how the other half lived. But the Mynndorffers were only scapegoats, and behind them lay the really sinister financial operations of Matthias Lang, an Augsburg small-time scribe who had made it via Royal Court service to ecclesiastical territorial ruler, Cardinal and millionaire status by 1515. It was he, as much as Maximilian himself, who kept a low profile when it came to dealing with the peasants once they had put themselves outside the law in an agony of righteous indignation.[10]

The rebels spread their organisation from Carniola westwards to Styria and Carinthia. Their attack on Maximilian's more rapacious officials soon developed into a major attack on more traditional landlords: noble, urban and ecclesiastical property and person. The latter called territorial assemblies and attempted to secure mercenary troops, which were, however, already badly needed on the Italian front, against France and against Venice. The delay that this caused enabled the peasants to capture and plunder castles, monasteries and a few smaller market towns. Town councils controlling the wealthier towns joined noble and prelate against the peasants. By late May 1515 Maximilian had handed over control of counter-insurgency measures to an experienced Venetian war general, Georg von Herberstein (brother of the more famous Sigismund, envoy to the Court of Muscovy), who raised several hundred hardened troops to be paid for by Inner Austrian territorial assembly tax grants. In this way the peasants were coerced to pay for their own suppression in piecemeal military operations, first in Carinthia, then Styria, and finally, with less success, in Carniola. Herberstein's political allies were Maximilian's Lords Lieutenant and leaders of the territorial Estates in Styria, Sigmund von Dietrichstein, and in Carniola, Hans von Auersperg. They were provided with commissars, who played for time by inviting the rebel leadership to present grievances addressed to Maximilian in person. Outside the Inner Austrian town of Gonobitz (Slovene Konjice), around Whitsuntide, three hundred peasant representatives, who were claimed to have spoken for 80,000 leaguist rebels (according to the commissars), presented their demands to Maximilian's men, Augustin Khefenhüller, Hanns Mannstorffer, Philip von Wichsenstein, and Nicklas Resch, to whom were added two loyal locals, 'not tainted by rebellion', namely Sebastian Gurk and Andre Hueter.

In a thirteen-point programme, which has only been preserved as minutes taken by their commissar enemies, the rebel leaders presented strictly practical, economic and legalistic grievances, which they expected Maximilian to hear in person. If that happened, they were convinced that they would find redress. Maximilian could not afford it: he abandoned them. His commissars, seen by the peasants as traitors and evil counsellors, had power over them now. It was only a question of time before the rebels would be defeated, their ring leaders placed on show-trial and the rank and file made to pay damages by even greater levies of arbitrary taxation. And so it happened.

The peasants complained, firstly, that they doubted whether the large amount of taxation which they had contributed over the last few years had ever reached Maximilian's coffers. They demanded audit, and wished to see Maximilian's original decrees ordering them to pay the huge sums that had been forced from them. This the royal officials had refused, and that is why they were up in arms – i.e. for Maximilian's and their own good. Here was a crucial political clash, over a policy difference. Secondly, they wanted a return to the customary level of labour service as one that did not interfere with their own farming activities. Thirdly, cost of copyhold renewal and of death duties should cease to be exorbitant, and fourthly, did Maximilian personally realise that local court fines had increased by ten to fifteen times, from about sixty pennies to two and three gulden per offence? Furthermore, the wrong people were being let off, provided they bribed the court officials. The peasants wanted more protection from Maximilian against common theft, petty crime, and even against *maleficium*, witches and the 'evil eye'.[11]

Rebels were not against royal government, indeed, they only wanted a more efficient exercise of it. Maximilian did nothing to provide them with it in 1515: centralisation was to arrive on his terms via unscrupulous prerogative officials recruited from the newly educated humanists of town and church, stiffened by the local nobility, and trained at his court and in his armies. His peasants had to learn that lesson the harsh way – by rebellion. Fifthly, the peasants complained on the one hand of receiving short measure at market, and on the other of unfavourably liberal weighing and assessing during tax-gathering. Above all, priests were now doing their own tithe-collecting, whereas it had always been left to the peasants to assess and collect by themselves. Sixthly, the royal customs had become excessive, as were, seventhly, the fines levied to enforce them. Eighthly, the new exchange rates accepted good coin and paid out in bad. What had happened to the good old 'black' coinage, asked the peasants? Ninthly, the poll-tax had increased three times from two pennies to two kreuzers or six pennies. Was Maximilian aware of that?

Tenthly, fish and water control, and eleventhly, forest law had been sharpened to husband the resources of landlords, to the detriment of tenants and ordinary folk. Twelfthly, the rebels complained: 'We poor people just do not obtain any redress either at law or outside it.'[12] Finally, if Maximilian did not soon mediate between the ordinary folk of country and market, and the richer townsmen, clergy and lords, then there would be an even more violent rebellion. If he now did something about redressing their grievances, then his Inner Austrian countryfolk would turn out to be his most loyal subjects and supporters. Considering the fact that Maximilian had always loved doing his own bureaucratic paperwork, as can be seen especially in chapter 12, it is surprising that he turned the matter over to commissars who were only interested in rescuing landlord property from more destruction, in compensation, and finally in teaching the peasants an unjust, brutal lesson never again to take the law into their own hands.

On Whit Monday 1515 the commissars dictated terms to the rebel leaders outside Gonobitz. Firstly, there had to be an end to all recruitment of peasants into the rebel league with cessation of secret society oath-taking. Then there was to be no harassment of landlords, whether burgher, cleric, noble or royal official. Secondly, peasant grievances were noted and they would either be sent to Maximilian, or to his Lord Lieutenant, Dietrichstein. This was cavalier treatment, considering that Maximilian had always thrived on a popular reputation for being accessible to all his subjects. In practice he was now nowhere to be seen. Thirdly, and fourthly, the property and castles of Cardinal Bishop Matthias Lang of Gurk were to be returned forthwith with full compensation. Fifthly, if any new rebel leagues arose as a result of these new fines, they would be suppressed by mercenary horsemen hired especially for the purpose by the commissars themselves. Sixthly, any burgher, priest or landlord forced to swear loyalty to the peasant league, was completely freed of any such ties. Seventhly, it was asserted that all three hundred peasant representatives had agreed to abide by these conditions (surely an unlikely proposition – but a clear indication that the commissars alone were in control of the channels of publicity and communication).[13]

In practice, the revolt was stamped out by General Herberstein's mercenaries, paid for by grudging tax grants from the territorial Estates, levied upon all the peasants and townsfolk of Inner Austria after the autumn of 1515. In Carinthia this became an eight pence a year poll-tax in perpetuity. In Carniola it was a levy of one gulden per hearth. In Styria, contributions were raised by troop billets in an *ad hoc* manner. Carniolan rebel slogans, in Germano-slavic dialect, are preserved in a popular song to commemorate the uprising: *Le uphup, woga gmaina, stara pravda,* 'Stick together, poor folks, uphold only the true law.'[14]

By not handling the 1515 rebels in person, other than by issuing a brief note in 1516 calling a final halt to the continued punishment of 'ring leaders',[15] Maximilian failed to provide good government for his ordinary countryfolk subjects. That fact contrasted markedly with his willingness at all times personally to handle the Bavarian Succession civil wars, by keeping the Swabian League and the Palatinate as much as possible from each other's throat. But why should it have become almost a platitude that peasants were not worth the same careful consideration as town councils, prelates and dynastic aristocrats? Maximilian spent his years of rule exploiting all the avenues of power, wealth and loyalty to him: the towns, their trade, manufacture and manpower; the mines and their hard-earned wealth; the dynastic system through marriage alliances and inheritance; and finally the peasants and their ability to pay more taxes. He was caught in the very machinery that he had been creating in order to help him in his ruthless businessman's rise to fame. Territorial assemblies led by nobles and prelates, who were also in a position to exercise power as his court officials, took over the messier side of everyday home affairs as regards tax-raising and law enforcement. The miners' strike of 1493 at Gossensass in the Brenner, as examined in chapter 9, will also show what was emerging here, namely that Maximilian was not prepared to rule the peasants without resort to brute force and coercion, which was itself to be provided by his warmongering, benefice-hunting and land-hungry courtiers. It was all epitomised by the Augsburg small-burgher's son, Matthias Lang, millionaire Cardinal by the grace of Maximilian, and through the sweat of his tax-paying subjects in the countryside.[16] Peasants were practical politicians. Their grievance, which led to rebellion, time and again, as exemplified in 1515 in Inner Austria, that a ruler must rid himself of evil and upstart counsellors and return to the honest ways of living of his own domain revenues, was indeed fully justified. The countryside could not pay annually increased taxes without exploding. In the 1490s that extra wealth for ambitious dynastic and military policies had to be sought in the mining industries of the Austrian Alps. There Maximilian found the ready cash he needed, but at a price. It was another low threshold of violence in labour relations, as the next chapter will show.

9

Mining and the Creation of Wealth

Around the year 1500 in the Alps so much of the wealth was tied up in the exploitation of mineral resources that mining communities were of crucial importance to the economic wellbeing of rulers like Maximilian and financiers like the Fuggers. This was especially the case in the Tirol, Inner Austria and the Habsburg satellite Archbishopric of Salzburg, where miners were the producers of strategic and precious minerals, which became immediately available to pay for ambitious patronage, diplomacy, wars and pleasures. Salt, silver, copper, iron, tin and lead were among the most lucrative mined materials of these regions. Maximilian himself went down to inspect the silver-ore seam at Rottenmann in north-western Styria, and wrote back, in his own hand, to his uncle Sigismund of Tirol, when he found enough there for up to six years' exploitation.[1]

The pay book (*Soldregister*) of the salt and iron mines at Hallein in the Archbishopric of Salzburg has survived for the year 1507.[2] It gives a vivid account of the wages and conditions of work, that we can take as indicative for Maximilian's own miners in Tirol, Inner Austria and the *Vorlande*. The salt-miners were paid for the year in a cash sum totalling just under 7000 pounds in pennies. On top of this, miners received unspecified payment in salt worth ten to twelve and a half pennies per *Fuder*. Scales of pay reflected the complicated division of labour. Thirty-two distinct occupations were described for this mining-township.[3] They begin with the warden (*Phleger*) at the top, and he alone took over five hundred pounds in pay (7 per cent of the total wage-bill in coin). Team-leaders were well paid. Two chief foremen

(*Gryesknechte*) netted just short of seventy pounds in cash earnings for the year. In 1507 the pound of pennies was accounted as equivalent in value to the Rhenish Gulden (fl.), and all payments were made in pennies of this sort. So the miner could become quite well-off, although it was no doubt a struggle of chance to arrive at the high station of works' official or foreman. Foremen's pay was certainly about twice that of an educated book-keeper or customs' official, four of whom were employed at Hallein in 1507 at annual rates of thirty-four to forty-three gulden.

In the four iron mines of Hallein the manager netted 176 fl., and his foremen received forty-six gulden a year each. Payment was made monthly in thirteen instalments a year with a double payment at Christmas. The total wage bill was here, however, less than 2400 fl., showing that the iron mines at Hallein were less lucrative than the salt mines in that year. Consequently, wages in iron-mining were lower than in the salt industry. The salt-pans were run by sixteen overseers with ninety men under them. When panning was in operation an overseer (*Perer*) was paid the equivalent of one gulden a week, and a manual worker received about one-third of the overseer's rate. The weekly wage bill during panning was sixty-eight gulden. This would have given an annual wage bill of over 3500 fl. at the salt-pans alone if a full rate of pay had been sustained over the year, but the actual annual overall wage bill was well under a half of this at 1500 fl. Thus, on average, the salt-pan overseer earned about thirty-three gulden a year, and his labourer about eleven gulden a year. The latter wage was still higher in money terms than that received by poorer peasants and labourers, but it was quite close to the hunger line, being about level with the earnings of poorer artisans and urban workers. No doubt the real difference lay in the number of fringe benefits, like rights to collect free fuel from the surrounding alpine woodlands, grazing for livestock, or even quotas of salt for the miners. For salt was a necessity not only for every diet, but it was also the only cheap spice and an effective preservative, especially for vegetables.

We may note that peasants, artisans, rural and urban labourers and their families were unlikely to have consumed meat regularly, considering the relationship between real prices and wages. With the miners of Hallein we can surmise that foremen, overseers and those in skilled jobs certainly earned enough at about thirty pennies or more per day to have afforded quite an acceptable standard of living. Also, the prospects of promotion to such a well-paid job were probably higher in mining than in any other kind of job available to the common man in the early sixteenth century. It was a career open to talent in a strikingly modern sense. In the Hallein salt-pans about one in six persons was an overseer with three times the pay of the other five. That is, one in six was taking home nearly thirty pennies per day on average, whilst the rest may have taken home somewhat under ten pennies a day. The latter was the rate that Lower Austrian skinners were receiving at about the time, and over which rate they would go on strike three years later in 1510.[4] No wonder that at this very time in prosperous east-central Germany Luther's father was rising successfully via a mining career from the younger son of a serf status to local town council burgher standing, sending his son into higher education and living in a house of stone in the County of Mansfeld.

Mining was a booming industry. It provided careers open to talent in the quite new manner of capitalistic self-help in late-medieval central Europe. No doubt mining was a badly paid profession for new entrants into it, but those who worked hard, had practical skills and survived the hazards to health in the open casts on the hill-sides, in the pans and foundries of the valley, or the underground shafts, were rewarded with a pay structure of great opportunity, rising, in the case of Hallein, from eleven to nearly seventy gulden a year. The only problem was that the miner was subject to direct market forces, depending on the ready availability of his ore at source, his finance and good luck extracting it, and on a price fixed by the pressures of monopoly financiers upon rulers. However, Hallein in 1507 was a success story, and the miner could and did do well, but he paid for this with a higher degree of economic insecurity and health hazard than usually pertained among common subjects outside the theatre of war, famine and disease. But the immediate problem was that because of its high profitability combined with high risk, mining was the plaything of Maximilian's financial yearnings, hopes and aspirations. We now turn to the Tirolean background, and then to an example of the volatile nature of labour relations during the change-over from Sigismund's more lax rule to that of Maximilian in the case of the 1493 strike at the Gossensass mine on the Brenner Pass.

In the fifteenth century alpine mining industries reached an all-time economic high point in technology, success and profit. The Tirol was at the heart of this industrial activity, which centred on the production of silver, copper, iron, lead, zinc and salt. Mining complexes were regionally grouped under *Berggerichte*, copying the local jurisdictions of town and country and preserving local autonomy directly under supervision of the territorial ruler's courts. Mining was treated as a prerogative of the ruler, who took high profits from the finished product without shouldering any of the risks of production.

In 1491 Maximilian I, as effective ruler of the Tirol, replaced Hans Vechlin and his Memmingen Company with Ulrich Fugger and his Augsburg Company in the financial exploitation of the silver-mines around Schwaz in the Lower Inn Valley.[5] Fugger agreed to pay the standard eight gulden for the silver mark at sixty kreuzers to the gulden. Of these eight gulden, the smelters would receive five, and Maximilian's exchange would pocket the rest. Maximilian was advanced 120,000 fl. in two instalments at April and Christmas 1491, which enabled him to meet the spring and winter quarter-days when creditors might otherwise have forced an exchequer-stop. For saving Maximilian from a bankruptcy at Innsbruck, Fugger naturally exacted a price.

For a start he monopolised Lower Inn Valley silver, although the copper industry was as yet still largely in the hands of the Baumgartners and others like the Herwarts.[6] After February 1492 Fugger promised to pay into Maximilian's Innsbruck treasury a regular 10,000 fl. a month without fail. This would be set against actual silver production to be accounted for once a year at Christmas. By the end of 1491 Fugger had probably guaranteed to purchase as much as 320,000 fl. worth of raw silver. If production actually came up to these high expectations then Fugger would pay Maximilian's exchange a new rate of five gulden to the silver mark.[7]

Yet the cost of the silver mark remained unchanged at 8 fl. In effect, Maximilian and Fugger agreed to increase production and lower wages in the mines, since their agreement meant that smelters were reduced to receiving three instead of the former five gulden for the silver mark. This represented an enforced cut of one-quarter in production costs, which was presumably to be cushioned by massively increased production, whereby the silver price held up but the miners and smelters received less for each ingot although they had the chance of earning more overall as the number of ingots was greatly increased. After 1495 production did in fact go up markedly but it hardly rose by more than 15 to 20 per cent, leaving a sensitive gap in production costs of 5 to 10 per cent (see below). The problem was that this also entailed a massive increase in hours and shifts worked, higher productivity and stricter quality control over the mined ore. In the 1490s there was no marked technological advance (as there had been in the 1470s when many new shafts were opened in the Tirol) to cover this rise in work norms for Maximilian's miners and smelters. Ulrich Fugger's new mining company was to transfer one-quarter of the existing production costs into Maximilian's pockets, and from there pay it to itself as interest on money advanced to Maximilian. The deal was justified by increased and cheaper productivity. Who thus paid for the new contract? It was the industry as a whole and the miner in particular. Unions, meetings and strikes could thus be expected to arise.

What was Fugger's reward from Maximilian? He was allowed two hundred silver marks a week free of all charges. The original advance to Maximilian was 120,000 fl. Hence, at the old exchange rate of three gulden to the silver mark, Fugger was receiving 2,400 fl. a month or 24 per cent interest per annum. No wonder Maximilian wished to reduce this or at least pass it on as a burden to the producers when it came to financing the regular 10,000 fl. a month in his treasury as from February 1492. Fugger seems to have refused to cheapen his rates since the deal eventually squeezed the industry itself to lessen costs by one-quarter, which just covered the Fugger interest rate. This may explain why Maximilian allowed Ulrich Fugger to start monopolising the Tirol silver industry since it cost the ruler nothing, and instead increased his gross royalties considerably. We must stop believing that the Fuggers exploited Maximilian because he knew nothing about finance. Maximilian was a ruthless businessman, quite prepared to sour labour relations with his miners in order to increase his revenues. How did deals like this actually affect labour relations in the mines? We must first set the scene and then see how an actual strike was handled by Maximilian's officials in the early summer of 1493 at the Brenner Pass near Sterzing.

In the 1490s six mining districts in all operated in north Tirol, at Hall, Imst, Schwaz, Zillertal, Rattenberg and Kitzbühl. A further seven districts were productive in south Tirol, namely Eisak (Klausen), Persen, Sterzing-Gossensass, Windisch-Matrei (Salzburg run), Etsch, Primor and Taufers. Translated into our terms at just under three and a half silver marks to the kilogramme ingot, Maximilian's accountants reckoned that silver production alone averaged over 9,000 kilogrammes a year between 1470 and 1494, rising to record levels at well over 11,000 kilogrammes a year between 1495 and 1519.[8] Leading smelters or *Silberbrenner* at Schwaz were as follows:

Cristan Taenntzl and heirs, between 1470–1535, producing 356,100 silver marks;
Hans Fugger and heirs, 1470–1530, 209,000;
Antoni von Rost, 1470–1513, 189,700;
Steffan Taenntzl, Hans Hartmann, Claus Schlosser, 1470–1512, 70,500;
Andre Jaufner, 1470–1511, 58,900;
Jorg *Perl*, 1470–1501, 117,400;
Virgili Hofer and heirs, 1475–1526, 305,300 silver marks.[9]

In an attempt to accommodate the grievances of smaller smelters on 2 February 1479, Archduke Sigismund decreed that a *Silberbrenner* should receive a guaranteed two hundred gulden per annum but not more.[10] At the same time the miners were to receive five more paid holidays added to the eleven already allowed. The favoured saints' days were George, Ulrich, Margreth, Mary Magdalene and Nicholas.[11]

The 1470s were an important time for establishing codes of conduct in the silver-mining industry of Tirol as the ruler's

exchange was moved over the mountains into north Tirol at
Hall in 1477. There were basically four distinct groups
involved in the industry; the ruler and his officials who
exercised supreme police and supervisory powers and also
granted out mining concessions as overlord and landlord who
received extensive royalties; the financiers and *Gewerken* who
bought the concessions often on a feudal-contractual basis,
and put up the money to exploit the ore; their managers,
foremen and bailiffs who supervised the work-force as *Hauer* or
Hutleute; and finally the hired miners (*Knappen*) and smelters
who worked the actual shifts at piece-rates in the mountains
and foundries.

Conflicts between work-force and management, *Knappen*
and *Hutleute*, were frequent. Official arbitrator between them
was the judicial officer or *Bergrichter* appointed by the
territorial ruler, and each of the Tirolean mining districts had
such an officer. It was his task to balance between excessive
demands of pay by the *Knappen* and excessive profits made by
the investors or *Gewerken*, in such a way that the ruler obtained
royalties of a consistent value from the industry. Thus it was
not a foregone conclusion that the government would always
support the bosses against the workers. Apart from the more
favourable conditions granted to the latter in Archduke
Sigismund's agreement of 1479, the *Knappen* could record the
following improvements. From 1474 management (*Hutmänner*)
were ordered to pay workers' wages within eight days of the
work done. The weekly wage had arrived. Deductions made
without prior knowledge of the worker were declared illegal.
From 1477 payment had to be made at the mine-head. No one
was permitted to hire unskilled workers, and managers were
forbidden to sell food and necessities, which had to be
provided by accredited merchants from the mining town.
From 1485 all hirings were to be reported to the *Bergmeister*,
and thereby recruitment of the labour force was taken over
effectively by the territorial authorities.

In the late spring of 1485 the Schwaz miners went on strike
against too many restrictive practices. *Knappen* marched to
Innsbruck, four kilometres away, to complain directly to
Archduke Sigismund, whose officials soon forbade them to
congregate in more than two or three in public. The miners

demanded half-shifts before all holidays and rest-days. This was granted in Sigismund's agreement of 25 June 1485, and the underground shift was limited to eight hours in each twenty-four hour day.[12] In return, the miners had to agree that anyone who complained of inadequate pay could be sacked forthwith. Yet miners were now expressly allowed to work old seams that the *Bergmeister*, on the advice of the *Gewerken*, had previously closed to them. This accommodated a major grievance of the *Knappen*, namely that the bosses and authorities had prevented them from private prospecting whereby they hoped to become entrepreneurs themselves. Mining in Tirol became a career open to talent under the rules of self-help for all and sundry in the industry by order of the ruler in June 1485.[13]

The *Knappen* also demanded more effective exercise of cheap law and order by the *Bergrichter*. Crimes against property and persons were to entail prison and the trip to the high court at Innsbruck was to be undertaken in the company of regular warders at just under two kreuzers a time. Yet workers, already called *arbaiter* in the records, had to swear an oath of obedience to their bosses (*Hutleute*) or be dismissed. Above all, miners were to receive job security even if there was no shift work for them.[14] All strikers were pardoned but no further assembly (*besaumlung*) was permitted on pain of life, limb and property. Yet where miners had grievances, the *Bergmeister* was to act as troubleshooter and organise meetings to settle the matter on the spot.

After Maximilian took over the government of Tirol from Archduke Sigismund in 1490 a harsher attitude towards the miners as well as to the industry as a whole appeared. As explained above, February 1491 saw Maximilian increasing his royalties by a quarter, selling out to the Fuggers at 24 per cent interest on silver revenues anticipated a year in advance. Something was bound to give. In the first half of 1493 the work-force at the south Tirolean mine of Gossensass withdrew their labour and barricaded mine and foundry (Plate 15). This working lay in the Brenner district, strategically across the main route between Schwaz, Hall, Innsbruck, Sterzing, Brixen (Meran), Bozen, Trient and Italy. That is presumably why Maximilian instructed his counsellors to act so harshly, out of keeping with previous government behaviour to miners' strikes in the 1470s and 1480s.

The records of this strike come exclusively from the government side. We do not know the names of the strikers nor their precise demands, although twenty-seven were captured and put on trial in Bozen after 13 July 1493.[15] This was after they were tricked into a meeting with Maximilian's counsellors, run by the chief military officer of the County, Dägen Fuchs, and the chief treasury official and salt-master, Lienhard Vells. Fuchs and Vells had appeared at the meeting with seven hundred armed men levied from the surrounding towns and villages. The troops had not been told for what express purpose they were being summoned, and they were stiffened by one hundred loyal salt-pan workers from Hall under the command of Vells.[16]

Gossensass was a large silver mine since it already had about three hundred *Gewerken* or investors in 1485, and from 1491 Maximilian's effective first minister, Bishop Melchior of Brixen, was beginning to invest in nearly a third of the mine's output, bringing him a handsome five hundred silver marks annually.[17] When the miners downed tools and demanded better conditions of shift-work, pay and holidays,[18] the investors and their hired managers turned the issue over to Maximilian and his military advisers. As it happened, Maximilian was at the same time planning to raise troops in Tirol to campaign against the Turks who had once again raided neighbouring Inner Austria.[19] He seems to have first used eight hundred of these levies to put down the strike, and then switched them to hunting down the Turkish slave raiders.[20] In punishing his own miners he was successful, but he failed to find any Turks in the ensuing campaign. Due process of law was ordered against the miners since it was a sole prerogative of the ruler to authorise meetings and unions, on pain of life, limb and property.[21]

Anyone accused of joining the union (*pundtnuss*) and going on strike (*ungehorsam*) was barred from further employment in any Tirolean mine. Blacklegs were especially praised and kept on the payroll.[22] All through the strike Maximilian and his officials played a double role. The miners were told to keep calm and present their grievances. The same was demanded from investors and management. Then, expressly in secret, eight hundred troops were hired from Tirol and the neighbouring tributary Bishopric of Trient, and Maximilian promised to pay for their upkeep and any damages. The documents record this bad faith and harsh behaviour of Maximilian's officials towards the striking miners at several points.[23]

It remained for Maximilian to set up the court that punished the ring-leaders as expressed in the officials' words, 'in order to have sound reason for applying the law and not fall into ill-repute. And whatever the law decides, is to be accepted swiftly and promptly carried out'.[24]

We may doubt whether Maximilian escaped ill-repute (*schimph*) in view of the earlier possibly more harmonious labour relations of the previous government. Maximilian's counsellors did not even list the miners' grievances here. They were only casually mentioned in passing, whilst preparations were made to smash the strike on the five following principles of action: preserve calm at the mine; secretly recruit troops who would be kept in the dark about their task; imprison all ring-leaders and make examples of a number of the rank and file; encourage blacklegs and ensure that no striker obtained another job; accept the assurances of investors and management that they could recruit plenty of alternative labour to restart the mine.

How many more strikes ended so unhappily as a result of the brutal and cynical behaviour of the authorities? Did the period around 1490 show a general hardening of attitudes towards labour by territorial governments which had not been in evidence in quite the same way in the previous generation? Was this due to a combination of increasingly productivity-orientated business methods, rulers' need for higher incomes for war, diplomacy, court and bureaucracy, and finally a rising surplus of labour as the population increased? Certainly the bad faith shown by the authorities in 1493 can not have helped them subsequently to retain loyalty in the face of Inner Austrian peasant uprisings in 1515, as has been shown in chapter 8, and the great upheavals to come in Tirol in 1525–6 under Michael Gaismair, the renegade official of a bishop. How many more strikes can be found in the fiscal archives of the period? From events like those at Gossensass in 1493 we can piece together the detailed labour relations that may well provide the clue to the great peasant war of 1525 in Germany and Austria.[25] We begin with a letter of Maximilian's commissars which sets the scene in laying plans to put down the strike to the advantage of the government.

From members of the Council at present still here, to those now at Linz [translated from Landesarchiv Innsbruck, Kopialbuch 16, ältere Reihe, 1493, fols. 106–8, undated, but probably from May or June].

Reverend Prince-Bishop, gracious lord,[26] noble and steadfast good friends, we send you our obedient and friendly service.

We have recently written and informed you by messenger that we have ordered Hilbrand von Gles, military commander in the Trento, to ride in person to the chief mining official and judge at Gossensass in the Brenner on behalf of the members of the union [*gesellschaft*] to discuss and negotiate with them, since they have handled matters in such a clumsy way by issuing threats, that even the management [*gwercken*], smelters and their foremen have nearly all left and dispersed.

We have also called upon Hans Fugger[27] with other local and mining officials to hear the views of the management, who have vigorously and not unreasonably complained according to the enclosed articles.[28] And we now have the best arrangements that could be worked out.

Namely, where the members of the Union have acted in dereliction of their duty, their activities will be strictly scrutinised.

Where the members of the Union have handed out punishments for incidents similar but less serious to those occurring in the reign of our gracious lord, Archduke Sigismund of Austria,[29] such action is to cease forthwith. All people in positions of authority in the mine must keep especially close control, since attempts to spread the strike seem to have been made after someone was hired at Sterzing [Vipiteno], and attempts are still being made to get everyone to stop work, which could lead to closure of all the mines.

To inform you on matters to be laid before His Majesty.

We advise that no one be sent in, nor should anyone be ordered to attend a hearing, since it is foolhardy to attempt to go in or leave against the strikers' wishes, and even if they were ordered to attend a hearing, they would forbid it and disobey the management. Hence it is best to send members of the Council together with the military commander of the Trento, as well as someone to represent the King, for which we recommend Herr Sigismund von Welsperg. They should take with them about 800 footsoldiers, to arrive at the mine as soon as possible and demand negotiations with the members of the union concerning wages, keep and other matters on the basis of findings made by the common assembly of the mine [*gemaine versamlung der Pergkwerch*]; to take into custody as many of the ring-leaders [*Redelfuerer*] as possible and take them out of the Brenner Valley and imprison them somewhere else.

Concerning the rest of the strikers who have equipped themselves with swords and joined the strike [*puntnuss*], they are to be banned permanently from the Brenner Valley and from all other mines in His Majesty's lands and territories, since the management says that it can hire enough alternative workers.

But you will also know how best to handle matters.

Let us know whether by day or night without delay what His Majesty wants us to do in this matter, since the management are here and are prevented from going into the mine, and the accounts need to be made up. In any case, where payment is not forthcoming the members of the union are blaming the management and demanding that the mines be handed over directly to themselves. We have suggested that all claims be shelved until they can be settled peacefully, and also ordered the military officials of the Trento to recruit 800 footsoldiers in secret, and to say when at the earliest they will be ready for use, that is, provided this meets with His Majesty's and your approval.

Yet those many miners who were not in the union and who are happy to work under existing arrangements should be kept in employment.

There follow the government's military preparations against the strike.

To the Supreme Military Commander, and to Herr Dägen Fuchs [translated from *ibid.*, fols 112–113, undated, but prior to 7 July].

Our greeting. Noble, strict, dear and good friend. We have received your letter containing your further advice concerning the matter of the undertaking against the members of the union in the Brenner. There was no need on our part since the matter has been handled on the direct orders of our most gracious lord the Roman King [Maximilian I] and the other counsellors with him, who are directed to give further advice.

Yet matters have been delayed for so long that we have accepted this advice in retrospect and invited the members of the union to a meeting arranged and promulgated for next Sunday after St Ulrich's day [Sunday, 7 July], according to the order which you received earlier that you should come together with Herr Dägen Fuchs and Herr Lienhard von Vells[30] with 800 armed, good men, 700 of whom the military officials have recruited from the towns and rural districts, and to inform these towns and rural districts that the men are urgently required by His Majesty also for the needs of their land and people, to be salaried by their own towns and rural districts, and provisioned by His Majesty. About this provisioning the said master of the saline [von Vells] has been instructed, and has promised to add 100 men which he will bring with him.

Fuchs and von Vells are to enter the meeting, remove and arrest the ring-leaders, and tell the rest of the union that especial note has been taken of the demands concerning shift-work, pay and salary, holidays and other matters, as notified from here by the mining management. Further more, they are to be thoroughly admonished by the chief master and judge of the Brenner mining region, who will accompany the two counsellors to the meeting, that our most gracious lord, the Roman King, is not satisfied but extremely angered by recent events. And those, who still refuse to work and decide to adhere to the decisions taken in

91

the previous common assembly [*gemainer besamlung vnd
sinodum*] of all the mines of this territory [Tirol], are each
and every one to be banned from employment in any mine
whatsoever.

And it is the wish of His Majesty that those of you who
came together and conspired to strike are not to be left
unpunished, although one should point out to His Majesty
that if the membership of the union or those on strike are
too large a number, then it will be necessary for the
commander of the troops to commission the recruitment of
further men. Herr Dägen [Fuchs] and Herr Lienhard [von
Vells] will let you know what is decided, and if necessary,
you will bring up reinforcements immediately, and
thereafter not only deal with the ring-leaders but the
rank-and-file accordingly. And in order that you may
recruit men for this purpose, we enclose herewith a general
open authority,[31] wherein you will know how to deal further
with the matter.

After a successful military campaign against the miners, the
government's lawyers instructed the commissars to hold a
show trial which would punish the ring-leaders whilst clearing
Maximilian.

Concerning the strikers [*vngehorsamen*] in the Brenner. From
the Roman Royal Majesty's *Statthalter*, counsellors and legal
advisers at Innsbruck, to the Supreme Military
Commander, Herr Dägen Fuchs and Herr Lienhard Vells
etc., dated Innsbruck on Saturday after St Margaret's day,
13 July [translated from *ibid.*, fols 122–3].

Our greeting. Dear and good friends.

We have received your letter concerning action taken
against the members of the union in the Brenner. On behalf
of His Majesty, our most gracious lord, we order you to take
several of the twenty-seven prisoners, mostly ring-leaders,
and arrange to put them on trial on an appointed day at
Bozen [Bolzano]. You should inform and invite the Regional
Military Commander, officials of the towns and rural
districts, and anyone else you regard as suitable. Appoint
someone to take evidence from the troops and let him deal
with the matter and find justice for or against.

The case for prosecution should show how the decisions of the last common assembly of all the mines were assessed and handled with timely advice by His Majesty, above all concerning pay and salary. But it turned out that no one went to work. They were not content merely to be disobedient but even held meetings without permission of the authorities; conspired to strike, for which there exists punishment of the body and confiscation of property; and enticed many others to join them, as you will find from the record when you meet in Council.

Leave the others in prison to await our further decision. You should collect any evidence [*kuntschafft*] which can be used to prepare cases against them, also requesting help from the judge of the Brenner mining region. However, where there is insufficient evidence for judicial proceedings against prisoners who also do not confess and own up to their activities, they are to be left. But those against whom there is sufficient evidence are to be told of it, in order to have sound reason for applying the law, and not fall into ill-repute. And whatever the law decides, is to be accepted swiftly and promptly carried out, in order to keep down costs, which will otherwise rise substantially where any case is prolonged. And we leave this in your hands.

These three documents have given us the clearest insight into how Maximilian handled labour relations that we so far possess from the archive evidence. It is not an edifying story. It corresponds with the understanding of thresholds of violence already gained in chapter 8 as regards the later handling of the peasants' revolt of 1515. These were the crises of his reign in the conduct of home affairs. Yet in the decision-making process Maximilian was at least very firmly served by his government officials, who were centred on the court or *Hofburg* at Innsbruck. We now turn to an examination of this power-house from a more domestic angle, followed by the conduct of practical policies in everyday mercantilist home affairs in chapter 12.

10

The Court of Maximilian and Bianca Maria

As shown in his itinerary, explained in Map 12.1, Maximilian stayed for twenty-two lengthier periods of time, amounting to anything from a week to several months, at the *Hofburg* or Court Castle in Innsbruck between the years 1489 and 1518. Perched on the edge of the town, near the fast-flowing River Inn, the court residence was started in 1420 by converting one of the heavily fortified burgher houses off the main square. When the Counts of Tirol became wealthier, as a result of mining resources exploited along the Inn Valley at neighbouring Hall and Schwaz, they acquired the streets and gardens to the north of their original town residence, which became the *Neuhof* or New Court. When the County was taken over by Maximilian in 1490, the retired ruler, Sigismund, moved to the original building of 1420. After Sigismund's death in 1496, it became Maximilian's treasury, ambitiously bedecked with a golden roof to protect sumptuously painted bay windows. This *goldene Dächl mit Erker*, now renovated, is today Innsbruck's main tourist attraction, depicting Maximilian, flanked by his two wives, Mary of Burgundy and Bianca Maria Sforza.

Maximilian himself supervised massive building works at the Court Castle precinct, where he had installed his new consort, Bianca Maria. Alterations began in earnest after 1495, reaching their height in 1510, when Dürer was invited to do sketches of the finished buildings, as vividly captured in the inner-courtyard atmosphere of Plate 16. In these fifteen years Maximilian turned the southern part or *Äussere Burg* into an arsenal and artillery store. The north became the *Vorder Burg* with rooms for public receptions and state occasions. The

94

Hofgasse or street between castle and town began to house courtiers, domestics and officials on a permanent basis. Queen Bianca Maria with her *Frauenzimmer* of ladies-in-waiting and female domestics was housed in the *Hintere Burg* across the courtyard, through a fenced-off part, approachable by covered walk-way, and also containing strong-rooms for the treasure. Beyond that was a jousting alley and a court garden, winding over towards the east.[1] Let us look more closely at these arrangements made for Bianca Maria; but first we must obtain the right setting by examining relations between her and Maximilian. The marriage was not a success.

Forceful women like Maximilian's daughter, the future Netherlands' Regent Margaret, must be set against those who were never given a real chance to develop their independence as competent *Hausfrauen*. The case of Bianca Maria Sforza (Plate 17), only married for her dowry, and for a fleeting political advantage in North Italy, is salutary. Such women were hot-house plants, heiresses, often very young at marriage and sternly ruled by housemasters and mistresses. Bianca Maria was totally unused to taking decisions. She was reared to become a selfish conspicuous consumer, as is shown in her correspondence, mainly with her husband. It deals with personal trivia, comforts and material worries. Her letters are a poor parody of what was always uppermost in her mind, and begin to tell us why Maximilian should have behaved so badly towards her. She was not the presentable, forcefully grand lady that Maximilian felt that, as head of the Habsburgs, he needed. Indeed, that task had been much more effectively carried out by Sigismund's last wife, Catherine of Saxony, who was to reorganise the Innsbruck *Frauenzimmer* before becoming a widow in 1496, and then, with Maximilian's blessing, getting remarried to the grandest of the generals serving under the Habsburgs, Duke Eric of Brunswick.[2]

In the first surviving letter, Bianca Maria writes from Worms on 26 March 1497 to say that she is very tired of the city and that its purveyors refuse her further credit. Will Maximilian please do something to remedy this situation before Easter? She has even had to pawn her linen and underwear. The embarrassment came as an anti-climax to the royal couple's first extensive travels together. Maximilian had taken Bianca Maria on an Alpine hunting holiday to the Valtelin and then they had moved on to Swabia, down the Rhine to Cologne and Brabant to let the Burgundian children meet their new step-mother. Maximilian then left Bianca Maria in Worms, where she was held in penury so that even Maximilian's loyal *Hofmeister*, Nicholas von Firmian, was scandalised. It finally cost Maximilian 1200 fl. to have his wife freed from her creditors, and she made her way back from Worms to Innsbruck via Ulm in the late autumn of that year.[3] Yet the Innsbruck treasury had also continued to pay Bianca Maria's expenses at Worms, and they were as high as 20,000 fl. in July 1496. In 1498 Bianca Maria was confined to Innsbruck, although she yearned to follow Maximilian on his travels, since it interrupted the boredom of her daily routine. She was only very occasionally allowed to do this. In 1499 the royal couple met briefly in Swabia at Villingen, from where they moved to Donaueschingen to feast, entertain and watch the jousting.[4]

In letters to Maximilian from Regensburg in November 1500, Bianca Maria asked for more money to redeem her personal belongings from local pawnbrokers, and for new materials to make towels and tablecloths. Much of her linen had been sold to pay overdue bills. The journey had started amicably in the early summer of 1500 with a stay first in Augsburg. Bianca Maria then went on to appreciate Regensburg considerably more than Worms, and in the following year, in allowing her a holiday at Passau, Maximilian came some way at least towards granting her wish to return to the Upper Danube Valley. The next attempt to make a success of the marriage seems to have come in the spring of 1504, which was spent in South Tirol around Meran, followed by a journey together with Maximilian to visit his favourite Tirolean hunting castles at Thaur, Melans and Imst. But Maximilian was soon off on his own to Kufstein, there to superintend siege troops in the Bavarian War of Inheritance. Left to her own devices, Bianca Maria fell into inaction and debt once more. From the Inn Valley, at the dramatic market-town of Rattenberg near Innsbruck, she wrote on 2 August 1504 in Italian asking for the return of clothes still in pawn at Augsburg. Maximilian gave up, and confined her to the

Hintere Hof (literally, 'back-yard') at Innsbruck. Marriage warfare was now almost total.

Bianca Maria retaliated. By March 1505 she had taken to her bed. Her *Hofmeister* informed Maximilian that she refused to follow doctor's orders, although she had first improved and only then relapsed into listlessness. The term used to describe her state was *Blödigkeit*, which was usually reserved for the condition of weak old age, or even senility. Did the thirty-three-year-old Bianca Maria suffer serious depression and for what cause? Was it all due to her neglectful, and aging roué husband? The *Hofmeister* implored Maximilian to write to Bianca Maria personally, ordering her to follow doctor's instructions. The marriage between Europe's 'first lady and gentleman' had finally broken down: it had never really got under way from the start.

At long last a new approach had to be pioneered. It was a financial one. Bianca Maria's sustenance was taken out of the hands of the periodically insolvent Innsbruck treasury. Her personal allowance was placed in the hands of a dynamic new treasury secretary, Ulrich Moringer. In a letter from Innsbruck, dated 29 January 1506, she ordered Moringer to pay a debt of 3,000 fl. owed to an Augsburg burgher, Benedict Katzenloher, in monthly instalments of 100 fl. as from next May until it was fully repaid, this being one-half of her monthly personal allowance. Perhaps Bianca Maria was not such a bad housekeeper if she was given only half a chance to prove herself. The problem may have been that Maximilian was just too impatient, domineering and unreliable for Bianca Maria to gain the confidence that a sheltered and pampered Italian woman needed in order to cope with the harsher north alpine German atmosphere of Tirol and Swabia. Above all, Maximilian never organised purveyance to court (*liferung*) without the great inconvenience and disruption of frequent cash crises. Hence it was no surprise that material relations between the two were doomed to go up and down like a yo-yo.

In the late spring of 1505 Bianca Maria suddenly began to heed her Italian medical adviser, Dr Wapista,[5] since he now obliged by recommending a change of air. Trent was first suggested, but then rejected because its climate was already too hot. Bianca's court ladies packed up too many belongings in their excitement to be gone from Innsbruck, and in June the *Hofmeister* forbade transport of all large chests. Personal clothes only were permitted. South Tirol was chosen, and local officials in Bozen and Meran sent provisions to Lienz in the far south-eastern corner of Tirol, where Bianca Maria was then allowed to holiday. The people of neighbouring Carinthia sent her supplies of fish, and Bianca Maria was happier than ever before. But she had had to suffer, or sham, depression and illness to obtain her rest.

The autumn of 1506 saw Bianca Maria in Styria, staying by the alpine mining community of Rottenmann. On the road to Augsburg she was informed of the death of Maximilian's son, Philip the Fair, and she was turned back immediately to Innsbruck, there to observe mourning. In 1508 Maximilian let her go to Constance, where he was assembling a Reichstag. She adored Lake Constance. She had more money and bought jewellery. She was altogether more cheerful. Her correspondence was now more sensibly divided between personal observations and money matters, the latter handled by the ubiquitous Ulrich Moringer. A new kind of begging letter emerged for Maximilian's personal attention. From Innsbruck, dated 26 July 1509, Bianca Maria requested the release from prison of a certain Nikolaus Spyss.

Bianca Maria had at last developed her own taste for travel and for the novelties it provided. For her, it was almost enough to go anywhere just in order to quit her *Frauenzimmer* at Innsbruck. Early in 1510 she was enjoying winter sunshine in Bozen, but when she wished to proceed to Trient and venture further into alpine Italy, she was ordered back to Innsbruck. The war with Venice was, after all, in full cry, which meant that Habsburg mercenaries had enough to do without the added duty to provide extra protection for a holidaying empress. Bianca Maria wrote in a fit of temper to Maximilian from Bozen on 14 January 1510, to say that she had her own important matters of business to conduct at Trient. Maximilian refused to listen, and she was hauled back to Innsbruck. In that year Bianca Maria used the Christmas festivities to over-eat. She died at New Year.

As has been said, during the earlier years of this second marriage, Maximilian's staunch supporter among the female members of the Habsburg family at the Innsbruck court was Catherine, in 1496 the widow of Archduke Sigismund, whom Maximilian had swiftly remarried on 29 June 1496 to Duke Eric of Brunswick, whilst he was serving in the Italian wars. Her entourage was more like that of a soldier's camp-following, and the head of Catherine's family, the Ernestine Saxon Frederick the Wise, suggested that her ladies-in-waiting be put under the supervision of Bianca Maria's *Hofmeisterin* and *Frauenzimmer*. Maximilian put the request into effect with a somewhat feeble joke, based on the interplay of the words *junkfrau* and *altfrau*.[6]

> For these same young women have a sensuous court life,
> which makes them forget all about marriage, and this
> means that they are no longer kept as *young*
> ladies-in-waiting but as *old* ladies-in-waiting, which is
> against the rules of the court, its decorum and charm, and
> really totally unpleasant.

Maximilian required a steady supply of young court ladies who could be matched above all with his military and diplomatic entourage. A reasonable turnover was essential for his standing as a patron of young men from well-off families in the region. Bianca Maria was not letting him have his way. To her, familiar faces meant security, although it did not prevent vicious quarrels and intrigues, especially among the Italian ladies-in-waiting in 1496 and 1500. Maximilian also considered long stays at court undesirable, since many ladies-in-waiting developed what he called *sbaczliebe*, that is, affairs of the heart, sparrow-like, and not dutiful. These affairs were frowned upon by the girls' families for the match was usually unsuitable, and not one in ten of them ended in marriage. They also damaged Maximilian's moral role, *in loco parentis*.

Yet Maximilian had a roving eye for a pretty face, and when in festive mood, he could show kindness towards Bianca Maria and her court. Information from his 'Book of Fishing' captures this sentiment. He instructs his officials:[7]

> When we return to living in our County of Tirol which we
> seriously intend from the autumn, together with our dear
> wife, the Roman Queen [Bianca Maria], by arriving at

99

Pulsan where we will go hunting after bears, wild boars and other game, as we did in the past year, we intend to stay with the people of Pulsan for some time. Since they do not have a town hall, it is our desire to have our house at the bridge extended by a large hall with further living rooms and bedrooms, where we and our dear wife, the Roman Queen, can hold dances and other entertainments for our enjoyment in the company of the members of both our courts [*vnser baider hof gesind*], and thereafter the local inhabitants can have the building as their town hall.

We have now seen that Bianca Maria was never given full control over her own finances and she was not allowed to plan her own budget. Consequently, she lived from hand to mouth with extremes of gluttony and luxury at one minute and pawning of linen to pay for purveyance at the next.[8] Unlike Maximilian, Bianca Maria was totally dependent on Tirolean treasury revenues. These were usually depleted in advance in order to meet debts incurred as a consequence of Maximilian's military exploits abroad or in the Reich. When the treasury was empty, Bianca Maria turned to pawnbrokers. When it was full, she feasted. Her court was expected to live on 900 fl. a month, and she had an extra allowance of 200 fl. a month. However, her charge on Innsbruck treasury revenues was a regular, fixed and expected one. By contrast, Maximilian's demands fluctuated wildly from under 200 fl. in 1506 to over 150,000 fl. in 1515. When Maximilian was in the Inn Valley the accountants estimated 300 fl. a week for the expenses of his table, yet this rate could hardly cover the costs of feeding more than two hundred people except on very rare occasions. Thus Maximilian was invariably pruning his dinner registers. Let us now turn to look in detail at this economic enterprise as a whole.

The court establishments of the ruler and his second wife, Bianca Maria Sforza, established in the *Neue Burg* at Innsbruck in 1497 employed a number of guards, artisans, labourers, domestics, journeymen and master craftsmen as well as the so-called higher and nobler sort, like officials, priests, choirboys, secretaries, ladies(and gentlemen)-in-waiting. The records that survive of the court and its economy from the last two decades of Maximilian's reign are relatively plentiful and they go into minute detail, something not so readily matched by the records of town, country and mining community.[9] As the court contained at any one time many more menial workers than members of any other group, it is essential for our picture of the common people under Maximilian's rule to use this evidence and let it compare and contrast with those common standards of life that pertained elsewhere in the late medieval and early modern alpine and Austrian lands.

Was the menial servant at Maximilian's court well off, or at least better off than common workers in town and country generally? How did the living conditions of menial servants at court compare with the conditions offered to the 'higher and nobler sort' also serving at court? Were the latter at all well off, and can we take their standards of life as indicative of burghers', patricians' and low nobles' own family economies elsewhere in the Austrian and German lands around the year 1500?

The first problem is to establish how many courts Maximilian kept at any one point of time. A substantial budget estimate of expenditure from the fiscal era of Georg Gossembrot in Innsbruck survives, undated, from circa 1500, a high point in Maximilian's career of extravagant expenditure and simultaneous fight to ward off bankruptcy.[10] Gossembrot is authorised to spend revenues from the Tirol, Lower Austria and the Austrian mines of 364,000 fl. annually. The Tirol is to provide for the upkeep of the Habsburg government at Innsbruck, as well as Empress Bianca Maria Sforza's court. Bianca receives 4,000 fl. a year pocket money. Her court servants are to cost no more than twice that – 8,000 fl. in annual keep. The Innsbruck government must make do with 20,000 fl. yearly, whereas, by way of comparison, debt repayment to the silver consortium of chief creditors headed by Fugger is over 170,000 fl. from this one source alone. Considering that Bianca Maria's Milanese dowry had been in the region of one million gulden some five years previously, Maximilian was indeed holding his second wife short of cash and comfort at this mere 12,000 fl. gross for the year.[11] At even the most modest of interest rates she was really entitled to at

101

least four times that amount as gross annual income. The 12,000 that Maximilian allowed turned out to be exactly the same amount that the emperor reserved for his own personal spending, as taken out of the revenues of lower Austria.

Gossembrot earmarked over 40,000 fl. for Maximilian and his peripatetic court, which was an establishment distinct from the Innsbruck government and from Bianca Maria's court, since Maximilian usually only spent a few weeks in any one year at Innsbruck. He was a compulsive traveller, and he seldom allowed his second wife to accompany or follow him.[12] The Lower Austrian government at Linz cost just under 12,000 fl. and building, artillery, hunting, shooting and fishing took up 24,000 fl. – twice as much as Bianca Maria's total court allowance. The rest comprised regular debt repayment from the domain treasuries of Innsbruck, Vienna and Linz, which, at 5 and 6 per cent interest, represented capital indebtedness in excess of one and a half million gulden. With income of 364,000 fl. and 1,720,000 fl. of debts, Maximilian had borrowed nearly five times his income. This placed his treasury in a difficult financial position, and treasurer Gossembrot was forced to make economies.

One such way was to cut the allowances of those least able to retaliate. This applies above all to Bianca Maria, who, unloved and unseen by Maximilian, was consigned to penury. She was kept so short of funds and provisions that twice at least the burghers of Freiburg-in-the-Breisgau and Worms forcibly detained her and her ladies-in-waiting until Maximilian had paid their bills. During the enforced stay in Freiburg in the late 1490s one court lady tried to put pressure on Maximilian to pay by contacting her lover, the influential Chancellor Cyprian von Serntein, and this letter, among others of a more intimate nature, has survived and is indicative of the frustration that Maximilian's finances could cause.[13]

> Dear Serntein. I send you herewith many very friendly greetings and wish you everything that is agreeable to you. And I do beg of you that you will use all your diligence so that we can get away from here and return home.
>
> Catterina von Schrofenstain

Some ten years later Bianca Maria's court was being refused dining facilities at Innsbruck and another lady-in-waiting wrote to Chancellor Serntein asking him to use his influence for her to be released from court service. Miss Sibila of Polhaim would rather have been dismissed from court than suffer the indignity of having her belongings mortgaged and then having to rely on meals from an inn-keeper. She claims, in a letter to Serntein, to have more confidence in him than in her brothers to act speedily on her behalf. She says that rather than stay with the empress she would like to accompany Serntein on his business journeys between Innsbruck and Füssen, where he was at that time chancellor to Maximilian's peripatetic court.[14] Miss Polhaim, however, remained in Bianca Maria's *Frauenzimmer*.[15] No doubt this was due to the fact that Serntein was married to Dorothea Perl, a burgher's heiress, whom he had snapped up before she was twelve years old in 1492, when he was already thirty-five.

In 1512, when Serntein, as chancellor, was helping Maximilian to run the Imperial Assembly at Cologne, he had left Dorothea at Castle Fragenstein near the Zirl Pass outside Innsbruck. Her letters to him from June to September 1512 relate boredom, lack of money, fear of catching plague (*rote Ruhr*), devoutness, and a vivid account of her emotional state during the birth and death two weeks later of their baby, Ursula. An elder child, a boy, had drowned prior to this date in the fast-flowing River Inn that runs under the Castle.[16]

Yet the testimonies of court ladies, as well as the shortage of money and supplies to Bianca Maria do not explain the real living standards at this court. They do, however, show that courtiers' expectations were sometimes in excess of the conditions they actually enjoyed. When Maximilian had settled his wife's court after 1496 together with Archduke Sigismund's widow, Catherine of Saxony, he tackled the problem with a set of minute and strict rules which left his wife with nothing to do except needlework, eating, feeling ill or intriguing with her servants, until her death on the last day of 1510. Then from 1517, for the last two years of his life, there was a further complication in that Maximilian had to make arrangements for his granddaughter, Maria, betrothed to the ill-fated King Louis of Hungary, later killed at the Battle of

Mohacs against the Turks in 1526, and for King Louis's sister, the young Anna, who was to consummate her marriage with the future Habsburg Emperor Ferdinand I in 1521. Setting up effective court households at various times for Bianca Maria and then for the two young queens, Maria and Anna, always remained an urgent dynastic matter of state for Maximilian.[17]

In seeking ways out of his financial embarrassments Maximilian turned to administrative regulations. An example is an undated instruction to his Innsbruck treasury, giving the finance officials there a free hand to raise money from mining assets in Tirol, Inner and Lower Austria to fund, among other things, the royal court (*Hofstaat*) at 13,200 fl. per annum for the next fifteen years. This itself represented a mere 10 per cent of the total annual expenditure from this one source. Maximilian promised to give his officials full powers over his finances and he promised to abide by their decisions. In case of war in the Tirol and *Vorlande* (lands exposed to French, Swiss and Venetian attack), even the 10 per cent regular expenditure on the court was to be redirected to covering any emergency military costs.[18] Maximilian further agreed not to issue any more credit notes to run on the Innsbruck treasury without the councillors' agreement, and if such notes were nevertheless issued then his treasury would not be required to honour them. Maximilian wrote:[19]

> And we promise that we will not burden our Tirolean treasury with extraordinary expenditures that are against this decreed establishment [*Staat und Ordnung*]. But if despite this extraordinary expenses or promissory notes on the Innsbruck government and treasury are issued, then they shall not be responsible and bound to accept these bills.

One wonders where Maximilian's concept of chivalric honour (*Ehre*) fitted that kind of financial deviousness.[20] Maximilian then personally initialled the *Ordnung* and Lord Marshal Paul von Liechtenstein, as head of the Innsbruck administration was detailed to operate the new system.[21]

Since money was so scarce, it was inevitable that every few years Maximilian should need to make further economies. His ambitious war policies and mercenary troop recruitment meant that he was having to make continuous reductions in home expenditure. His court felt the cold austerity measures perhaps most keenly of all. At one point he cut Bianca Maria's establishment down by a quarter from 196 to 148 persons. Forty-eight courtiers and court servants were sacked. Bianca Maria's chamberlain dispensed with the services of two ladies-in-waiting, two organists, dwarfs, a medical doctor and a substantial number of men and women menials from the house, yard, stables and kitchen.[22] Even at around 150 persons the court remained quite sizeable, considering the Austrian territorial resources that had to be marshalled to feed it. It was, however, a scandalous show of poverty for an empress who was supposed to hold court as the wife of the first ruler in Christendom – at least according to the ideology of the Holy Roman Empire to which Habsburg Maximilian sub-scribed. If we look in more detail at this court of about 150 persons from the chamberlain right down to the lowliest stable-boy and scullery-hand, we will find that budget arrangements were made to the last candle-end, measure of wine, and slice of bread by the accountants.[23]

The court was divided into five departments under the masters of house, yard, stable, kitchen and wardrobe. Among others there were four washer-women for the ladies' fine things, two chaplains with two servants, Master Rupert the furrier with one assistant, three door-keepers with two assistants, three lutanists, three drummers and pipers and the master of the stable with one assistant. Then came seven noble pages, two silversmiths, one assistant to clean the silverware, a candlemaker and two accountants, four cooks, with four domestics, three stable-hands, eight wagoners, one teacher of dancing, four guards, a gardener, two fools and various cleaners and porters. They were carefully assigned specific keep and places at certain dinner tables in the main hall.

The empress sat at high table (as did subsequently the young Queens Maria and Anna) with *Hofmeisterin* Paula. At the next table the Lord High Steward presided over the heads of the household departments, including the personal servants and domestics of the empress and later of the queens. This group included the Italian tailor. At subsequent tables sat the noble pages, ladies, common servants, guards and porters. Chamberlain Nicholas von Firmian (Plate 18), his wife and daughter presided at the table of the ladies-in-waiting, which included two further tables for their own personal servants. An extra table accommodated a number of favoured servants, including the ladies' tailor, musicians and guards of the inner chambers. This was the inner court.

The outer court comprised the cooks' table, which included the accountants, and the kitchen and table hands. Thereafter came the cellarer's table with the stable servants, unruly folk needing the chamberlain's personal supervision to preserve decorum and discipline in the hall. A table was set aside for servants' children. Those detailed to do the rough work of hewing, fetching, carrying, hygiene and cleaning, including the wagoners and woodcutters sat at the outdoor servants' table. Next in the list was the chaplains' table which included the choirboys, no doubt regularly smarting under the rude proximity of the preceding table, sandwiched as they were between the outdoor servants and the cooks' extra table for kitchen boys, which also accommodated more washerwomen, porters, the carpenter, a Hungarian wagoner and, surprisingly, the dancing teacher. At the time that this seating plan was drawn up the Hungarian wagoner was ill and given his food in the town.[24] Fourteen tables in all were provided.

Rations of wine were dispensed five times a day, although not to everyone. At dawn the empress and later the queens received two measures each. The wagoners, kitchen staff and rough servants were the only others to receive wine this early. No doubt they needed it to start their early morning chores, and to keep them company empress or queens were given a liberal quantity, which may suggest that these ladies used wine also for washing and personal hygiene. One wonders about its quality: was it vinegar? At breakfast everyone received a measure of wine at table or place of work about the court. Between the morning and evening meal a number of people received an extra measure, notably the kitchen staff to cheer them through their preparations for the evening meal. At supper everyone received another measure at table. Finally a number of people received a night drink (*Schlaffdrunck*). It was handed to those who had late duties, such as door-keepers, guards, tailors and assistants who were working on, but only to the drummers and pipers when they were *not* giving an evening dance concert. The ladies-in-waiting and all senior court officials were also favoured with a *Schlaffdrunck*. In all, over 300 measures of wine were consumed daily, and this gave more than two measures of wine per person per day, varying from a maximum of six measures for Bianca Maria down to a minimum of two measures for the common servants.

There were only two set meals a day at court. At these meals rolls of fine white bread (*semeln*) were given primarily to the senior court officials and personal, indoor servants. The rest made do with black bread made from rye. At nine thick slices to the loaf, black bread was issued four times daily – with the soup at the daily main course, for breakfast and for supper, and with the night drink. Again only those who were eligible for the extra measures of wine received extra amounts of black bread. In all over sixty loaves of black bread and 140 white rolls were consumed every day. It provided about one-third of a black-bread loaf (three thick slices) and one white roll per person per day. But the privileged and their indoor servants obtained considerably more fine bread than the outdoor servants. However, two measures of wine and two slices of black bread were the minimum official ration for anyone working at court. No one starved, although by no means everyone grew fat, which after all made sound economic sense.

During the half-year from late September until mid-April the court consumed 103 candles nightly. In summertime the rate was thirty-two candles a night. Average consumption for lighting was one-third of a candle per head per night, ranging from fourteen candles nightly in winter in the empress's rooms down to two per night for the accountants. The majority of people working at court naturally received no lighting allowance, although one must take into account a fair amount of night-work (tailors, accountants) and amusement (musicians) as well as devotions (chaplains, choirs) and guard duty.

The court stabled forty-two horses including the cart and draught-horses, as well as riding beasts. This worked out at one horse to every four persons. Stabling costs were understandably high in an age when it took more to feed a horse (reckoned at half a *Star* of oats per day) than a domestic servant, and when horse-power was a crucial factor in defence and communications. Maximilian held Bianca Maria's court in very short supply and only increased the number of horses when the court was moved or when pomp and circumstance demanded.[25]

Despite all these minute regulations in the service of stricter economies, Maximilian was informed that 336 persons were still claiming daily meals at Bianca Maria's court, which was well over twice the number officially accounted for.[26] When a second count was made and recorded later in the same set of documents, the number had come down dramatically to an acceptable 191 persons. There was no mention of alms to beggars or court charity feeding. Perhaps in this sector Maximilian was quick to make real economies, although the Innsbruck government handed out just over a hundred gulden worth of charity a year in weekly instalments. This, however, seems to have been the limit here at least of Maximilian's regular duty to the concept of good works, although the matter will be dealt with more fully in chapter 11.[27]

Was a court dinner worth having? A number of the menus of empress's and the later queens' court have survived.[28] Menus were divided into three classes. The best foods went to the empress and queens and to their ladies-in-waiting. The chamberlain and inner court servants ate according to the second menu, and the outer court were given a third menu of rough fare. There were only two meal-times, at nine o'clock in the morning and at four o'clock in the afternoon. It was forbidden to receive meals in private chambers unless the individual was ill or indisposed. This rule applied also to Bianca Maria, who was to be seen to preside in person at all meals like any lady of a household. On fast days and Fridays only one meal was allowed. There were two basic types of meal; firstly, meat with soup as either game with pepper and cabbage, or veal/lamb fried in batter or in a pie with pastry; secondly, either fresh cooked fish with cabbage, or salted herring/stockfish with vegetables and soup. To all these dishes came wine and bread as already outlined above. A typical diet at court on a meat day was thus,

Breakfast: meat and soup, fried or game, cabbage, porridge,
              bread, wine.
Dinner: cooked cabbage or beets, stew, salted calf's head,
              or similar dishes according to season, choice and
              availability, bread, wine.

A typical Friday menu consisted of salted fish (stockfish), soup, cabbage, vegetables, bread, wine.

From this we see that those in the first-class menu certainly lived well, but diet was none too varied, nor were meals turned into marathons of gluttony by providing too many unnecessary courses. However, dairy products and fresh greens were notably absent: everything seemed to be well-cooked and well-spiced, an understandable measure of safety possibly further enhanced by the disinfectant properties of the relatively great quantities of weak alcohol (wine or even vinegar) that were consumed.

Clothing was issued twice yearly. Each person in court service was entitled to one suit every summer and winter. A pair of slippers for indoor wear was to be supplied every three months and outdoor shoes every four weeks. Early modern footwear was not long-lasting and the court would no doubt lose face (and the empress lose credit from her purveyors) if its servants walked abroad ill-shod and in tatters. In the last two years of life Maximilian tried to save too much money by cutting court clothing rations. Immediately after his death in January 1519 court officials led a strike demanding arrears in supply of clothing as well as pay. They refused to disband or to hand over Maximilian's personal effects and property until they had been paid in full. They claimed that each was owed two coats, two pairs of breeches, and two jerkins. They had received only one green winter coat in two years' service.[29] They wrote to the arbitrator handling the case for young Archduke Ferdinand and King Charles:[30]

> Well-born, noble, stern, highly-learned gracious lord. After
> we have humbly notified to both of our gracious lady
> Queens how our Court clothing allowance is in arrear, so
> their majesties have directed us to Lord Chamberlain von
> Firmian in order that we shall be supplied and paid. Now,
> gracious Lord, we write to you that we have not been

supplied nor has his late Imperial Majesty's last wish in this matter been carried out. Thus we humbly beg of your grace to recognise our needs and just claims that the clothing still owing to us be provided, since a number of your grace's servants have had similar claims satisfied and we wonder why this has not happened to us as well, seeing that we have always carried out our duties faithfully.

[signed]

Both our Lady Queens' most humble
Officers and Court servants

Court service was not necessarily a sinecure. Leonhard Vischmaister served for six years at eight gulden, two suits of clothing and one pair of boots yearly, totalling 102 fl. in money terms. Of this he only received five gulden in pay from Maximilian. To obtain this position he had lent forty-six gulden of his own money to the emperor which had not been repaid. Claus Botzen had also served six years and had only received two suits and twenty gulden pay during this time. As a liveried servant, Botzen had been promised eight gulden annually in cash and eighteen gulden worth of clothing. Servant Liendl had been hired with his wife and she had served indoors for five years without receiving her full pay. Complaints such as these are scattered throughout the archives.[31]

Because court service provided food, shelter and clothing, the money element in a job there was naturally relatively small. Annual rates of pay ranged from the chief cook at twenty-six gulden down to the stable-hands and porters at six gulden. The annual salary bill of Bianca Maria's court was less than 1500 fl. and this included the salaries of top court officials like the chamberlain who netted between 150 and 300 fl. every year. On average, chamber-servants received eight gulden a year and master craftsmen twenty gulden. Chaplains, lutanists, accountants, stable-masters and master-cooks also received twenty gulden. Ladies-in-waiting were promised surprisingly little. At between ten and twelve gulden per annum, they no doubt relied on their noble families to make them an extra allowance.

The range of pay at court, especially for craft and menial or unskilled and apprenticed tasks, was thus marginally lower than in the mines, agriculture or towns, when compared with our previous surveys. Whereas a miner's range of pay was eleven to seventy gulden in Hallein in 1507, that of a court scullery hand rising to chief cook was six to twenty-four gulden. At court no doubt security and good conditions, livery and perquisites made up for the discrepancy, but ultimately, working at the Habsburg court was probably just like most jobs anywhere else at that time, since rates of pay were uniformly minimal, although they were above the starvation level. Was a position at Maximilian's court hotly competed for or not? The evidence so far suggests that even menial posts had to be purchased with bribes worth up to five years in expected salaries. At court a prepared dinner was always available, but life there was institutional, regimented and public. The worker on day-rates in town and village may have enjoyed his privacy, which rapidly became a useless luxury at times of dearth, bad health, high prices and underemployment. At such times families sought the service and protection of a lord and his household on any conditions that he might have cared to offer. The wise commoner, given the chance, would have seized the opportunity to invest in court service, even if salaries and clothing rations were hopelessly in arrears at the courts of Maximilian and Bianca Maria around the year 1500 in Austria. An example of this is the prosopography of a chambermaid in the next chapter which gives a first insight into the provision of old-age pensions in Maximilian's Tirolean household, as we now turn to look at the socio-political treatment of *menu-peuple* in Maximilian's Renaissance Austria.

11

Menu-Peuple

As we have seen in the last four chapters, each of the major walks of life presented its own hazards. City life was subject to paternalist regulation of business, craft and retail opportunities, leaving little room, legally, for private initiative. With chronic under-employment rife, any further crisis could readily turn individual family privacy into misery. Peasant life entailed over-taxation and over-exploitation, by a myriad of landlords, of limited, inflexible amounts of agrarian produce. The consequence was a high level of rural violence. Mining was certainly an enterprising career, producing its own hazards at work, both technically, and in the field of labour relations. Hence the attraction of domestic service in the household of any landlord, priest, burgher, official or noble. The ultimate in security was to be employed at Maximilian's own Court Castle in Innsbruck. There were no shortages of applicants, place-hunters, scroungers, and those hanging-on in hope of a vacancy. That is why Maximilian could get away with the taking of bribes in return for the privilege of holding a very menial job which hardly ever received regular disbursement of the agreed salary and livery. But what of those who needed aid genuinely, because of illness, misfortune and old age? Maximilian's social policy was his Christian charity. What did it do to aid the *menu-peuple* under his rule?

The Innsbruck chancellery granted the following pension on 22 April 1492.[1]

> Margreth Wuestin. We recognise and openly proclaim in this letter that we have acknowledged herewith the honest Margreth, widow of the late George Wuesten, for her long

and regular service which she rendered to the late gracious Eleonore, born of Scots, Archduchess of Austria, of praiseworthy memory, in her Grace's chamber, that the next *Scheffel* of salt which becomes available in our panning-house at Hall be given to her weekly, or its equivalent in money. We order our faithful counsellor Lienhard Vellser and any subsequent salt-pan supervisor at Hall that you provide Margreth with one *Scheffel* of salt or its equivalent in money when available every week without fail.

It was an instruction by Maximilian to his Innsbruck counsellors to arrange for payment of a pension to a former domestic servant of Princess Eleonore. The sixth child of King James I of Scotland, Eleonore died eleven years previously (Innsbruck, 20 November 1480) as the wife of King Maximilian's cousin, Archduke Sigismund, who retired from governing the Tirol in March, 1490. What insight does this document provide into the terms of employment enjoyed by a domestic whose mistress was a Scottish princess and ruling duchess in the Alps during the middle of the fifteenth century? Who was Margreth Wuestin and what was she being promised by King Maximilian in 1492?

The first clue is with her former employer, to whose life a dissertation has recently been devoted.[2] Princess Eleonore was probably born in 1433, brought up at Linlithgow and orphaned in 1445. She was sent to the French royal court from where she was given in marriage to Duke Sigismund of Tirol in 1448. Sigismund was twenty-one and Eleonore sixteen years of age, but the marriage that lasted until Eleonore's death was childless. The story that they had a son, Wolfgang, who died young, was an invention of the Innsbruck chronicler, Gerard de Roo, who in 1592 misread the gravestone at Stams of Sigismund's elder brother, Wolfgang, who died in infancy in the 1420s.[3] Yet Sigismund was reputed to have been a womaniser.[4] He sired so many bastards that the Innsbruck chancellery insisted on a list of his authentic natural children before Maximilian was asked to provide for their well-being out of treasury revenue in 1492, just at the time that old domestic servant Margreth Wuestin was promised her pension.[5]

Eleonore kept a lively court. She was fluent in German and French, and a keen huntress. She travelled often and helped to found the first library in Innsbruck castle, where she had a *Frauenzimmer* of about fifty ladies-in-waiting. It was probably here that Margreth Wuestin found employment. Eleonore's habit was to reward courtiers for faithful service with pensions out of the salt-pans in the nearby town of Hall in the Inn valley. Thus the widow of her former doctor, Hans Speck, was granted a substantial rent of fifty *Fuder* of salt a year in 1475, over thirty times as valuable as Margreth Wuestin's promised salt-rent in 1492.[6]

This suggests that it was still the custom after seventeen years to reward faithful court servants from the same source of revenue. Was Maximilian being particularly sensitive to the memory of his late kinswoman, Eleonore of Scots, whom he probably met but once as an adolescent in the mid-1470s, or was he just making use of a social service for widows and old-age pensioners among Innsbruck court servants? Furthermore, what did Margreth Wuestin's promised income actually amount to in 1492?

One *Scheffel* of salt was perhaps twenty litres dry volume of granulated salt. Its value was just under ten kreuzers, according to Vienna *Bürgerspital* prices of 1493.[7] In 1491 Maximilian's Tirol silver deal with the Fuggers quoted the Rhenish gulden at sixty kreuzers.[8] A mid-day meal consumed by a well-off burgher and banker like Fugger cost about four kreuzers, reckoning one kreuzer per dish. Twelve kreuzers worth of salt was consumed in one meal by about 140 courtiers and court servants travelling with Maximilian through South Tirol in 1510.[9] It was considered possible to live on an income of forty gulden a year.[10] That was over forty-six kreuzers a week. Margreth Wuestin was being granted under ten kreuzers a week. Was this the basic old-age-pension of late fifteenth-century Austria? If so, then it was a pittance. Yet Margreth Wuestin had to be more than grateful for Maximilian's intervention on her behalf. It was proof of King Maximilian's meticulous attention to his writing desk, and a credit to the officials in his Innsbruck chancellery and treasury, one of whom was Lienhard Vellser (the very person who was to put down the Gossensass miners' strike in

1   Young Maximilian hunts backyard ducks, from the *Historia
Friderici et Maximiliani,* composed after 1497

2 Boxwood carving portraying Dr George Tanstetter, formerly
Maximilian's physician, *circa* 1521 with his son

3   Maximilian in 1518, by Albrecht Dürer

4   Frederick III *circa* 1452, ascribed to the Barbarini Master

5 Antler candelabra with attached busts of Maximilian I and Charles V backed on to each other, *circa* 1516

6 Double portrait medal of Emperor Frederick III and King Maximilian I, *circa* 1490

7   Maximilian, South Netherlandish School, after 1510

8 Maximilian in his travelling clothes riding on the road to
Augsburg, *circa* 1510, by Hans Holbein the Elder

9　Maximilian on 12 January 1519 at Wels: the Mask of Death

10 *opposite*　Effigy of Empress Eleonora, Maximilian's mother, completed in 1469

11　Maximilian's sister, Kunigunde, aged fifteen, School of the Schottenmeister, 1480

12 Maximilian's daughter, Margaret, subsequently regent of the Netherlands. Flemish portrait of 1483, when she was three years old, just before her ill-fated betrothal to Charles VIII of France

13 *opposite above*   Archduke Sigismund at his devotions in retirement after 1490, ascribed to Ludwig Kronreiter

14 *opposite below*   Personal letter of King Maximilian to Archduke Sigismund from Graz, 8 August 1490

15 *above*   Gossensass miners at work after 1490, altarpiece ascribed to Matthias Stöberl of Sterzing

16   Courtyard of the *Hofburg* at Innsbruck, *circa* 1498 by Albrecht Dürer

17   Bianca Maria Sforza, Maximilian's second wife, portrayed after
more than ten years of childless marriage in 1505 probably by
Bernhard Strigel, the Habsburgs' favourite family artist

18   Lord Lieutenant
of Tirol and
Chamberlain of
Bianca Maria's court,
Nicholas von Firmian,
circa 1498, Italian
workmanship

19   Effigy of
Archchancellor
Berthold, Mainz
Cathedral, after 1504

the following year). Just two months before promising Margreth Wuestin her pension, Maximilian had appointed Vellser as one of his four chief treasurers at Innsbruck, at a time when the king was struggling to preserve the Austrian Tirol and the *Vorlande* especially in Swabia from disintegrating under the weight of former Archduke Sigismund's debts and mismanagement.[11]

How old was Margreth Wuestin in 1492? She had served many years in Eleonore's chamber and we may surmise that she was appointed as a young woman when the princess arrived as a bride in Innsbruck castle in 1448 or shortly thereafter. Perhaps she was about Eleonore's own age when appointed, which would have made her sixty in 1492, truly a high age for a woman who had married and worked at menial tasks. Comparing the lives of Eleonore and Margreth, the roles seem to be reversed from the stereotype that one might expect. The chambermaid lived to a ripe age, married and probably bore children, outliving her husband, George. Her employer died eleven or more years before her, married but was barren, and was outlived by the husband, Sigismund.[12]

Did Margreth Wuestin receive her pension from Maximilian? She may well have done, since her fellow employee in Eleonore's *Frauenzimmer*, Waltpurg Kölpöckin, widow of Wolfgang Windeck, was granted sixty marks Bernese a year by Maximilian to bring up her son, payable quarterly from customs revenues as from 14 September 1493.[13] Peter Rueger, an old retainer to Sigismund, was also granted a salt-pension identical to Margreth Wuestin's on 20 January 1493, this time payable immediately since the death of a certain Schmägl had created a vacancy. Sigismund's fire-stoker, Sebastian Dreyer, was also pensioned at the same rate.[14] Salt pensions seem to have been standard practice and a number were used as the basis upon which to organise the retirement of court servants.

What everyday retail prices did Margreth Wuestin contend with, assuming that she received just under ten kreuzers or forty pfennigs per week in old-age pensions. In 1493 Maximilian's Innsbruck counsellors issued a table of maximum prices at the urgent request of the Estates made at the territorial assembly of 1492 in Sterzing.[15] Rye or black bread retailed at around one kreuzer for the two-pound loaf, and the

Innsbruck pound weighed a substantial 560 grammes.[16] Margreth Wuestin probably bought her bread in half-pound loaves at one *fierer* (farthing or quarter-kreuzer, the same as one pfennig). She may also have yearned for the typical basic fare of her former employers in the *Frauenzimmer*, namely fine white bread at around two kreuzers for a three-ounce roll. Did she treat herself to one just occasionally? Although meat prices were not standardised, the cheapest fish retailed at three kreuzers per pound with carp at four, bream at five and eel at six kreuzers. When it came to luxuries such as fish and meat she probably only ate scraps on rare occasions. Comparisons with present-day retired people on minimum pensions are probably not too far out of place.

Yet we must reckon that by the standards of the time, Margreth Wuestin was probably rather well off – one of the lucky few who had served at court. What of cleaners and menials who had not worked for such august employers? How did they fare? The labour relations of everyday existence in late medieval and early modern Europe need to be rediscovered from the fiscal archives, and they can be reconstituted with the help of biographical techniques applied to the *menu-peuple* like Margreth Wuestin of Innsbruck, one-time servant to a fifteenth-century Scottish princess. An indication of what was in store for the ordinary person, who had not made provision for himself or herself in old age or illness, can be given through examining the arrangement made by Maximilian, as a charge on his Tirolean revenues, for his own personal spending, and for his wife, Bianca Maria; comparing all that with the alms they allowed out of the same treasury for beggars at their castle gate.[17]

Alms were distributed daily from the court mill-house in the form of bread, meat and vegetables, according to a register roll-call, naming the deserving poor, who were also paid a dole of one pound in pennies every week. What remained as surplus was then left for the unregistered poor. Non-local and sturdy beggars were not advised to show their faces. In his decrees, Maximilian only recognised as worthy the local resident poor (*Hausarme*), and pilgrims. In 1496 he had ordered his Innsbruck treasury to give 100 fl. a month to these two categories of beggars 'for the sake of God'. In 1506 that

Menu-peuple

Maximilian's Innsbruck pocket money			Bianca Maria's Innsbruck pocket money	
	fl.			fl.
1500	2,242		1502	17,333
1502	5,000		1503	13,000
1506	184		1504	13,000
1507	821		1506	4,192
1509	4,796		1507	10,171
1510	4,588		1509	6,016
1511	1,840		1510	2,074
1512	6,619		(posthumous debts;	
1514	75,265		1511	12,289
1515	150,079		1512	4,109)
1516	20,692			

Their alms for Innsbruck's poor

	fl.
1506	904
1507	1,400
1509	1,300
1510	1,300
1511	1,300
1512	1,300
1513	1,300
1515	1,372
1516	1,359

had been officially reduced to 25 fl. a month, although in that year Maximilian for the first time approved of the distribution of food every Saturday in the Innsbruck suburbs. Perhaps he had tired of seeing unregistered beggars at the gates of the *Hofburg* in the old town itself. There remained the problem of assistance payments to the genteel poor as well as to retired servants. These payments were considerably more *ad hoc* than were the regular alms. Each case was treated on its merits, along with provision for widows and orphans, as *Gnadengelder*, starting at 2500 fl. a year in the 1490s and reaching about 15,000 by 1514. For example, the treasury recorded: '[1501] To the children of the late Wolfgang and Walpurga von

117

Windeck, namely Sigmund, Ulrich and Magdalena, 60 fl. for the next three years. [7 August 1511] To the poor carpenter's wife, whose husband was killed by a tree, graciously given two gulden.'

As Maximilian aged, so these expenses grew in order to take into account an increase in retirements and old-age pensions. After Bianca Maria's death at New Year 1511, Maximilian was concerned about her reputation and good name in posterity. Effectively, that meant honouring her debts. He ordered:

> Since we are dedicated to the well-being of our wife's soul
> by honouring all her debts which she contracted during the
> whole of her life in order to protect her memory from gossip,
> we request you [Paul von Liechtenstein] to call a meeting of
> all our treasury councillors to inquire into, and
> subsequently pay, all valid claims.

We now have some indication of the kind of business that Maximilian personally handled. As a paternalist at the peak of a feudal hierarchy he clearly took responsibility for matters of welfare, both great and small, concerning family, kin, court and servants. His duties here were less burdensome and time-consuming than in the military sphere. The impression that does emerge, however, is that he may have been rashly impetuous, but he had a sense of responsibility appropriate to his calling as an overlord in feudal Germany.

Yet it was only when Maximilian was being pulled up short by the prospect of his own impending death that his piety turned to more expensive forms of charity, which would glorify his name and also win him a place in heaven, when his soul should pass before God on the last day of judgment. His last will and testament made the provision outlined below for a lucky few of the *menu-peuple*. It should be understood as natural that, as a traditional Christian ruler and calculating businessman, Maximilian should feel a need to show his repentance by establishing alms-houses for the common poor in his will, in order to prompt the inmates to pray for his soul, for, as we have seen, he had upheld a system which heavily burdened the labourers and peasants in his realm.

On 30 December 1518, shortly before his death, Maximilian had dictated his last will, 'between twelve and one o'clock in the night at Innsbruck', to his private secretary Hanns Vinsterwalder.[18] It is a conventional document in that Maximilian is at pains to atone for his sins by means of chantries which would ensure that regular masses were sung for his soul. The will provides insights into the late medieval ruling-class attitude towards poverty and good works. Obsessed with the need for his name to last for ever, Maximilian linked his piety with provision of charity. Good works would atone for his actions in the eyes of God and posterity. Among other arrangements, eight poor hospitals were to be founded, one in each of his provincial capitals, in Innsbruck, Vienna, Linz, Graz, Sant Veit, Laibach, Breisach, and the eighth in his beloved Augsburg. In thus catering for the urban poor, Maximilian chose his locations very carefully in order to glorify most effectively his name and dynasty. The fact that he went into the closest details over these arrangements is yet another indication of his passion for rules and regulations, on this occasion indulged in even at death's door. The problem was that he expected far too much for the money that he was prepared to invest – truly a problem that Maximilian had always faced in life and which he optimistically took with him to the grave. In his will he sought to associate a select few of the deserving poor with his good name in posterity. Was he then merely expressing the pious sentiments that were expected of a Christian ruler, or did he also experience a real need to repent for having burdened his common subjects with twenty-five years of personal rule? If we examine his proposals more closely it can be seen how puny in quantity yet perceptive in quality his arrangements were.

Maximilian directed that each of the eight poor hospitals was to be endowed with one thousand gulden capital in perpetuity for the upkeep of its inmates. The money was to be taken out of local domain revenues at 5 per cent annual interest. The revenue needed for buildings and essential services was to be collected from other securities that were safer than domain revenues, for the latter were open to frequent alienation. Out of this perpetual fifty gulden net annual income each poor hospital was to pay for a priest to read mass for Maximilian's soul. It thus seems that uppermost in Maximilian's mind was his desire to be remembered by posterity. The next priority was to provide social and medical care for the poor inmates, expressed as follows by the emperor himself: 'Then, in each of these hospitals there shall be a large room and chamber with bedsteads for the poor, and in each bedstead a straw sack shall be made up and kept.'

Each establishment was to employ a warden, cook, cellarer and other servants for daily needs. Each poor inmate should be given every morning and every evening vegetable pottage (*gemuess*) and sufficient bread, plus a measure of soused (*gsotten*) water, flavoured with honey and berries. Bread, vegetables and sweetened fruit-juice would provide a worthy diet for sick and ailing common people, compared with the diets for urban and rural labouring families. In theory this arrangement was all very fine, but Maximilian's real appreciation of the needs of the poor and afflicted must be contrasted with the knowledge that his small charity grant of eight thousand gulden would not go very far towards satisfying the needs that he stipulated in his will. In return, Maximilian expected the prospective recipients of his charity to pray for his soul. Whenever they received his bounty, they should thus remember what a good ruler he had been. All this consolation Maximilian wished to buy for eight thousand gulden, a sum that two decades previously he had been spending on his falcons and falconers in one year alone.[19] The old emperor thought that a rent of 400 fl. per annum was enough to secure for all time the memory of his charity and goodness throughout Austria.

Having made arrangements for the provision of a reasonable diet, Maximilian turned to the question of clothing for the prospective inmates. This time he equipped his last troop, not of proud Landsknechts, but of derelicts and beggars, some of whom, one may speculate, would probably be old campaigners from his earlier wars. The clothing ration was, in theory, very generous. Each inmate was to receive two smocks a year, of single cloth in summer, and double cloth in winter. Four times a year they would be provided with a long shirt and one pair of shoes. Each winter they would also be given an overcoat. Maximilian then instructed that his plans be scrutinised by accountants and in this he showed a last passion for administrative detail as he set up annual audits (*jährliche Raitung*) for his posthumous almshouses.[20]

Never a man to ignore the impact of the visual image as propaganda, Maximilian decreed that each almshouse should have a portrait statue of him holding a candle, in front of which masses were to be sung to the glory of God, Maximilian and his patron saints, George and John the Evangelist.[21] And he ordered all his government, court and local domain officials to remain at their posts after his death until these measures had been carried out by his successors.[22]

> Biography is limited by the fact that universal movements intersect in the individual life; if we are to understand them we must seek for new foundations outside the individual. It is not possible for biography to become scientific. We must turn to new categories, shapes and forms of life which do not emerge from the individual life. The individual is only the crossing point for the cultural systems and organizations into which his existence is woven; how can they be understood through him?[23]

Let us turn to how Maximilian conducted his practical politics, since we now have some idea of the people over whom he exercised dynastic power 'by the grace of God'.

12

Practical politics

The 1490s were the crucial decade in Maximilian's career when he came into his own as sole federal ruler of Germany and overall head of the Habsburg dynastic complex centred on the Tirol and Eastern Swabia at Innsbruck and Augsburg. At this time, between the age of thirty and forty, Maximilian was at the peak of his power, energy and personal drive. The Burgundian wars of his youth were drawing to a close, with the successful capture of Franche Comté from the French Valois at the end of 1492. The Italian Wars had not as yet fully drawn him and his far too limited resources into a long conflict with Venice which was to mar the last decade of his life. The 1490s were his halcyon days, opening with the transfer of Tirolean government from the incompetent Archduke Sigismund to himself, and ending in painful defeat at the hands of the Engadin Swiss in 1499. By that time Maximilian had personally entered the tournament jousting lists for the last time, and was to turn increasingly to his court humanists, poets and artists in nostalgia for the exploits of his youth and highest manhood. These were a myriad of journeys, feasts, campaigns, marriages, hunting, shooting, fishing and jousts, *welsch tournay und teutsch stechen*. After 1500 Maximilian became the propagandist of his own life and exploits, creating myth and cult out of his autobiography. As we have seen in chapter 2, he worked hard at his own image, wishing to become an official folk hero, seeking the admiration of the marketplace, cottage and terrace as well as of pulpit, manor house, town hall and chancellery. We may thus regard him as a refined Germanic prototype of Rabelais' Gargantua and King Picrochole rolled into one person.[1]

We will look at his work-routine, then see him handling federal, Reich affairs, especially as exemplified at the Reichstag at Frankfurt in 1489, and finally give cases of Tirolean and Austrian Habsburg domestic, territorial politics. In this we shall show firstly, what the practical, day-to-day actions and personal constraints of rulership amounted to, as a physical burden of responsibility on Maximilian. Secondly, we wish to determine policies, as immediate reactions to circumstances were routinised administratively. Thirdly, this will clarify some of the problems of comprehension that the modern reader has when trying to make sense of a politician like Maximilian, who had no real ministerial machinery, and who dealt with all matters, great and small, at random, and according to urgency and whim from minute to minute.

Maximilian's political routine was not firmly established until after he took over the Tirol in 1490. From then on his life revolved around nine basic types of activity, involving personal attention to an endless amount of paperwork. In his Austrian domains no hunting castle was complete without the writing desk in his personal chambers, however sparse the rest of the furnishings.[2] He organised military campaigns, fortifications and defence accompanied by an aggressive, opportunistic foreign policy. He organised Austrian dynastic territorial politics as well as German imperial federal politics through a variety of treasuries, chancelleries, parliaments, *Landtage* and Reichstags. He dealt with privileges and confirmations stemming from his high jurisdiction as German King. By way of contrast to that, he had to satisfy his creditors and look for new sources of finance. Maximilian had to keep a watch on the federal peace and try to minimise feudal civil war by arbitrating in perennial conflicts over inheritance, debt and high jurisdiction among Germany's leading noble and urban families especially in the South and West. As ultimate feudal overlord he also had to regulate family and dynastic affairs among Habsburg kinsfolk and related dynasties. He had to take ultimate responsibility for all appointments, apportioning and supervising of counsellors, secretaries and servants in his various regional and personal establishments. Finally, he took great pains to regulate his own entertainments, feasts, food, travel, culture, hunting and court culture.

123

The daily routine of written work was sorted by his chancellor and secretaries into six sections according to which type of seal, signet or signature was to be used. Correspondence was conducted in German, Latin and French, although Maximilian did most of his own writing and annotation in German.[3] *Diplomata* were formal agreements on parchment (*epistolae patentes membran.*). Secondly, there were *Patents*, concerning feudal matters (*epistolae patentes chartac.*). Thirdly came *Instructions*, and fourthly *Papal letters* (*epistolae claus. membranc.*). The most time-consuming and personally exhausting for Maximilian was, fifthly, his correspondence dealing with administration and finance (*epistolae claus. chartac.*), linked to the Instructions and also, sixthly, to *Drafts* (*concepte*) which were usually loose sheets with large margins, often corrected in Maximilian's own, forcefully chunky, upright hand.

Although he was loyally aided by a quite bewildering array of chancellors, treasurers, courtiers, envoys, secretaries, scribes and domestic servants, both peripatetic, like himself, or fixed in one town or castle as at Innsbruck, Maximilian spent most of his working life composing and checking through drafts which usually became *epistolae claus. chartac.*, that is, the instructions of his own territorial administration and fisc as folded letters, signet-sealed with address and addressee on the outside. The character and style of the man is most immediately captured in his fleeting comments on these draft letters, occasionally supplemented by the personally scribbled note, letter or memorandum, which are Maximilian's personal *autogramme*. The basic point here is that Maximilian was a politician with many schemes, always impatient, always in a hurry, generally over-ambitious. Hence, his archives have a breathless, chaotic and unexpected charm of their very own, more suited perhaps to the speed with which modern politicians have to react to pressure groups and their media than to an earlier epoch. To that extent, Maximilian was very quick to adapt the printing press to administrative and official governmental purposes. He was not afraid of producing red-tape, and therefore of receiving it back by return. By the 1490s his war propaganda, writs to parliament, demands for taxation and allied judicial business were all becoming adapted to the printed formula, leaving his officials with more time for other business as they now merely had to fill in name, address, date and amount where appropriate.[4]

An example of Maximilian's impetuousness is contained in a draft letter to his future chancellor, Cyprian von Serntein, from the field of battle in North Italy, 26 August 1496, as he blamed his military failure on the lack of loyal financial support from his Innsbruck administration. 'I strictly order you to carry this out quickly for they should be told quite clearly where they stand. We are bogged down here and dancing to a piper on one stilt.'[5]

Maximilian had three signatures. Firstly, *M.RO. Kunig p.m.p.* appeared under his rare private and personal letters. Secondly, he used what was called the large hand-sign (*grosse Handzeichen*) which spelled out *Maxis* with an elaborate flourish, followed by *sps (subscripsi)*. The small hand-sign (*kleine Handzeichen*) was *per regem per se* which he kept even upon taking the title of Holy Roman Emperor in 1508, although thereafter he did occasionally substitute *per cesarem per se*. In 1497–8 and in 1500 Maximilian had to agree that his great officials, above all Elector Frederick the Wise of Saxony, be allowed to sign letters in his name. By this time he was clearly feeling the strain of routine paperwork and had given strict orders forbidding his officials to importune him with special pleas. Territorial political matters were increasingly steered towards his Innsbruck administration, and so after 1497 the signature *per regem* no longer automatically implied Maximilian's personal presence for the actual preparation of that document. However, *per regem per se* did guarantee his direct involvement.

Attempts were continually made to sort his affairs into three overall compartments, namely imperial affairs (Reich); dynastic and territorial princely matters (*Fürstenhäuser*); and personal, court, household business (*Hof*), but he never succeeded in being so bureaucratically neat. Since Maximilian was hardly ever solvent for more than a few weeks or days he was always robbing Peter to pay Paul, which quickly resulted in a bureaucratic muddle that only Maximilian in person could unravel. The more that happened, the more he set himself good resolutions and planned marvellously elaborate departments and institutions, only to see them break down as of necessity during the next credit or cash crisis.

A whole variety of chancellery business was automatically signed and sealed in Maximilian's name. If his council of administration made the decision, the signature was *commissio domini regis in consilio*. If the decision came as his direct verbal command, the matter was signed *commissio domini regis propria*. If the decision was the result of an indirect instruction, the name of the relevant official was also added, *per dominum N*. At Innsbruck there were five administrators, collectively called *Statthalter und Räte* who handled fiscal matters in Maximilian's absence. They were Bishop Melchior of Brixen, Herr Marten von Polheim, Heinrich Prüschenk (Graf zu Hardegg), Walter von Stadion and Hans von Landau, serviced by the secretaries, Casius Hagkeney and Blasius Hölzl. Between 1498 and 1502 all these officials used Maximilian's signature with their own counter-sign.[6]

After Maximilian's temporary eclipse and near-bankruptcy in 1500, the Nuremberg federal regency administration issued letters until March 1502, countersigned by Archchancellor Archbishop Berthold of Mainz or by Waldemar of Anhalt, prepared by secretary Sixtus Ölhafen. Some of these letters were issued without Maximilian's knowledge or approval and they were a major cause of the notorious rivalry between him and his Archchancellor.[7]

Maximilian had to keep making new rules of administration for himself because he could never stick to any arrangement for very long. Necessity and temperament were hopelessly enmeshed here. Business was mixed with pleasure at all times and mighty matters muddled with minutiae. There were also his loose notes or schedules (*lose zettel*), a typical example of which is:

Michel, Freiherr zu Wolckenstein.
We order you to act upon our completed citation as our judge to find a legal solution to the dispute between our fellow ruling prince, Duke Wolfgang of Bavaria, and Wolf von Freyberg. Herein you will do our earnest bidding.
Given at Innsbruck, 5 August 1510.

per regem per se

Another lose note in Maximilian's handwriting was in fact nothing more than a luncheon voucher, showing that impulsive King Maximilian had time for everything.[8]

> Zyprian von Serntein, our Chancellor.
> Our earnest command is that you immediately order sustenance to be provided for the servant of Count Lienhart zum Hag, the holder of this note, in order that without any delay he can ride on to his master concerning the Hungarian business. Herein you will do our earnest bidding. Given at Trient, 29 July 1511.
>
> per regem per se

Maximilian was setting up the Hungarian-Habsburg marriage alliance. He did his own paperwork. He liked to make all his own arrangements at the dynastic level, delegating nothing.

However, the chancellery used various forms to relieve him of routine business such as confirmations, domain and tax matters. The three most common formulae were *commissio domini regis propria, in consilio* and *ad mandatum dominin regis proprium*, with substitution of 'imperial' for 'royal' after 1509. Maximilian also used the technique of producing draft letters whilst on his travels, signing and directing them to Innsbruck by dispatch rider for government processing. These letters were then sent with place of origin as Innsbruck, whilst Maximilian was miles away, as happened, for example, whilst he was visiting Thérouanne in Artois during late August 1513. After 1507 Maximilian showed signs of bureaucratic tiredness and he began to use a stamp instead of his handwritten signature or sign. The fashion soon caught on at court and Chancellor Serntein had a stamp of his own, but also used Maximilian's. Some parts of his patrimony Maximilian visited less frequently, above all parts of Lower and Inner Austria, where the Viennese chamber of accounts and Neustadt prerogative court almost invariably handled his correspondence, orders and patents on commission. All this entailed a remarkable trust giving considerable freedom of action to actual officials locally and regionally in charge, yet it was also the great age of unofficial enrichment by rulers' favourites: in Maximilian's case, the Sernteins, Liechtensteins, Prüschenks, Waldaufs and Stadions to name only a few, for no one who could help it condemned himself to live on an inadequate official salary.[9]

Maximilian was a royal locust. With his entourage averaging well over a hundred persons, he ate up more in cash equivalent in a day than could a priest or local official in six months. Maximilian rated as a somewhat dowdy and moth-eaten patron when compared with his French, Italian, Iberian and Netherlands counterparts. On 6 January 1510, Maximilian and an entourage of 140 persons ate in Bozen, South Tirol. Their bill (*Küchenzettel*) came to just under 20 fl., showing that dinner could cost an average eight kreuzers per person when Maximilian was on his travels, *and* celebrating Epiphany.[10]

> 4 capons – 49 kreuzer [kr.]
> 9 chickens – 56 kr.
> 2 hares –24 kr.
> milk – 19 kr.
> vinegar – 9 kr.
> salt – 12 kr.
> barley – 12 kr.
> fine flour – 7 kr.
> lard – 2 Rhenish Gulden [fl. rh.]
> One *star* of white peas for His Majesty's own mouth – 1 fl. rh.
> Sauerkraut – 12 kr.
> beets – 8 kr.
> apples – 8 kr.
> onions – 8 kr.
> cabbage – 6 kr.
> pears – 8 kr.
> wood – 48 kr.
> Two pigs turned into sausages at His Majesty's command – 5 fl. 14 kr.
> Sausage skins – 12 kr.
> Cumin seeds – 14 kr.
> 400 pounds of beef and veal at one kr. per pound – 6 fl. 40 kr.
> Total   19 fl. 13 kr.

The bill for drink has not survived. On the next day food costs were just under 16 fl. 1510 was a particularly hectic year for Maximilian and his entourage. They stayed in 117 towns and castles, traversing Tirol, Alsace, the Black Forest and Swabia.[11]

In tracing Maximilian's itinerary it is often thought sufficient to give merely a deep impression of his restless character but in this he was really only very traditionally feudal. Yet in the regions of Innsbruck and Augsburg as from 1490 he did have his favourite places of residence and they were reasonably close to each other. But it was never the case that Maximilian had *one* capital city from which he governed and in which he permanently resided. He was a truly old-fashioned German king, always on the move, as had been his father before him. October 1477 saw Maximilian in Bruges, aged 18, as an Archduke of Austria, already two months married to the heiress of Burgundy and confirming Burgundian fiefs as feudal overlord. At the same time, financial problems were becoming the major concern of his lifetime, as he ordered treasurer Nicolas Prevost to pay the Bishop of Metz 3,000 fl., using the creditworthiness of his wife to still the demand. The itinerary is a first reasonably full survey of his whereabouts from some of the sources and literature.[12] Map 12.1 is also an attempt to list some of the places in which he stayed, as Maximilian ranged from the Pas de Calais to Szekesferhervar in Hungary, from Frankfurt to Rougemont in Franche Comté, and from Amsterdam to Pisa. He knew Brabant, the Rhine Valley, Alsace, Swabia, Tirol, Upper, Lower and Inner Austria like the back of his hand.

Maximilian's restlessness increased with age and was exacerbated by his political failures in Reichstag affairs especially linked to his campaigns in Italy (1496 and 1509) and Hungary (1506). The last ten years of his life were spent tearing up and down the Rhine and Danube, into the Netherlands, criss-crossing Alsace and Swabia and exploring Franconia, Bavaria and his Austrian lands, including the first of several daring winters on the move, traversing the Alps, in South Tirol, Salzburg, Carinthia, and Styria (1511–12). Even the itinerary simplifies Maximilian's movements especially from 1509 whereafter he seldom spent more than one night in

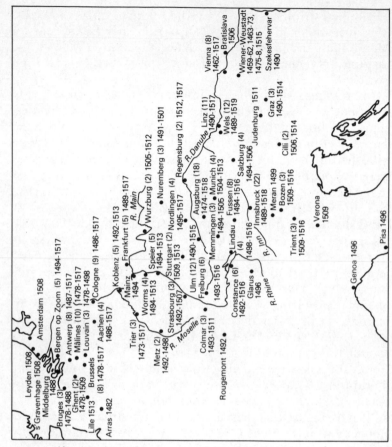

Map 12.1 Maximilian's itinerary (listing place, number of times visited – counting once per year only – and the years of first and last stay. The list is not complete; it gives an impression only)

130

ITINERARY

1486 *January* Cologne
 April Aachen
 August Bruges
1487 *October* Brussels
 November Antwerp
1488 *August* Middelburg
 October Mâlines
1489 *May* Innsbruck
 July Frankfurt
 December Wels
1490 *May* Ulm
 June Linz/Danube
 July Graz/Styria
 August Vienna
 November
 Szekesferhervar/Hungary
1491 *January* Linz
 February Augsburg
 March Nuremberg
 September Ulm
1492 *February* Innsbruck
 April Augsburg

 June Ulm
 July Constance
 August Strasbourg
 October Koblenz
 November Metz
 December
 Rougemont/Franche
 Comté
1493 *January* Altkirch/Alsace
 February Colmar
 March Freiburg-im-Breisgau
 May Augsburg
 July Linz
 September Innsbruck, Hall,
 Schwaz, Kufstein
 October Vienna
 November Graz
 December Vienna
1494 *March* Salzburg, Innsbruck,
 Memmingen, Füssen
 May Kempten, Pfaffenhausen
 June Worms, Speier, Mainz,

 Cologne
 July Aachen, Maastricht
 August Mâlines, Antwerp,
 Mâlines, Louvain
 October Antwerp
 December Bergen-op-Zoom,
 Mâlines'
1495 *February* 's Hertogenbosch,
 Maastricht
 March Aachen, Cologne,
 Bonn, Worms
 October Frankfurt-am-Main
 December Nördlingen
1496 *January* Augsburg
 February Schwäbisch-Werth
 March Füssen
 April Augsburg
 May Ulm, Augsburg
 June Ulm, Augsburg,
 Kaufbeuren
 August Glarus,
 Schlunders-im-Veltlin,

Thun-am-See
September Viglerano, Tortona
October Genoa, Pisa
November Vico Pisano
December Innsbruck
1497 *February* Überlingen
May Kaufbeuren, Füssen
June Hall, Innsbruck, Füssen, Kaufbeuren
July Imst
August Innsbruck
1498 *April* Füssen
May Ulm
June Wolfach, Freiburg-im-Breisgau
October Metz, Louvain
1499 *February* Mâlines
March Cologne
April Freiburg-im-Breisgau
May Tettwang, Lindau
June Nauders, Meran
July Lindau
September Augsburg
November Innsbruck
1500 *January* Wels

February Innsbruck
March Augsburg
September Telfs, Stubach, Innsbruck, Steinach
October Donauwörth
November Nuremberg
December Linz
1501 *January* Wels, Linz, Wels
March Salzburg, Innsbruck, Augsburg
April Donauwörth, Nuremberg, Augsburg
May Landshut
June Hall/Tirol
July Augsburg
September Innsbruck
November Augsburg, Nördlingen, Öttingen-im-Riess
December Ehingen
1502 *July* Ulm
August Augsburg
September Innsbruck
November Schwäbisch-Hall
1503 *January* Augsburg

March Antwerp, Bergen-op-Zoom
June Breisach, Waldshut, Füssen
August Stams, Imst
September Fragenstein, Innsbruck
October Stams, Imst, Füssen, Kaufbeuren
November Mindelheim, Augsburg
December Ulm, Ehingen, Biberach
1504 *January* Leutkirch, Memmingen, Zirl, Innsbruck, Fragenstein, Zirl, Imst, Augsburg
May Dillingen
June Innsbruck
July Augsburg, Reutlingen
August Constance
September Munich, Schwaz, Rattenberg
October Outside Kufstein, Rosenheim

November Innsbruck, Salzburg
December Kufstein, Reichenhall, Wels
1505 *January* Gmünden, Rottenmann, Innsbruck
February Reutte, Memmingen
March Constance Villingen, Gengenbach
April Hagenau, Weissenburg/Alsace, Strasbourg
May Cologne
June Düsseldorf, Cologne
July Antwerp
August Aarschot, Mâlines, Brussels
October Diest, Andernach, Gelnhausen, Würzburg
November Ebersdorf, Osterhofen, Passau, Wels, Linz
1506 *April* Bruck/Mur
May Vienna
July Bratislava
September Cilli

October Knittelfeld
November Salzburg
1507 *January* Innsbruck
March Strasbourg
April Constance
September Innsbruck
1508 *January* Sterzing
February Neustift
March Innsbruck, Mittenwald, Partenkirchen, Schongau, Kaufbeuren, Augsburg
April Esslingen, Ulm, Blaubeuren, Speier, Landau, Wetzlar
May Birkenfeld, Kochem, Andernach, Linz/Rhein, Cologne
June Boppard, Kreuznach, Oberwesel
July Koblenz, Andernach, Cologne, Duisburg, Xanten, s'Hertogenbosch
August Doordrecht, Leyden, Amsterdam, Haarlem,

s'Gravenhage
September Brussels, Mâlines, Antwerp
October Doordrecht, Rotterdam, s'Hertogenbosch, Breda, Antwerp, Mâlines
December Bergen-op-Zoom, Mâlines
1509 *January* Brussels
February Ghent
March Mâlines, Antwerp, Bergen-op-Zoom, Breda, s'Hertogenbosch
April Xanten, Duisburg, Cologne, Koblenz, Rüdesheim, Worms, Speier, Stuttgart
May Ulm, Kaufbeuren, Kempten, Stams, Innsbruck
June Sterzing, Bozen, Trient, Arco
July Feltre, Bassano
August Outside Padua

133

October Vicenza, Camisolo, Custozza, Verona
November Trient
December Bozen
1510 *January* Brixen, Sterzing, Innsbruck
February Stams, Kaufbeuren, Mindelheim, Augsburg and surroundings
July Munich, Weilheim, Füssen, Lermoss, Fragenstein
August Innsbruck and surroundings, Landeck
September Bludenz, Feldkirch, Bregenz, Lindau, Über-lingen, Constance
October Radolfszell, Villingen, Freiburg-im-Breisgau
November Breisach, Ensisheim
December Colmar
1511 *January* Freiburg-im-Breisgau
February Ensisheim, Colmar
March Breisach, Schlettstadt, Oberehnheim

April Gengenbach
May Ulm, Munich, Braunau
June Rosenheim, Kufstein, Rattenberg, Hall, Innsbruck
July Telfs, Sterzing, Brixen, Bozen, Trient
August Pergine, Trient
September Bozen, Bruneck, Lienz
October Sterzing, Steinach
November Innsbruck, Sterzing, Lienz, Ober-Drauburg, Greifenburg, Gmünd
December Murau, Judenburg, Rottenmann, Aussee, Ischl, Gmünd, Wels, Linz/Danube
1512 *January* Wels, Linz, Buchheim, Landau, Regensburg
February Ochsenfurt, Würzburg, Frankfurt-am-Main
March Wiesbaden, Koblenz,

Trier and surroundings
May Namur, Brussels
June Mâlines, Antwerp, Turnhout
July Diest, Maastricht, Jülich, Cologne
October Neuss, Cologne
November Andernach, Koblenz, Kreuznach, Alzey, Neustadt, Speier
December Weissenburg/Alsace
1513 *January* Landau, Reichshofen, Hagenau/Alsace
March Speier, Stuttgart, Ulm, Augsburg
April Mindelheim, Landsberg
May Kaufbeuren, Augsburg, Mindelheim
June Ulm, Esslingen, Stuttgart, Speier, Worms, Darmstadt, Frankfurt-am-Main
July Bingen, Koblenz, Bitburg, Namur, Brussels, Oudenarde

August Bailleul, Aire,
Thérouanne, St Omer
September Aire, Lille, Tournay
October Ath, Mons, Namur,
Kochel, Bingen,
Frankfurt-am-Main
November Miltenberg,
Rothenburg-ob-der-
Tauber, Dinkelsbühl,
Nördlingen, Donauwörth,
Augsburg
December Munich
1514 *January* Benedictbeuren,
Mittenwald, Seefeld, Zirl,
Innsbruck, Hall, Schwaz,
Rattenberg, Inn-
sbruck
February Kufstein, Gmünd,
Wels
March Enns, Steyr, Wels,
Gmünd, Braunau
April Passau, Linz, Wels,
Linz, Enns
May Krems, Vienna,
Reichenau, Murzzuschlag,

Graz
June Windischgrätz, Cilli,
Krainburg, Laibach
July Graz, Leoben,
Rottenmann, Gmünd
August Wels
September Rosenheim,
Kufstein, Innsbruck and
surroundings
1515 *March* Reutte, Füssen,
Augsburg
April Ulm, Krumbach,
Mindelheim, Buchloe
May Augsburg, Buchloe,
Weilheim
June Mittenwald, Innsbruck,
Kufstein, Wels, Linz
July Enns, Vienna,
Wiener-Neustadt
August Krems, Enns, Wels,
Rosenheim, Kufstein
September Innsbruck and
surroundings
November Lermoss, Augsburg
December Ulm, Memmingen,

Füssen, Lermoss, Feldkirch,
Bregenz, Lindau, Ulm.
1516 *January* Augsburg,
Kaufbeuren
February Füssen, Landeck,
Imst
March Bozen, Trient, Lake
Garda, Caravaggio
April Terzolas, Trient, Arco
May Trient, Bozen, Glurns
June Landeck, Immenstadt,
Tettnang, Constance
July Bregenz, Sonthofen,
Füssen, Lermoss
August Innsbruck,
Fragenstein, Reutte
September Füssen,
Kaufbeuren, Füssen,
Kaufbeuren, Augsburg
October Augsburg,
Kaufbeuren, Füssen,
Reutte
November Bregenz, Lindau,
Constance, Freiburg,
Breisach

December Hagenau
1517 *January* Trier, Maastricht, Diest, Turnhout
February Mâlines, Antwerp, Brussels, and surroundings
April Breda, Antwerp, Bergen-op-Zoom and surroundings
May Maastricht
June Aachen, Cologne, Frankfurt, Mergentheim
July Nördlingen, Augsburg
August Ingolstadt, Regensburg, Passau, Linz
September Krems, Vienna and surroundings
December Enns, Linz, Wels, Linz
1518 *January* Wels, Braunau, Freising, Augsburg
February Augsburg and surroundings
August Augsburg
December Innsbruck
1519 *12 January* Death of Maximilian in Wels on his way to Vienna to organise a crusade against the Turks

one place, although many of his trips were local, as for example in the spring of 1512 when he explored Trier and its surrounding village and riverside towns. Some of his travel ling was now clearly aimless, as, for example, in September and October 1516 when he set out several times from Füssen to Augsburg, tracing and retracing his steps along a road which had become his substitute for a back-yard. In these last years he also tended to avoid the large cities themselves such as Innsbruck and Augsburg, Linz and Vienna, preferring rather to stay in the hunting castles and markets in their environs. Lack of funds certainly only explains half the story for this restlessness, for he still had to pay for his court and administration centred above all on Innsbruck. Keeping on the move had become an ingrained way of life which he could not arrest despite the aches and pains of increasing age and despite the Habsburg dynastic successes of his last years, which took the pressure off his daily routine of politics and paperwork. Maximilian had become a traipser around – in his own slang – an *vmbzotler*, a habit which got worse with age.

Maximilian's travels served several major purposes. They were personal, recreational and representative journeyings within and across to his own territorial patrimony in Austria, Swabia and Alsace. Then he travelled for wider dynastic and military-diplomatic purposes, up and down the Rhine and Danube, as far as Hungary in the east, Franche Comté in the west, Artois, and Amsterdam in the north-west, and Pisa in the south. Yet for his endless schemes, wars and campaigns, whether against the French, Venetians, Hungarians, crusad-ing in the Balkans or to settle internal German squabbles, as in Württemberg or Bavaria, Maximilian was dependent on extraordinary tax levies from his Habsburg territories and above all, for their legal justification and overall financing, from federal tax grants which needed to be negotiated with his fellow territorial rulers, lay and ecclesiastical, great and small, noble and burgher, urban and rural, in the German empire. His Imperial Assemblies, Reichstags, were crucial to the development of early modern German federalism in matters of law and order, and civil and fiscal legislation, troops, supplies and money. His great Imperial Assemblies from Worms in 1495, to Augsburg in 1518, created a state, however loosely organised, that lasted 300 years until the Napoleonic era.

What were Maximilian's responsibilities in the empire after he was elected king in 1486, and what revenues could he call on to carry out his royal tasks? At his Aachen coronation in March Maximilian made the customary royal promises to uphold the Catholic faith, protect churches, rule the German empire with justice and uphold its laws, shield widows and orphans from harm and remain true to the Pope and the Roman church. Thereafter 350fl. were thrown to the crowd and the royal party, including the old Emperor Frederick III, the Electors and princes retired to a fifty-course meal with 32 meat dishes, guarded by 2000 horsemen in sumptuous livery. The streets were filled with royal soup kitchens, and from the fountain in the main square spurted three jets of red wine.[14] The Habsburgs combined German tradition and Burgundian conspicuous consumption.

What could Maximilian expect in soldiers and taxes to defend his new kingdom, its churches and inhabitants? Indeed, did they really need defending? That aspect of the coronation oath was not spelled out. In fact, he could expect nothing. Federal taxes would have to be obtained after months of hard bargaining at Imperial Assembly level, arguing the merits of each case of political emergency that Maximilian and his counsellors drafted, for uncustomary grants of soldiers, stores and money. Territorial rulers and their subjects were liable to no regular federal taxes in 1486. Maximilian spent a lifetime trying to change this, and although the 'common penny' poll-tax did not outlast the 1490s, two other federal taxes did. They were the *Kammerzieler*, a small biannual tax paid by territorial rulers' treasuries for the upkeep of the *Reichskammergericht*, or imperial treasury court of appeal, and the all-purpose schedule for providing soldiers and military pay based on monthly quotas, regularised asan administrative system for fighting imperial wars, especially during Maximilian's Italian and Venetian wars, and finalised in the *Matrikel* of Charles V, from the Imperial Assembly of Worms, 1521.[15]

Between 1486 and 1518 Maximilian held over 20 full-scale Reichstags or Imperial Assemblies, and many further *ad hoc* meetings with territorial rulers, discussing more specific, technical, executive and less weighty problems of the German federal state.[16] As shown in Map 12.2, Reichstags were held all over the Holy Roman Empire. Most were held in Maximilian's name, conducted by his commissars, who presented his case, usually for more soldiers and money, to the territorial rulers or their representatives. At some of these meetings Maximilian appeared in person. Technically he held

Reichstags were held at:	Lindau (1496–7)	Gelnhausen and
Frankfurt-am-Main	Worms (1497)	Würzburg (1502)
(1486)	Freiburg-im-Breisgau	Cologne (1505)
Nuremberg (1487)	(1497–8)	Worms (1509)[17]
Frankfurt-am-Main	Worms (1498–9)	Augsburg (1510)
(1489)	Cologne, Überlingen	Trier, then Cologne
Nuremberg (1491)	(1499)	(1512)
Koblenz (1492)	Augsburg (1500)	Worms (1513)[18]
Frankfurt-am-Main then	Nuremberg	Mainz (1517)
Colmar (1492–3)	(*Reichsregiment*) (1501)	Augsburg (1518)
Worms (1495)		

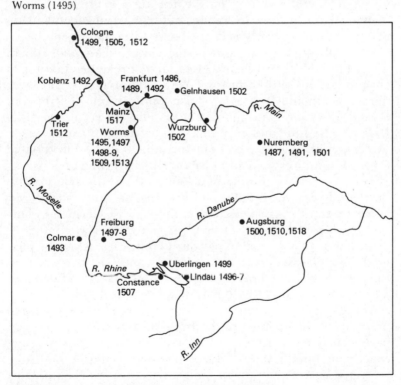

Map 12.2 Maximilian's Reichstags, 1486–1518

the six assemblies up to 1493 jointly with his father, the aged Frederick III, who disliked any attempts by territorial rulers to influence imperial policy in return for tax grants. Up to 1504 Maximilian also had to negotiate with an effective reforming party of territorial rulers, led in the Imperial Assembly and secretariat by Archchancellor Berthold of Mainz (Plate 19). Berthold's active political life spanned 14 of these assemblies, yet during Berthold's last years Maximilian clearly had the upper hand in defining the competence of federal institutions, effectively routing the reforming party in 1503 after the failure of the *Reichsregiment*, a federal caretaker government, set up (in Maximilian's name but against his wishes) at Nuremberg after the Augsburg assembly of 1500.[19] Maximilian's five last assemblies were clouded by his Italian wars and shaped imperial institutions and fiscalism, giving the form of the German federal executive for the next three centuries.

The strengths and weaknesses of fiscal arrangements made at Maximilian's twenty or thereabouts Imperial Assemblies in the era of *Reichsreform*, and of the Burgundian and Italian wars, 1486–1518, are clearly essential to any understanding of early modern German history. Yet the sources are scattered, patchy and mostly lost, whilst publication of Imperial Assembly records in this era has only covered the years 1488–90. In June and July 1489 Maximilian appeared before the Imperial Assembly at Frankfurt-am-Main and negotiated for federal military aid and taxes for the first time in person.[20] It was the real beginning of a long and stormy relationship between King Maximilian and his chief subjects, the *Reichsstände* or territorial rulers and authorities of Germany. This relationship was above all fiscal. It centred on Maximilian's continual pressing need to pay his mercenaries, which he justified by claims that his policies, and debts, were in the service of the German empire, for its needs and defence. The records of the 1489 Reichstag demonstrate this.[21]

On 20 June Maximilian arrived in Frankfurt-am-Main to prepare for the opening of the Imperial Assembly which had been called for 7 June, and which was then ready to start exactly one month later.[22] There was high water in the Rhine for it had been a rainy spring and early summer. Maximilian's contingent included his Wittelsbach brother-in-law, Duke

Albrecht of Bavaria, at Munich, who ingratiated himself by paying most of Maximilian's dining bills. The presence of Albrecht in the Habsburg entourage underlined the rifts in the Wittelsbach dynasty between Munich, Duke George of Lower Bavaria, and Elector Philip of the Palatinate at Heidelberg. Maximilian's main opponents were the Wittelsbach middle Rhineland contingent led by the Palatinate who showed up at Frankfurt on 29 June. Alongside, but distinct from them, because of mutually irreconcilable regional Rhineland rivalries, came Elector Berthold of Mainz, the executive organiser, as Archchancellor of the Reichstag. He had no following among the important princes and prelates and instead turned to Mayor Seckingen of Strasbourg, successfully building up a party for himself among the imperial cities. Whereas Maximilian wanted Reich military and monetary aid in putting down the French-backed revolt of Flanders and Brabant, which effectively entailed another war with France in the Netherlands and along the whole sensitive frontier from the Channel via the Ardennes through Lorraine and Alsace into Franche Comté and ducal Burgundy, the Palatinate wanted Wittelsbach territorial aggrandisement along the middle Rhine, and Berthold of Mainz wished for institutional reform of the Reich with judicial and legislative arrangements for internal security and peace. To this came the brief of the Bishop of Eichstätt who represented Emperor Frederick III especially in his demands for Reich aid against King Mathias Corvinus of Hungary who had conquered Lower Austria and was holding Vienna. Frederick III refused to make concessions in the administration of the federal institutions of the Reich in order to obtain aid and therefore stayed away from the Reichstag leaving Maximilian to balance between the grievances over maladministration of internal security voiced by Berthold and the imperial cities, and the rigid but ineffective prerogative rights and principles of his aged father, the emperor. A French embassy also appeared, having first come via the Palatinate court at Heidelberg in order to test the strength of German national feeling, convinced that it was running high after the recent imprisonment of King Maximilian by the rebellious pro-French burghers of Bruges. This feeling Maximilian exploited to the full at a memorably stage-managed session of the three curiae of Electors, princes and prelates, imperial cities, comprising in a quite new manner the Reichstag held in Frankfurt's *Römer* on 10 July 1489. Maximilian avoided appearing personally on that day. Instead, his closest confidant, Veit von Wolkenstein, who had been imprisoned with him at Bruges, painted a sombre picture, backed by the Bishop of Eichstätt, of the French and Hungarian forces lined up from the west and south-east against the Habsburg-Burgundian dynasty in particular and the Reich in general. The assembled territorial rulers and representatives sat in embarrassed silence as Haug von Werdenberg, veteran leader of the Swabian League, took up the cry from among the crowd in the hall. Haug asked for 20,000 men to silence the Hungarians and rescue Austria, and another 20,000 to punish the Flemings and their backer, King Charles VIII of France. Haug remembered how with a small Reichstag commission he had helped to set up an army in 1474, and he offered to do the same again now. Eichstätt also stepped in, generously as it now seemed, asking for a mere 20,000 men in Emperor Frederick's name, suggesting that an immediate levy of 6,000 horse and foot soldiers would do for a start, but refusing to say whether they would be used in Austria or in the Netherlands. The Electors, princes and prelates then agreed to appoint a committee of twelve to settle the details. No one dared to oppose whilst Maximilian rode high on the crest of a wave of national feeling. Berthold muttered his demands for a more effective enforcement of the 1486 Reich Landpeace by emperor and king in return for any support of Habsburg policy by Reich troop grants but was only listened to by the cities' envoys, whose informal leader, Mayor Seckingen of Strasbourg, was also reacting against the exclusion of all imperial cities from the secret committee. For the great constitutional innovation of this Reichstag had been to allow the cities to form their own curia, a third Estate, deliberating as a closed group for the first time ever. The Electors, and princes and prelates argued that many imperial cities had still sent representatives with powers too limited for decisions to be reached without first referring back to their city councils. That would take too long and it would also break the secrecy of any arrangements in the making. There was, however, some satisfaction in the way that the Electors and princes and prelates dropped that flamboyant fool, Haug von Werdenberg, from the Committee, after an initial proposal for his inclusion.

Another concession that Maximilian made to his followers which enhanced his national public image was of a ritualistic kind. Within the Christo-pagan ruling cosmology of the time the wet early summer was not a good omen for a successful Reichstag, let alone for a fruitful harvest, as the summer solstice appeared and the sun began its retreat once more towards the southern hemisphere. The Frankfurt records report:[23]

> Item, on the birth of St John the Baptist's eve [23 June] our gracious lord the King asked his grace Albrecht of Bavaria to prepare a bonfire. It was made on the top of a hill as follows. In the middle a wooden pole forty feet long was stuck into the earth, ringed by six logs, leaned up to it, between which straw and branches were packed. Our lord the King himself lit it.

A good harvest was thus prepared in the best manner of agrarian magic by the head of state.

The deliberations of the 1489 Reichstag lasted only from 7 July to 23 July. The grant for 6,000 troops was decided within four days. The rest of the time was spent in haggling over individual assessments and the general ways and means of payment. By 18 July the news had broken that Maximilian and the French ambassadors had reached a temporary truce. Charles VIII had abandoned the Flemish rebels to the tender mercies of Maximilian's generals like Eric of Brunswick and ecclesiastical rulers like Bishop Henry of Cambrai. Just before this there had been one final hiccup in the arrangements when Maximilian refused the 6,000 and held out for 10,000 men. It caused a rift between the king and Eichstätt as the emperor's representative, which was healed by Papal Legate Peraudi, who persuaded Maximilian to come to arbitration with King Mathias Corvinus of Hungary at Linz on the Danube in the following September. Peraudi wanted peace between France, Germany and Hungary in order to set up a crusade against the Turks to be led by Pope Sixtus from Rome in 1490. A feeble attempt by Berthold of Mainz to demand the restarting of a federal law court to enforce internal security, headed by himself and the territorial authorities of the Reich on commission from the Habsburg monarchs, was scotched by Maximilian, who rightly refused to ruin relations with his father at this early stage, on any matters whatsoever which might decrease royal and imperial prerogatives.

On 23 July Maximilian approved the quotas for 6,000 men to campaign in the Netherlands for six months. Two days later he made a separate and unofficial deal with the Electors, and with the few princes and prelates closest to him to commute their quotas to money payments enabling him to hire 2,000 Landsknechts from the Swabian League and Swiss Confederation via his swashbuckling friends Haug von Werdenberg and especially Tscherli von Wyl for a two months' campaign. He illicitly employed the open administrative system of the Reich tax schedule covering all the territorial authorities in Germany, by placing it in the hands of a fiscal commission with legal powers of coercion centred in the wealthy imperial city of Frankfurt. It was only one of a series of stratagems used in obtaining money for Maximilian's war policies. Already before the Reichstag had even met, Maximilian had anticipated any revenues that he might expect from a Reich grant by exempting Salzburg and its six client bishoprics from attending. A number of other territorial authorities were granted similar privileges, above all Liège, the loyal Netherlands, Luxemburg and parts of the Lower Rhine. They paid to be quit in advance, as did the Duke of Jülich (for a loan of a mere 1500 fl.), who was far from friendly towards Habsburg aspirations in his part of the world. Others like Christoph of Baden obtained exemption by entering Habsburg service, in his case as Viceroy of Luxemburg.[24]

It was very surprising, therefore, that this underhand and unofficial money demand should make just short of 10,000 fl. paid by 125 out of the 328 territorial authorities whom Maximilian petitioned on 29 July, three days after the Mainz Archchancellery had issued the final official report of the Reichstag proceedings and decisions.[25] Maximilian had no permission from the Reichstag to levy money in this manner for officially he had only been promised troops and not cash. The fact that 38 per cent of all the territorial authorities in the Reich nevertheless paid up was a most promising sign for the future and encouraged Maximilian to continue to call more Imperial Assemblies, especially since he had not as yet made a single firm promise to institute *Reichsreform* in return. His vigorous but essentially piecemeal approach to reactivating Reich politics was paying off in terms of an increase in royal, pragmatic power at the expense of institutional reform as desired and directed by anti-monarchical, oligarchic groups of territorial authorities at Reich federal level. But the latter were to wreak their revenge and reach a first high point under Archchancellor Berthold of Mainz from the 1495 Reichstag at Worms to his death in 1504.

After the events of July 1489 in Frankfurt-am-Main it was clear that the Old Reich had a new head of state with a new approach to federal politics. Maximilian's genius was to involve as many territorial authorities as possible in the external trimmings and trappings of Habsburg policy in order to spread the responsibility and load for further military and financial support of these aims. His was the pragmatism and appeal to national feeling and public opinion which was the hall-mark of Renaissance humanism. The major example of this lay in the inclusion once and for all of the imperial cities as a third Estate in the Reichstag. Maximilian was now creating a new system with the help, at first unsuspecting and unwilling, of the majority of the important territorial authorities in the south and west of Germany. A closer analysis of those present or represented at the 1489 Reichstag, and of its aspirations in levying the tax grant of 6,000 soldiers for a campaign of six months in the Netherlands, above all buries two old myths, despite the fact that Maximilian undermined the process by anticipating the grant and making his own *ad hoc* arrangements for it. Firstly, the imperial cities were not over-assessed by the Committee of Electors, princes and prelates. Their quota was approximately one-fifth of the whole, for which modest assessment Elector Berthold of Mainz could, unopposedly, claim most of the credit in the eyes of the imperial city councils. Secondly, the Reich tax-granting schedules, although antiquated, inaccurate and incomplete

145

could be revitalised and operated to threaten neighbouring rulers like the Kings of France and Hungary to raise troops quite quickly in an emergency as part of a concerted federal effort. There was a 90 per cent assessment resulting from a 27 per cent turnout, although this hides the fact that most of the larger territorial authorities came or were represented.[26] Those who tended to stay away were the smallest counts, lords, prelates and imperial cities.

The Reich system was working as effectively as could be expected, but it might never have happened if the burghers of Bruges had decided to kill Maximilian instead of letting him go, knowing full well that he would not keep his promises, made under duress to them in 1488. The Reichstag of 1489 was a lesson to Charles VIII of France that Maximilian was once again his main rival in Europolitics. About one hundred territorial authorities comprising well over two hundred leading politicians and civil and military servants were present in the negotiations at the *Römer*. Observers from France, Rome, Milan and Brittany also appeared. Many counts, lords and knights came in the entourages of the greater princes. The largest contingents were those of Maximilian and of the Elector Palatine, representing the rival dynastic leadership of the Reich between Habsburg and Wittelsbach.

We now move from federal to territorial home affairs, by examining examples of how Maximilian tried to tidy up law and order when he came to power in the Tirol after 1490. He introduced a type of government at a wider territorial level which had previously been evident only as an urban, town-council mercantilism. Everything to do with prices and wages was to be regulated. Law-courts were to follow written rules and they began to keep better records. The age of modern bureaucracy had dawned. The following selection of documents from the Innsbruck archives gives an insight into this process. A suitable start can be observed with the reappointment of the hangman, a social outcast and job-specialist paid as modestly as any curate (by way of comparison) and available on loan (at a price) to local Austrian nobles and clergy needing his services in the exercise of their own criminal jurisdiction.[28]

Table 12.1 Maximilian's Frankfurt Reichstags, 7–26 July 1489

| Political groups of territorial authorities | Taking part | | | Total assessed | Total listed | Those taking part as % of those assessed | Those taking part as % of those listed | Those assessed as % of those listed | Military levy | | |
	In person	Represented	Total						Horse	Foot	Overall %
Electors archbishops and bishops	9	11	= 20	40	51	50	39	78	350	1477	30
Abbots and prelates	3	—	= 3	46	54	7	6	85	27	172	3
Princes, counts, lords	12(+29)[a]	7	= 48	139	150	35	32	93	556	2273	47
Imperial cities	—	23	= 23	71	74	32	31	96	318	971	20
Totals	(53)	41	94	296	329	32	29	90	1231[b]	4893	100
										6124	

[a] In the entourages of the mightiest rulers.
[b] Actually 1251.

147

To acknowledge that we have reached a new agreement
with Gilg von Ro, the hangman, that he will cover the
executions of all our courts from Steinach to the Eisack, the
Etsch, Vinschgau and Nauders, and be paid inclusive of
livery, sustenance and all incidentals 80 Rhenish Gulden at
our pleasure from our customs revenues at the Tell. If he
executes anyone from the courts of prelates and nobles or
where someone has personally brought an accusation which
has not been lodged by us, then the hangman is to be paid
at the rate of six kreuzers per mile plus two pounds of
Bernese pennies for food and livery each day that he has to
wait before carrying out his task. For each execution he
shall receive ten pounds Bernese and a rope and gloves
without fail. We order all prelates, commanders, courts,
lords, knights, esquires, bailiffs, district judges, judges,
customs officers and local officials to give the executioner
his fees without delay. That is our earnest wish. Innsbruck
on Saturday before the Sunday of Quasimodogeniti, the
first after Easter, 1496.

A harsher style of government had been promulgated in the
new law of the land (*Gerichts- und Landsordnung*) of 1493 which
covered bakers, millers, butchers, fishmongers, vintners,
inn-keepers, grain, cattle and wood merchants. Prerogative
court justice was to be cheap and equitable. Gambling was
curtailed and punishments standardised.[29]

We send our gracious good will to all our dear, loyal
notables, counts, free lords, knights, esquires, bailiffs,
district judges and judges, who are hereby warned that
whereas in the past after searching and pleading for the
common welfare not only of our subjects but also of the man
who handles trade and manufacture and such who deal in
goods and retail with others like wine-shop and inn keepers,
bakers, millers and butchers, by whom no one should be
cheated in their common dealings, so we have issued this
ordinance. Yet after many decrees and acts to further
justice and fair trade were promulgated such as the law of
crimes whereby murderers were declared outlaws and
traitors, etc., but to little practical effect, we have carefully

considered how the law should hereby in future be more
carefully enforced.

Bakers
The fine wheaten roll shall not be baked from stale or
sprouted matter and where the cost of the corn is between
20 and 24 kreuzers per *Star*[30] the well-baked roll will weigh
2½ ounces (5 *Lot*), proportionally increasing to 3½ ounces
(7 *Lot*) when corn prices are down to 14 kreuzers.

The 2½ pound rye loaf shall retail at one kreuzer when
rye costs one pound of Bernese pennies per *Star*
proportionally decreasing to 2 lbs in weight as rye prices
rise to 16 kreuzers, when the farthing loaf will weigh 5
ounces (10 *Lot*).[31]

Bakers are forbidden to decrease the weight and quality
of any bread that they sell in the countryside. Since bread
must be readily and cheaply available everywhere, these
regulations must be enforced in all towns and villages. To
ensure that this is done we order the printing of this decree,
and so that it shall be obeyed more effectively, authorised
people must be appointed in all localities to inspect the
newly-baked bread. Any bread that has not been inspected
must for God's sake [*vmb Gotzwillen*] not be offered for sale
or bought. Above all, foreign-baked bread that is imported
into the towns and villages must always be carefully
weighed and inspected. Those who come from abroad to
market bread, wine or flour and sell from one morning to
the next, saying that they can not keep prices down any
longer, shall be provided with approved measuring bowls
by two market inspectors in order to keep to the above
rates. Sour-dough bakers are not to gain more than
six-farthings from one *Star* of grain that they bake. The
miller is to receive 1½ lbs and certainly not more than 2 lbs
out of every 30 lbs of flour that he grinds. All this is to be
observed on pain of 25 pounds Bernese pennies fine, to be
paid immediately.

Butchers
All bailiffs, judges, mayors or councillors must enforce this
decree by inspecting and assessing the value of meat at all
times. Best beef must not be sold for more than one kreuzer

per pound. No home produced cattle are to be sold abroad and no innkeeper or other inhabitant shall be allowed to purchase meat unless it comes from a local butcher within one mile of the town or village where he lives. Innkeepers or others who live in the open country may purchase only enough meat for their own needs and not for resale. A calf or lamb that remains unslaughtered after it is four weeks old and yet is sold for meat shall lead to the fining of buyer and seller. Village butchers must comply with the regulations of their nearest town as regards quality and weight of meat sold. Anyone who is convicted of slaughtering ailing cattle and selling unwholesome meat is to be punished not lightly but severely. All towns and villages are to appoint officials to reweigh meat on sale, and where they find fault to impose fines of 25 pounds Bernese, to be paid immediately.

Fishmongers
All fish caught in the Inn Valley and up to Sterzing [Vipiteno] shall be sold as follows,
Eel, 1 lb for 6 kreuzers, maximum 7 kreuzers,
Bream, 1 lb for 5 kr.,
Carp and tench, 1 lb for 4 kr.,
River-skate, 1 lb for 3 kr.,
Trout and grayling, 1 lb not over 7 kr.
At Matrei and Steinach all fish is 1/2 kr., and in Sterzing 1 kr. per pound more expensive. The weighing of fish for sale must be carefully supervised on pain of a fine of 25 pounds Bernese. The inspectors of bread, meat and fish shall be sworn in to reweigh, examine and assess all goods without any let, hindrance or deviation from these rates. And where they find fault and report it to the authorities, they shall be allowed to keep one-third of any fine to compensate for the extra work that it causes them, but not to the detriment of any freedoms and jurisdictions of towns and local courts.

Innkeepers
No wine-shop and innkeeper who has not previously been inspected and sworn in by local wine assessors in town and country shall be permitted to sell wine. The inspectors must not grant a licence unless they are satisfied with a trial

dinner of four good meat dishes for 4 kreuzers, and a meal containing two fish and three other dishes for approximately 6 kreuzers. Where fish is not available an alternative non-meat meal of five dishes costing 5 kreuzers must be tasted. Concerning the provision of fodder in town and country, it is to be sold by using only an approved measuring bowl at 12 to the *Star* costing the innkeeper 9 or 10 kreuzers but not more. Each measure can then be retailed at one kreuzer.[32] If fodder has to be bought at a higher price, then the local inspectors must be called in to fix the retail price per measure. If any traveller demands one or more *Star* of fodder, the innkeeper shall provide it at a maximum profit of 3 kreuzers per *Star* and not more. For each stabled horse, for the day and the night with fodder included the cost is 2 kreuzers.

All wine-vats will be filled by sworn inspectors using approved measuring cans, sealing the vat and marking the quantity. Pre-purchase of wine is forbidden to anyone who lives where it is grown unless he is a bailiff, judge, local official or otherwise authorised to deal in wine, and they only shall be allowed to buy, produce and market grapes and wine. The same applies to grain which is only open for purchase from the field by locals to cover their own household needs. Cattle may only be purchased, slaughtered and salted to cover immediate needs, and it is forbidden for unauthorised persons to sell it in the countryside. The same applies to wood.

From now on the administration of justice will be kept to the minimum cost and exercised by educated officials and scribes who will keep records [*Redner vnd gerichtschreiber*] and who will be salaried in order that those using the court are not burdened, and that no one shall be denied a judgment because he is poor. Justice is now open to everyone and marketing is to be supervised in order that our subjects do not run to our regents and councillors with any plea that can be decided by our local officials.

Crime and punishment shall be controlled as of old custom and the more courageous are to be exhorted more than has occurred in the past to help prevent many irregular judgments which distort justice, and which failed up to now to punish evil-doing. Where anyone has been judged an outlaw, the decision is to be publicly announced on three days running and only on the third day is sentence to be enforced. Murderers and outlaws [*todsleger vnd absager*] are to be hunted down more diligently and where they are caught, they are to be brought swiftly to justice. Anyone who aids such people will also suffer their punishment. In the case of murderers we have forbidden that any safe conduct [*glait*] be issued within a year of the deed, and this does not mean that after one year we accept responsibility for ensuring that the guilty party has been reconciled with the friends of the victim, nor that they have accepted his offer of compensation, and we are not bound to give the murderer protection or access to the country, all of which rights we reserve at our pleasure.[33]

Henceforth no one is allowed to carry dice since such games do great mischief among the idle and unemployed [*muessiggeer*]. And those who pay no taxes and have no personal belongings shall be more closely watched. All according to need and fairness as laid down in the laws of the land and of our cousin and previous ruler, Archduke Sigismund, that you promulgate this decree publicly and undertake to carry out our wishes contained in it. Let no official be lax in imposing, collecting and accounting for any fines whether they accord with the letter or are imposed in the spirit of this decree, on pain of our serious displeasure and punishment. Given at Innsbruck on Sunday Judica [2 March] 1493.

To show that he meant business, Maximilian suspended the first of the corrupt judges left from the previous, more lax regime of Archduke Sigismund. This order came a mere seven weeks after the above decree.[34]

We Maximilian etc. inform you, Hans Hagel of Telfs, that because of the irregular judgment that you gave at your last criminal court hearing concerning Hans Zeuner and another locksmith, when you made your decision on oath as if you did not understand the plea of the other, which anyone with common sense could have comprehended and given a just pronouncement upon, that we suspend you from taking any further criminal or other cases until further especial notice from us on pain of our displeasure and punishment. Innsbruck, Friday after Misericordie [21 April] 1493.

After improving his chances of increased revenues from the regulation of civil and criminal jurisdiction, Maximilian began to tackle the problem of tax evasion. Unpaid taxes from South Tirol were recouped from towns and territorial nobility by surcharging their salt imports at 4 fl. per *Fuder*.[35] Further problems arose when Trient and Cremona refused to contribute quotas to the Sterzing territorial assembly grant of 50,000 fl. Maximilian ordered the confiscation of their wine . exports northwards as from the following autumn, to be implemented by his customs official, Simon von Thun, and by barring their trade through Maximilian's customs posts. The customs exemptions of all local noble families, except for one not in tax arrears, were cancelled and instructions to this effect were issued to twenty-six customs posts, warders and local officials.[36]

Maximilian made no concessions. He was prepared to fine noble families as strictly as any other subjects in order to obtain his exchequer revenues in direct and indirect taxes, and in *dons gratuits* from territorial assemblies. His ultimate sanction of closing the roads against those who failed to pay taxes was, however, destructive since the action could generally disrupt existing trade and increase the cost of necessities such as salt, grain and wine, which ultimately harmed everyone in the region and made the laws on prices, retail, wages and marketing unenforceable. By taking such crude, punitive action, Maximilian destroyed his own chances of good government. Discrimination was thus carefully practised in order to minimise this wider problem. In an instruction to his customs official, Pancratz von Spaur, dated Innsbruck, Tuesday after Whitsun, 1493, Maximilian ordered.[37]

Remember to let the people of Nons import what grain they need from mainland Venice, but levy the new surcharges on all the rest in the Etsch Valley [since only Nons had paid its

taxes] but do not use confiscation or prison on Neuspaur
just because of their refusal to pay.

One may wonder if this confused approach towards delin-
quent locals was effective and whether Maximilian could
actually do anything at all to coerce them. Another paradox
lay in his complaint that crime was continuously on the
increase, especially murder. Cases were very profitable to his
treasury, yet on the other hand they led to feuds and
undermined the efficiency with which he could keep the peace.

As a result of tax-collecting methods that were too
rapacious, such as hastily increased customs levies and
high-handed action by his officials, Maximilian was faced
with passive resistance, especially from small landowners in
the Bishoprics of Brixen, Trient and Chur. A case was the
rebellion of 'the landlord up at Metsch who will fortify himself
in Chur Castle'. All Maximilian could do at that stage was to
order his military official at the Etsch to ensure that the rebel
obtained no fire-arms or provisions, to starve him out and
send him under guard to Tirol. Maximilian might threaten to
disrupt trade but he could ill afford even the rebellion of minor
lords, let alone the disruption of marketing in any of his
territorial towns and villages. The embargo against Trent had
been imposed in April 1493 and by June of that year had
already been lifted as regards wine, although extra charges
were kept on salt and grain. Obtaining extraordinary taxes
was an extremely wearisome and hard-headed business, and
the *Kopialbücher* show that Maximilian and his high officials
spent more time on such items of business than on anything
else.[38]

We now have some understanding of the real Maximilian at
work in matters of routine, both public and personal. In all his
tasks he was fully in charge of the issues, and he was behind
the decisions taken. He took his administration seriously and
felt personally responsible to such an extent that he never
really succeeded in delegating authority at all effectively or for
any length of time. One must admire the tenacity of his senior
territorial and court officials, such as Paul von Liechtenstein
and Cyprian von Serntein, who stayed with him for life.
Another basic factor which complicated all his affairs was

Maximilian's incessant, restless travelling. Under these circumstances, one of the largest items of internal government expenditure became the postal system. Instructions were swiftly given and easily written but terribly expensive to post in terms of time, men, horses, food and equipment. All Maximilian's treasury accounts itemise the expenses incurred by this service, day by day, as *Bottenlohn*.

A restless but thoroughly feudal, paternalistic and conventional ruler of the period of transition between scholastic and humanist times, Maximilian was a truly Renaissance and gothic figure as his practical politics show. We may conclude our survey of this opportunistic monarch with the roving eye by translating the documents dealing with his far-fetched attempt to obtain the throne of Sweden and the fealty of the Prussian towns after 1489, when he was German King but with little actual land of his own.[39] The matter was pursued again as a result of the imperial assembly at Nuremberg in 1491, and in June, Georg von Turn, Maximilian's 'adviser to the Kingdom of Sweden, and from there to Prussia, Russia, Livonia and elsewhere' was issued with letters of credence.[40]

> We Maximilian etc. acknowledge that we have now instructed our dear, loyal counsellor, Georg von Turn, with an especial task in the Kingdom of Sweden. We have ordered him to the same Kingdom to negotiate with its prelates, nobles, towns and others together or separately to find ways and means as to how the Crown of Sweden might come into our hands and power. He has grasped our instructions and commands, with which he is fully conversant, and that he may carry out and conclude our wishes even more effectively, we have given him total and complete power to act on our behalf.
>
> We have also consciously and by virtue of this letter given him, Georg von Turn, full powers to negotiate in the Kingdom of Sweden with those of the clergy, nobility, towns and others together or separately on our behalf uprightly, and to undertake to accept and carry out all that is required to secure the Crown of Sweden in our hands or in those of our son, Archduke Philip of Austria [subsequently Philip the Fair of Burgundy]. Where advised

as necessary he will exercise all his energies to bring about a
common assembly of all places in the Kingdom with whom
he shall negotiate with full authority. If it is the will of God
that the Crown of Sweden shall pass to us or our dear son,
Archduke Philip, then Georg von Turn is empowered in our
place and in our name to take the necessary oaths of duty
that are requested and to promise not to harm but to keep
them in all their customs, freedoms and rights, as is deemed
just and necessary.

And what he will say and do on our behalf it is our good
wish to let it stand firm and unbroken without any damage
to him. Should he require more powers we give them to him
as if they were written here word for word. All given in good
faith as attested by this letter.

Georg von Turn was from a petty noble family in the
Bishopric of Brixen, South Tirol, and he was also instructed
by Maximilian on 5 September 1489 to conduct an embassy to
Prussia.[41]

We Maximilian etc. acknowledge that we have now sent
our dear, faithful counsellor, Georg von Turn, on several
important matters concerning us and the Holy Empire, to
the honourable, spiritual and devoted noble, and our dear,
faithful mayors, councillors and commons of the towns of
Danzig, Marienburg, Marienwerder, Thorn and Posen,
and also to other prelates, nobles, towns, castles, markets
and communities in Prussia which in the past have been
taken away by the King of Poland. We have ordered him to
negotiate and to exhort them to submit and to come to us
and the Holy Empire. We have thus given him our
command and instruction and in order that he may more
effectively carry out our wishes, we have given him our
whole and complete power by virtue of this letter, so that
they may submit to us, the Holy Empire and the German
nation [*damit Sy sich an vnns dasselb heilig Reiche vnd dewtsche
Nation ergeben*].

Where they agree to submit to us and the Holy Empire,
Georg von Turn is to take their fealty in our name, and he is
to confirm their freedoms, rights and customs without
diminution. He is also empowered to act further in our

name as he thinks suitable [*was Jn gutbedunckht*] and necessary, and we will honour and keep all that he undertakes. If he requires even more authority, we hereby confirm with this letter that we have sanctioned it.

But what was behind all this ceaseless practical activity? Upon what cosmology, upon what view of nature, upon what mentality was it based? We now turn to the most difficult of all tasks, and that is to explain the material and mental world that Maximilian found himself born into, and then operating within, in terms of his own hopes and fears over the facts of weather, harvest and health, realities which he and his subjects faced almost helplessly, from year to year. Maximilian resorted to conventional Christianity, mixed with medical, gnostic and faith healing, as we have seen in chapters 2 and 11. It was combined with three-monthly, smaller weather prognostications, drawn into one great annual set of predictions, usually handed out at New Year, an ordinary example of which we reproduce in full in chapter 13. It emanates from the chancellery records of his Tirolean kinsman and hunting companion, Archduke Sigismund. First, however, we open the next chapter with a survey of natural conditions which dictated the pace of life to one and all, high and low, in this era of pre-industrial production, and of pre-diagnostic, pre-clinical and pre-antibiotic medicine. We then show that in such an insecure and capricious place, the ultimate threshold of violence was seen to reside in the world of God, the Devil, belief and science. Our *Practica* from 1491, to come in chapter 13, is thus an example of built-up confidence in astrological forecasting that conventional rulers at all times have felt necessary, to boost their ambitious egos in the face of heavy, everyday, grinding responsibilities. Maximilian was no exception, nor was Archduke Sigismund. One of the latter's *practica* has been chosen, because it has not been published before, and it was also produced mainly in response to Sigismund's well-known anxieties about Maximilian and his future.

13

Necessity and Mentality

The weather, health and harvest conditions in later fifteenth-
century and early sixteenth-century Germany, which Maximilian lived through, are summarised for the reader to
ponder as follows.[1]

1459   Frost from Christmas until 8 March. Cold and wet
from January until April, and also May. Very cold
around Christmas. Frost and snow on 21 May. Fruit
crops frozen.

1460   Hard winter. Danube frozen and open for wagon traffic
from 13 January to 23 April. Rhine frozen down to
Cologne. Cereals expensive in Brunswick. Plague
straight after Christmas, affecting strong men but
seldom women or children. Great frost followed by
great drought. Dearth, and very cold from 2 to 22
February. The Easter vintage turns out very well,
substantially marketed in Augsburg. Hot summer.

1461   The lake at Überlingen is frozen until 23 April. Cold
spring, and the vines had hardly started growing by
Ascension Day. Cereals expensive.

1462   Great plague with 10,000 deaths in Nuremberg.
Abundant crops of apples and chestnuts, but the
grapes wither on the vine. Apples and pears cheap.
Tumbling and red dysentery in Augsburg. Harsh frost.
Roses flower twice.

1463   Great plague in Augsburg, Nuremberg, Brunswick,
Magdeburg. Wormed fruit, expensive. Plague from
July to September is said to have killed 10,000 people
in Görlitz. Prices reasonable.

1464 Much snow. Plague. Many caterpillars. Hard winter.

1465 Lake Constance frozen on 21 January, the lake at Überlingen on 2 February. Earthquake on 11 October. Plentiful fruit and grape juice. Dry summer. The grapes freeze on the vine on 4 October. Cold autumn.

1466 Tumbling dysentery in the autumn. Whooping-cough in Augsburg.

1467 Wet summer. Fruitful year. Good crops of bullaces, plums, pears, apples, cherries, nuts, morellos in Bavaria. Plague in Ulm and Memmingen. Roses flower twice.

1468 Comet after Michaelmas but not easily observed. Harvest damaged by rain. Heavy snow-fall on 4 October. Cold, wet summer with a late, poor harvest. Watery walnuts, unripe, sour grapes in Saxony. Dearth after 27 October in Thuringia, Mark Brandenburg and Franconia. Autumn plague in Frankfurt. Snow and floods after 4 October in Thuringia hindering the harvest. Oats were not brought in until shortly before Christmas. But the unusual weather did not last long.

1469 The coldest winter in living memory. Good harvest. Water shortage, and the River Oder could be forded. Cold weather from 4 December to 4 March. Hard winter with snow until 6 May.

1470 Earthquake on 16 February. Rainy summer, rich harvest. Good autumn, warm until 19 November. Fish expensive. Roses blooming until 10 November.

1471 A good, warm, dry, peaceful summer of the sort that comes once in a hundred years. Melons and fruit very tasty. Warm spring after 10 March when the violets begin to flower. Wild roses bloom twice. Cherries ripen by 9 June and the first apples and pears 24 June. Early harvest ended by 1 August. Flowers until 8 December. Very little snow and ice during the whole winter.

1472 Comet observed in the west on 21 January in the sign of Taurus, the Ram and Scales. Good year for wine. Drought. Cheap wine and corn. Wine harvest unusually plentiful on 30 August and 1 September. Summer plague in Einbeck and Göttingen. Winter plague in

Hildesheim. Plague in Erfurt, Nuremberg. Comet after Epiphany [January] observed, rising and falling, for eight days.

1473 Wine harvest on 9 August. Very good, strong wine. Wine and corn inexpensive. In Austria the strongest wine of the century, only drunk diluted with water. Dry, hot summer with no rain at all. Summer plague in Brunswick. Dry spring with much wine in the Breisgau, Alsace and Switzerland.

1474 Less plentiful harvest. Plague in Halberstadt and Lüneburg, in Nuremberg and Görlitz.

1475 Locusts in Saxony, Styria, Trient, Brixen, Italy, but not Venice, and Nuremberg.

1476 The Danube is frozen. Earthquake on 23 August. Coldest winter for fifty years with snow from 30 November until early April

1477 Hard winter from 11 December until 1 March.

1478 Locusts from Hungary to Bohemia, Saxony, Friuli, Bozen and Trient, Italy.

1479 Very dry summer. Dry spring with no rain between 22 February and 12 May, and then none until 24 August. Caterpillars damage the harvest. Very good wine, so-called brother's wine, even better than the 'king's wine' of 1443.

1480 Dearth.

1481 Plentiful, but sour wine.

1482 Plague in the Archbishopric of Salzburg with 4,500 deaths. Dearth in Nuremberg.

1483 Very mild winter, no snow. Dearth in Magdeburg. Dying in Nuremberg. Wet winter without snow.

1484 Plague in Brunswick and especially in Einbeck. Dry summer. Dying in the countryside especially among young girls between Whitsun and Martinmas. Plague in Glogau.

1485 Eclipse on 17 March. Barrenness in Austria. Plague in Dortmund.

1486 Many die of scurvy in Brunswick.

1488 Very cold. The River Oder open to wagons.

1489 Sunday after Epiphany massive snow-fall.

1490 High snow, as tall as a man. Dearth. Around

Christmas more snow than for twenty years past. Dry year. Coldest spell for fifty years starts 21 December.

1491   The Rhine freezes at Basel on 20 January, and on 26 January at Cologne. Snow at the beginning of May with frost on 9 May. Vines and fruit frozen. Dearth. Snow and cold after 1 May. First warm days after 17 and 18 June. Dearth in Westphalia. Lake Zürich frozen over.

1492   Cattle plague. Butter and meat expensive. Dry summer.

1493   Great plague in Worms. Rampaging infection in Dortmund, Wesel and Deventer.

1494   4 May the vines and all the fruit frozen. Great plague in Nuremberg.

1495   The fruit freezes from 13 July until 13 December. 300 people die in Landshut. Good, inexpensive harvest but plague in Dortmund. Until Martinmas 2,000 deaths. Dry year. Second blossoming of hawthorn, wild roses, trees and cornflowers in September and October.

1496   Summer dying in Zittau, 3,000 deaths. French sickness.

1497   Warm winter, much snow and rain. Chicken-pox.

1498   Cold winter until 25 March with few warm days before Whitsun. Rhine frozen and open to wagon traffic.

1499   Over-abundant wine harvest in Austria. Cold winter. Snow forty times consecutively. Adequate harvest of cereals and wine.

1500   Plague in Germany. Good wine but not much of it. No shortage of fruit and grain.

1501   Rain and fog. Fruit unripe. Wine sour. Hailstone damage around Zürich. Elbe floods on 16 August.

1502   Harsh winter in which birds and wild animals freeze. Foliage diseased in March. Snow in mid-May. After St John's (24 June) heatwave and forest fires. Trees die of drought. Widespread hailstorms. 5000 die of plague in Basel. Price rises throughout the year.

1503   Trees freeze in harsh winter. Much ice. Very hot summer, drought and price rise. Heatwave from 16 May to 2 July, and even to 10 August. No rain over Lake Constance in four months. Onions withered.

Forest fires, followed by early plentiful harvest.

1504 Unusually cold winter. Hot dry summer. Little rain between April and July. Rivers dried and were easily forded. Early autumn with abundant wine harvest. Some shortage in Alsace.

1505 Spring frost damage to vines. Good harvest. Low prices. Massive vintage in Alsace. In some places it was given away. Plague of boils in Zug.

1506 Winter frost damages vines and splits trees. Good summer, ample harvest. Wormy fruit. Prices rise due to exports. Heavy rain with flooding in September/October.

1507 Mild winter, with first snow settling in March. Flowers blossom in February. Young foliage damaged by pests. Plentiful, sour wine. Widespread hailstone damage in Breisgau and Württemberg.

1508 Raw, cold winter until March. Late fruit blossom. Mice eat seedlings and cause poor harvest. Plentiful, good wine.

1509 Long, severe winter. Heavy snow after New Year, melting without flooding. Larks caught in their thousands. March started dry and warm, followed by frost and snow. Drought hampered milling and summer hay was scarce, although autumn harvests were sufficient.

1510 Winter corn froze in March. Plentiful, good vintage. Hailstone damage in Alsace on 31 May. Rhine in flood. Widespread plague with attacks of coughing illness called *gruppi* and *pfypsi*.

1511 Hailstorms and floods spoiled the harvest. Rhine in flood in July. Many bridges down. Lake Constance higher than at any time in ninety years.

1512 Water shortage in Zürich until May. Unseasonal snow-storm in the Rhine Valley on 31 May damaged the vines. Poor harvest. Price rise.

1513 Heavy snowfall on Shrove Tuesday, lay till mid-Lent, followed by dry, warm weather until 23 April. Then came a cold spell, although vintage still turned out plentiful. Overall, moderate harvest. Prices remained high. Early, harsh winter.

1514 Rhine froze right across. Storms and earth tremors in January. Very late spring after 6 May. Adequate harvest.

1515 Warm winter, cold summer. Rain from 25 May to 24 August. Flooding. Late harvest, some of it ungatherable. Fruit unripe. Sour wine.

1516 Cold winter, vines frozen. Snow on 25 April, followed by drought. No hay. Dearth followed by plague. Price rise, but excellent Rhine wines, as good as the vintages of 1479 and 1504.

1517 Cold winter, blowy spring. Forty hoar frosts until 10 June. Hailstorms and dearth, followed by heat wave and summer drought. High prices despite adequate corn harvest. Mysterious epidemic of headache, fever and loss of appetite causes 2000 deaths in Basel.

1518 Long, cold winter. Dearth until harvest-time. Warm, dry summer yields cereals and wine in excess. Sweating and dancing sickness in Alsace. Plague in Basel.

1519 A plentiful year for cereals, wine and fruit, but plague widespread.

The close relationship between climate and health of crops, animals and humans was strongly felt. Life was near the farmyard and the growth cycle depended on the vicissitudes of temperature and humidity.[2] God was indeed the all-mover and yet he gave signs through nature and time which could be judged by observing the sky. Written record and statistics were not part of this early world of meteorology and astrology. The wise sayings of woods and fields among the populace had their counterpart in the almanacs which fixed Easter and regulated church life as well as the fertility rites of season and agriculture. All came together in the New Year prognostications, predictions or *Practica* of Saturnalia and the zodiac. Time and weather were the prime movers of life and death, health, fertility in the fight for sufficient sustenance. These forces could be personalised, as in the dance of death, or cautiously harmonised with current Christianity and a schoolman's learning.

The *Practica* of 1491 translated here is crude and commonplace, and it captures the mood of the 1490s in Maximilian's Austria.[3] It seeks to pander to Archduke Sigismund's anxieties at having handed his Tirolean government over to his younger kinsman, Maximilian. That it survived in pristine condition in the archives indicates that it probably never reached its destination, but was caught up somewhere in the chancellery and filed, although we cannot be certain. A similar prognostication has survived for 1492, to which the same author, Schynnagel, appended a begging letter to Sigismund.[4]

> On next Sunday after the Purification of Mary (2 February) I will sing my first mass and it is my very humble plea to Your Grace that you will help me with a hundred gulden for this, in order that I can celebrate my first mass in a worthy manner and also pay off my debts that I made in Rome so that I do not fall into rack and ruin.

Schynnagel had nothing further to report from Rome, 'other than that we Germans are very much despised by the foreigners', and he gave a warning that serious troubles would befall King Maximilian in 1492 especially as regards his conflict with his father, the old Emperor Frederick III, about which Schynnagel was prepared to say more, but not in writing.[5]

Practica for 1491[6]
To the Most High Ruling Prince and Lord, Lord Sigismund, Archduke of Austria, Styria, Carinthia and Carniola etc., my most gracious Lord, I, Marcus Schynnagel, doctor of the free arts and especially of Astronomy, offer my submissive, willing service.

Most Gracious Lord, take this as true that the King who rules in heaven and earth through his all mighty creation, dazzling us humankind in this earthly kingdom, giving his mighty protection that we may live in orderly ways to strive in time towards his godly will, doth favour all the ruling princes, sincerely desiring to grant, as is natural according to each kind and virtue, a happy government [*glücklich regiment*] by which they may here and now be praised and in their time be raised above.

Wherefore, notwithstanding my drily learned art, Your Most Gracious Highness, who, for the greater expansion of

the Christian people, are adorned for the sake of others in
the Empire with the Archducal throne of princely rule, has
been most praiseworthily recognised as benefiting from the
natural fortune of heaven as is shown in the signs of the
planets and creatures, each and every one after their own
nature, for the good or ill of living creatures and especially
of mankind in general and primarily to strive and to give an
account for the pleasure and further consultation of Our
Gracious Highness, yet all quite naturally in order that the
power of God, which is not subordinated to nature but
rather is above it, and which in regard to our work and duty
is not changed or condemned, concerning which your
selfsame humble Christian servant serenely knows and has
up to now adhered to and will always keep (God willing).
Hence I draw my conclusions concerning the
aforementioned, God-created signs of nature and their
development in the coming New Year as herein follows.

After the birth of Christ 1491, Golden number Ten,
Sunday letter B, Roman interest number Nine, between
Christmas and the Night of Lent seven weeks and one day
will be 'Allelulia' ended on Sunday before Candlemass [2
February]. The same time will be very cold with snow and
wind. Yet Jupiter the indulgent planet will give much
mildness and it will be fine and clear. The first Sunday in
Lent before St Matthew's Day [25 February] will at the
same time be very cold with some wetness. March will give
some mildness with warmth. Easter [3 April] is on Sunday
before St Ambrose [4 April]. During this period it will
become warm and fine. Rogation week on Sunday after
Saints Philip and John [1 May] will have very unstable
weather with wind and wetness. Yet Jupiter will give some
warm, fine days. Ascension day is on Thursday before St
Servatius [13 May] when there will be fine weather. Yet
Saturn will in this period prevail upon several planets to
give some cold spells with rain. Whitsun is the Sunday
before St Urban [25 May] and in this period there will be
unsettled weather. Yet Mars, who will dominate at that
time, will provide some very warm days. Advent is Sunday
after St Catherine's [25 November] at which time it will be
cold with snow and wind.

165

Concerning the division of this Prediction into twenty-one parts or distinctions.

The first distinction is about the great configuration in this year which itself is in five parts. The *first* is the fourth view of Jupiter and Mars on Saturday before St Valentine's [14 February]. The *second* constellation is again the fourth view of Jupiter and Mars on Sunday after St John the Baptist's Day [24 June]. The *third* is the fourth view of Saturn and Mars on Thursday after St Bartholomew [24 August]. The *fourth* is the resistance of the opposition called Jupiter and Mars on Tuesday before St Catherine's [25 November]. The *fifth* and last is the conjunction of Saturn and Mars on Friday after Christmas.

In this year these configurations will cause a number of strange surprises with great uproar on the land and in the towns, which will occur between dawn and midday.

The second distinction concerning the ruler of this year. Following the advice of the ancients, Haly, Leopold and Ptolemy, I predict that the angry, fiery and quarrelsome planet Mars will be with the help of the Sun, master of this year, which will result in much uproar and commotion [*aufrur vnd vfflouff*] among the people, and much anger and hatred in accord with Mars' nature and as is his wont so this year will tend towards greater warmth and heat rather than to cold and rain. This should lead to a good, calm year with all the crops.

The third distinction of the four developments and significance of this year namely concerns hot, cold, wet and dry, which results from the other planets associating together. This year will be more warm and fine than cold and wet but Sun and Moon in conjunction in the middle of the sky at the 28th degree in Pisces before the opening of this year will bring wet weather with heavy rain between midday and midnight with strong gusts of wind which will make it dangerous this year to venture out to sea. However, Mars, who is master of this year and who will be included in the figure of the conjunction, will be seen in the middle beneath the Earth in the house of the Sun before the start of this year and will move across, giving great warmth with thunder and lightning and powerful rays which will cause concern.

166

The fourth distinction concerns the four seasons of this year, namely spring, summer, autumn and winter. Spring, because of Mars and the Sun, who are its masters, will be fine and warm with lightning. But Mercury, who will become active and displace the Sun in the first point of Aries, will, in his ascendancy, cause considerable darkness with black cloud, fog, wind and rain. However, Mars, who will dominate the whole year, will restore calm. The Sun will suffer some cold, rain and wind due to Saturn and Venus who will dominate but Mars, who will be found in the middle under the earth in the house of Mercury, will give great warmth with thunder, lightning and hail. The autumn will be dominated by Jupiter and will give much fine and warm weather. However, Saturn will begin to dominate the conjunction before the entry of the Sun at the first point of the Scales between the figure of the 7th house and his own house, and will give cold, rain and biting winds. The winter will be dominated by Saturn and the Moon and I judge that it will be a cold winter with much snow and wind in the air. But Mars who is included in the figure of the entry of winter in the 7th will give some fair and warm weather.

The fifth distinction, concerning the eclipse of the Sun, will come on the 8 May, namely on Sunday after Saints Philip and John in the 16th degree in Taurus near the dragon tail, starting two hours and three minutes after midday, reaching its peak three hours and eight minutes after midday, and ending four hours and thirteen minutes after midday, coinciding with the rising sign from the east, the Scales in the 8th degree covered with eight spots.

Now Haamar and Tyberiades, writing on Ptolemy, tell us that when the eclipse of the Sun occurs in the seventh house it will bring death, and gloom will spread among the high and mighty families with much sorrow and depression so that many will surrender their lives to death in the year. Many will also perish by the sword. And Albateg speaks in the fourth that when the dragon's tail occurs in the eighth, one will relinquish much to the powerful with great ill-will. And Ptolemy speaks in the fourth chapter of the second of his four books that the most powerful affliction is due to the

increase and decrease of the sun. But unfortunately
Messahala in his letter about the seventh says that this does
not have to be, since the eclipse of the sun alone can cause
mistakes and vexation but also much adroitness. And the
authorities speak in the fourth chapter concerning the
repetition of the years, that the sun is the soul of the world,
and the moon the body. When they are hindered, then the
air is also hindered, and so one must fear that in this year
there will be great reverses and disturbances between the
powerful and at the same time also between the poor
inhabitants of town and country, for there will be between
them great betrayal and falsehood with great deception.
And an extensive great dying with spilling of blood is to be
feared.

The sixth distinction concerns the three races, namely of
Christians, Jews, Heathens-Tartars-Turks.

The Christians, through the influence of the planet
Mercury, will in this year go greatly in fear of God. They
will experience changes [*wandelschafft*] above all in spring
and they will have good fortune in trading and owning
foreign goods. In the summer they will be fortunate with
their children. In the autumn they must fear death, plague
and sorrow. In the winter they can expect good cheer and
health.

The Jews through the influence of Saturn will have in this
year much illness, senility and little luck. Their faith will be
weakened and they will have much sorrow. Many will be
expelled and uprooted, and one will kill many with fire.

The Turks and Tartars will be greatly on the move in this
year. They will proceed against the Christians and rule
mightily, for which they will have much good fortune. In
summer they will have health and good cheer. They will
plot to undermine the Christians but in autumn they will
suffer a great reverse. In winter they must fear serious
illness and sadness.

The seventh distinction for this year concerns the crops in
general according to the propriety of heaven which I have
found in the figure according to Messahala, Leupold and
Ptolemy, etc. I judge that this year will be fruitful in all
crops and their quality I judge according to Hallus and
Leopoldus. Corn, rye, wheat (from which one bakes bread)

will grow well. It will not be expensive, but rather of good value and adequate. Crops of barley will be in danger of receiving damage especially around midnight but otherwise they will be cheap. Oats will be expensive this year. The vines will grow well and will produce enough wine which will be inexpensive and of good quality. Honey and beeswax will be expensive. Onions, apples, pears, hazelnuts, beets [*erdöpfel*], plums, melons etc., will be adequate but it will be especially dangerous to overeat in this year. Sugar will suffer some damage but it will not become expensive. Saffron will be cheap to buy and healthy to use this year. Ginger will increase in price. Long and short pepper will be cheap. Carnations will receive damage in this year and will increase in value. Muscat and cinnamon will remain moderately priced. Oil will be more expensive. That is what is predicted.

The eighth distinction concerns peace and war in this year, for which I have studied the figure of heaven with especial diligence and have found that the planet Mars will be the father and master of all the wars in that year, somewhat tempered by Saturn and Jupiter who will produce considerable disturbance and conflict in the form of war and riot [*vffloff*], and great bloodshed is to be feared. Oh, what great falseness and baseness there will be in this year! Seldom will anyone defer to his superiors and the smaller man will commonly despise the greater man by wishing to raise himself to the level of the greater, as Abraham Ebeneezer says in the fourth, when Mars is in the ascent in the figure of the entry of the Sun against him, then many heads will roll and many hangings will take place. Dynastic ruling princes will have better luck than their ecclesiastical counterparts. Ecclesiastical rulers will be seriously obstructed by them. And Adila says that when the part of the towns falls in the twelfth at the house of Mercury it will cause great unrest in several towns. The commons will turn against their authorities and thus cause much damage and misfortune especially between sunset and midday. Therefore, watch out for the planet Mars, who is the ruler of this year, stirring up enmity at his fourth appearance. He will cause several towns and lands great damage and great unrest. Thus the powerful should beware of the time between 8 February and 12 April, and again between 25 June and 5 August, and again between 21 November and 3 December. In these periods several towns will be troubled and so be cautious and prudent.

The ninth distinction concerns illness and plague. I draw attention to the entry of the sun in the first sign of the Ram, and also in the eclipse of the Sun I find, according to Ptolemy, Hallus and Albubertus, etc., that many illnesses and ailments will come in this year in the form of red dysentery and great aching of the head with sweating sickness and fourday fever, as well as colic. Hence it will be necessary to heed the doctors, to visit them and take advice from them in this year. But I have searched with all my diligence and found that bleeding will be quite beneficial for the head, lung, liver and generally. Avoid Turkish baths in this year. Also avoid fatty foods. All mutton and pork is unhealthy and above all unsalted fish and small woodland birds. Water fowl should be avoided if they are not healthy. Equally, avoid red wine unless suffering from dysentery. Herbal wines will be beneficial to drink. One should savour plenty of spice which is good in food. Saffron will be especially good sprinkled in all kinds of food. One should keep warm.

Now I have examined the signs and discovered that in this year in several lands and towns there will be great plague. Death will reign above all around midday, and more so at sunrise than at sunset. A great and powerful lord of high lineage will give up his life to death, as will also one or more high and mighty lady. This will be caused by the tail of the dragon which will appear with the planet Jupiter in the middle of the sky in the house of kings and ruling princes.

The tenth distinction concerns our holy father, the Pope. I have found that according to the nature of his election, His Holiness will stand in this year in the eighth, which is death and sorrow, and he will have little good fortune. He will be loaded down with hatred and it may even be feared that he will be poisoned. Several Cardinals will give him much opposition but in the summer he will improve his standing with good fortune and cheer. In the autumn he will have great sorrow and opposition, and perhaps it will then be feared that he will succumb and give up his life to death. In the winter he will have good luck.

The eleventh distinction concerns the Cardinals. According to Albubetrus, I have found that they will be factious and in disagreement among themselves and they will not be subdued, but will give rise to great ridicule from which they will suffer. Many of them will give up their lives to death.

The twelfth distinction concerns the Estate of the Clergy, and all those who have the fear of God, namely archbishops, bishops, abbots, priors, deans, etc., and the common clergy in general will suffer much envy and hatred from laymen in this year. They will be greatly despised. That will be caused by Jupiter who is hindered by the tail of the dragon in mid-sky, but according to Haamor and Tyberiades they will have some good fortune in their dealings with the common people and will amass many benefices. But it is to be feared that many will give up their lives to death.

The thirteenth distinction concerns the Estate of our most gracious Lord, the Holy Roman Emperor, etc. [Frederick III]. I have found that His Imperial Majesty will stand in the second, which is that of property and sustenance. His Majesty will have great good fortune with property and will gain many foreign lands. Whatever he undertakes will be fortunate, but he will be burdened with serious illness and weakness of old age. His Majesty will easily become angry and will undertake a large amount of travelling from which he will obtain great good fortune. But between 9 February and 6 March, 20 April and 16 May, 19 September and 5 October, and 3 December until 9 January His Imperial Majesty will have very little good fortune; it will all be against him.

The fourteenth distinction concerns our most gracious Lord, the Holy Roman King, Maximilian. In this year I find that His Royal Majesty will have mighty good fortune, a thousand times greater even than in 1490. His Majesty will gain many lands and towns, and will be loaded with mighty riches, new inheritances and friendships. Everything that His Majesty undertakes will turn out ready made for him

171

[*vingfertig*]. But beware serious illness from 16 June to 8
July, 1 August to 1 September, and 1 January to 28
January. His Majesty is totally forbidden to undertake
anything new in the months of June, August and January,
and the following days of the week, namely Mondays and
Saturdays, which are totally forbidden.

The fifteenth distinction concerns our gracious Lord,
Archduke Sigismund of the House of Austria, etc. Using all
my diligence, I have discovered that the figure of this year
will be the entry in the point of the Ram, etc., and that His
Grace will be found in the second house which is of property
and sustenance. Whereupon I judge according to Haamor
and Tyberiades in the fourth book, tenth chapter, that His
Grace will have full good fortune with a timely harvest
and luck in mining. In this year His Grace will have happy
and good relations with kings, ruling princes and the
powerful. But Mars, who will be found in the ascendant,
will give rise to some anger to His Grace, but as Mars
wanes so the anger will diminish and His Grace will enjoy
peace and happiness. His Grace should guard against illness
and old age in the periods from 27 January to 1 March, 2
April to 3 May, and 1 August until 5 September. His Grace
is warned to be careful in February, March and August.

The sixteenth distinction concerning the Estate of kings,
ruling princes, high-born lords, and all those who are
descended from noblemen will be found in the seventh
house of dissension and war. I have studied the figure of the
sky and have found that some of the princes will be in the
twelfth which is public enmity, envy and hatred and
imprisonment. According to Albubetrus, this will give rise
to great discord with envy and hatred between themselves
as each wishes to be more powerful than the other. In the
summer they will have great good fortune and happiness.
In the autumn they will have illness and indecision, and
many will die. In the winter they will hunt for new
friendships, happiness and luck.

The seventeenth distinction concerns the Estate of knights
who will be influenced by Mars. All those who are involved
in warfare such as mercenaries, doctors, goldsmiths,
surgeons, barbers, blood-letters, and all those who deal in

metalwork will be fortunate in this year. Many will be knighted and they will find plentiful sustenance. But many will perish and die.

The eighteenth distinction concerns the Estate of wives and virgins. It is to be noted that women and effeminate men such as singers, harpists, painters, lutanists and the unchaste in this year will be smitten with deadly sorrows, with heavy illness. They will be fortunate in finding occasional sustenance, and they will seek to increase their circle of friends. They will have good luck with their children.

The nineteenth distinction concerns the common Estate of merchants who will have much trade far and wide in this year with good fortune, especially in the spring in their own sustenance through buying and selling. In the summer there will appear envy and hatred, and many will be destroyed by bad fortune. Their position will improve in the autumn, but in the winter they will suffer illness and indecision.

The twentieth distinction concerns the common Estate of the people, who comprise the poor that toil heavily, such as millers, fishermen, sailors and the peasant-folk, etc. In this year they will become more fearful of God and will hold Him in esteem. They will have good fortune in finding their timely sustenance, but they will also be subject to much illness and indecision with considerable dissension. Otherwise they will be lucky in all their enterprises.

The twenty-first distinction concerns mines that contain mineral ores such as gold, silver, copper, lead, etc. I have found in the figure of the sky in this year that many new mines will be opened due to new finds giving much good new wealth and happiness to many.

Most Gracious Lord and Master, crude people [*grobe menschen*] acting from either great foolishness or through malice, will denounce this, my prognostication, as tempting Almighty God, since he alone makes good or bad weather and since my art does not obey his Godly will, so I can make bad weather myself. Thus evil thoughts will drive me to death. I am persecuted and blamed for all manner of natural occurrences which I will refrain from mentioning now, in order to avoid rebellion of the masses [*der groben luten vffrur*]. In order that God in Heaven and I on earth shall not be blamed in pointing to that which God in his almightiness commands nature itself to carry out, I will regard these prognostications as for the time being sufficient, and I remain at all times at Your Grace's command and further service.

The eclipse of the Sun is on 8 May 1491, three hours and eight minutes after midday.

We have now come to the point of asking, finally, how it was that in three generations the Habsburgs, as an impecunious and middling sort of German dynasty, came to take central and western Europe by storm in a mere eighty years from the shadowy reign of Frederick III to that of his great-grandsons, Charles V and Ferdinand I? The answer lies in the reign of Maximilian I, his style, personality and practical confidence in himself and his dynastic mission. So what was his *Domus Austriae*?

14

Domus Austriae: What was the House of Austria?

Habsburg Castle lies roughly half-way between Basel and Zürich in Switzerland. Its owners were Counts and also Landgraves in Alsace. After the destruction of the Hohenstaufen in the mid-thirteenth century, a vigorous upper-Rhinelander, Rudolf of Habsburg, had himself elected Roman King, defeated the Bohemian King Ottokar in Lower and Inner Austria, and in 1282 enfeoffed his son, Albrecht I, as the first Habsburg Duke of Austria, Styria, and Carniola. In the fourteenth century the Habsburgs tended to be eclipsed by the Wittelsbach Bavarian and Luxemburg-Bohemian dynasties in their mutual competition for election to the Roman royal and imperial crowns. The Luxemburgers held lands in the Netherlands, as well as Bohemia. The Wittelsbachs controlled Bavaria and the Palatinate and for a time parts of the Netherlands with Hainault, Holland and Zealand. Both dynasties fought over the Mark Brandenburg and the County of Tirol, with the Wittelsbachs giving way to the Luxemburgers who in their turn handed their inheritances on to the Habsburgs in the south and the Hohenzollerns in the north by the early years of the fifteenth century. The fate of the County of Tirol is indicative of the massive dynastic rivalry during the fourteenth century. Between 1335 and 1341 it was Luxemburg, 1342–63 Bavarian Wittelsbach, and after 1363 Habsburg. In just over a century, from being Swiss-Alsatian, Upper-Rhenish castellans, the Habsburgs had moved into Lower Austria, taken up service and dynastic ties with the Luxemburgers and beaten the Wittelsbachs over control of the Tirol. Between 1250 and 1350 the Habsburgs made a name for themselves as dynastic adventures in the northern alpine region.[1]

From 1350 to 1450 they consolidated their hold as territorial rulers in the region and evolved the notion of the House of Austria.[2] During this period the concept remained very ambiguous, meaning at one point the ruling family only, and at other times only the land, its territory and permanently resident nobles, burghers, clergy and their tenants.[3] The first reference in the archives comes from 1306 where *domus nostra* is used by the Dukes of Austria in their Habsburg family negotiations with King James II of Aragon in fixing up the first 'Spanish marriage' of the dynasty: that between Duke Frederick (III) and Princess Isobel.[4] *Domus Austriae* is first used in about 1360 at the imperial Luxemburg court of Charles IV in papal correspondence pointing out kinship with the Habsburgs.[5] By the early fifteenth century the chancelleries of the Habsburg rulers all vie with each other to establish a natural, organic link between the ruling family and the territory it rules. This task is made difficult by the lack of any rules of primogeniture over the various branches of the Habsburg dynasty. It is a problem which also beset their rivals for control over the Reich federal system as elected Holy Roman Emperors and Roman Kings, who split into the Wittelsbachs of Upper Bavaria, Lower Bavaria, and Upper and Lower Palatinate, with no lasting dynastic co-operation between the three groups.

It was the Holy Roman Emperor, Frederick, who ruthlessly disciplined his Habsburg family in such a way that the doctrinaire notion of primogeniture could pragmatically and more flexibly be circumvented and rejected in favour of a mystique of supra-territorial Euro-dynastic family co-operation for primacy. The policy was quite consciously manufactured with enormous success between 1450 and 1550 by Frederick III and his son Maximilian I, and then kept traditionally and self-evidently alive by his great-grandsons Charles V and Ferdinand I. Although stemming from the intra-German dynastic rivalries of the fourteenth century, it was a unique and very unconventional central European solution to the problem of how to reconcile biologically chaotic dynastic politics with a more rational, finite and continuous territorial state development. Frederick III and Maximilian I succeeded in this task so well that by the time of

Maximilian's death in 1519, the notion of the House of Austria could be talked about as referring to the 'highest dynasty in Christendom', almost as if it were a self-evident platitude.[6] Yet the origin of this grand claim lay in the personal note-books of an ambitious young bachelor and it was barely some eighty years old. It was the scheme of the twenty-two-year-old Archduke Frederick, who wished to call himself the dynastic head of four Habsburg family branches, namely his own, and those of Ladislas, Albert and Sigismund, which would then hopefully unite Tirol, Alsace and East Swabia, Lower Austria and Bohemia in support of his own Inner Austrian power base to claim the imperial throne when, in due course and by biological good fortune, it should become vacant.[7] In the short term this plan led to violent wars within the Habsburg Austrian dynasty since there were several Habsburg aspirants to the imperial crown in the 1430s. Frederick III lost Vienna first to another branch of his own family, and then to Hungarian troops. He further denied an inheritance to his family ward Ladislaus Posthumous, and attracted the undying hostility of his cousins ruling the Tirol. Archduke Sigismund, who was childless, nearly gambled away Tirol to the rival Wittelsbach rather than let Frederick inherit it. It was only the charm and tact of Maximilian I who held the family together and led to a reunited dynastic rule in the 1490s.

The ideas for establishing the notion of the House of Austria as a major force in German dynastic and European state diplomacy all came from Frederick III, but he lacked the pragmatic ruthlessness and drive to implement them. In that process he was fortunate in his son, Maximilian, whose dynastic-diplomatic ambitions linked the Habsburgs with the Valois Burgundian inheritance, with Castille-Aragon and with the Bohemian-Hungarian Jagiellos. The concepts were those of the father; the execution that of the son. By the 1450s Emperor Frederick's strategic plans were all laid. Firstly, he needed to take over the senior position within the Habsburg family. Secondly, he had to link the House of Austria with the Habsburg family such as to make them synonymous or organic within himself, his son and their progeny. The Habsburg House of Austria was thus right from the start a propagandistic euphmism to provide political leadership and simulate territorial state unity which was otherwise lacking. So *Haus Österreich*, which had meant dynasty only or territory only, was now bound together to produce political loyalty to ruler and administration. From the 1450s, Frederick was hiring scholastic chroniclers as well as Italian and Italianate humanists to propagate this new style of political loyalty by making it look traditional, ancient and even biblical. What started with authors like Aenaeus Silvius and Thomas Ebendorfer in an attempt to instil loyalty to the Habsburgs in the Holy Roman Empire at federal, Reich, and territorial, *Land*, levels, was continued via the classicists, historians and orators of the humanist universities and courts under men like Celtis at Ingolstadt, then at Vienna. It overreached itself with Conrad Peutinger's scheme in 1516 to raise Maximilian's Archduchy of Austria to a kingdom, for it seemingly lacked nothing that was needed to qualify easily as a monarchy.[8]

Having united family and territory into an effective state, Frederick would then use its economic and administrative power to revitalise the federal Reich under his personal leadership, establishing his own progeny as the natural rulers of central Europe not by dogmatism but by example. In this way, lack of primogeniture in the Habsburg territories would be cancelled out by holding the crowns of Germany and the Holy Roman Empire. Lack of prerogative power as kings and emperors would then be overcome by having a strong territorial base. Frederick lived long enough and avoided wars for merely short-term advantages to be able to move through a period of serious material weakness in the 1460s, 1470s and 1480s, to a position of great potential political strength. He had identified the major problems of German politics as the inability to stomach doctrinaire and brutal solutions in the grand manner of England or France: no national unity; no subordination of dynasty to fixed, traditional territorial boundaries and limits; no primogeniture: no over-mighty subjects who could be curbed by the royal prerogative law of necessity, public safety and treason. Frederick found solutions to these problems in an admittedly selfishly dynastic but also consultative, supra-national manner by manufacturing his

178

own myth, namely that the House of Austria was naturally ordained by God to rule in Germany as the highest family in Christendom. He progressed during his long life (1415–93 by politicising family (Habsburg), house (Austria), land (territorial possessions), and election (Holy Roman Emperor). Maximilian's friendship and close kinship with Duke Albrecht of Upper Bavaria at Munich further helped this myth (despite Frederick's initial oppostion) in that it divided the only dynasty who could have provided the Habsburgs with serious rivalry and opposition on its own terms – the Wittelsbachs. They were held further in check by developing the Württemberg–Swabian–Alsatian region under the Swabian League as a pro-Habsburg buffer between the opposing poles of Wittelsbach middle-Rhineland, and Swiss Confederal upper-Rhineland bases of power especially in the years 1489–1506 under Maximilian's management.

What is a country: what was Austria? Under Frederick III and Maximilian I the notion of the House of Austria was consciously created by these rulers themselves in order to build a political system under the serious handicap of unshakeable, narrowly German principles of federal election and of dynastic partible inheritance within a wider European world where primogeniture, unity and centralisation over a limited, fixed territory and its regular, productive inhabitants had become a much more efficient and powerful way of running politics and society. 'Austria' proved that a spuriously traditional pragmatism was indeed viable in contradistinction to the unified nation state, the latter operating with its rulers and subjects dragooned into seemingly harmonious continuity over time and space like a piece of clockwork in mathematical set-theory. By working out an alternative that rescued the feudal, elective, contractual and dynastic freedoms of an older set of principles, Frederick III consciously created a political system which nearly drove the nation-state out of business by way of dynastic marriage expansion in the sixteenth and seventeenth century. What Frederick III originated, Maximilian developed and fixed as a personal link in the political chain of Habsburg, Austria and Old Reich. It was an original feat of conscious cultural creation through politics and propagandistic management, bequeathed to

179

Charles V, Ferdinand I and their children in Madrid, Vienna, Prague and Brussels. It was soon to prove successful as the curiously complacent self-perpetuating and self-evident myth of the Habsburg court in Europe when in fact it was little more than well-believed hot air.[9] When, on 3 June 1509, Maximilian wrote to instil some energy, confidence and courage into his counsellors at Worms, who had just failed to obtain a Reichstag tax grant, he was still very much involved with the rhetoric creating the Habsburg Austrian myth of rulership:[10]

> The Estates [i.e. German territorial rulers and authorities of the Old Reich who had elected, crowned and sworn fealty to Maximilian as one of their own number, mutually raised as leader over them] should in all fairness remember that as ruler of Austria and Burgundy, I have had to bear and suffer many long years of heavy expense, burden and effort in countering the opposition of the French, Swiss, Gelderlanders, Hungarians and Turks. I have survived them all through my own strength and inherited treasury wealth, and against all such threats I have always thought it most essential to retain my Houses of Austria and Burgundy, forging them into a shield to protect the Reich from the attacks of the above.

Maximilian was once again sabre-rattling and exploiting German xenophobia to provoke an open and cumbersome political machine into giving him troops and money for his war against Venice. The more youthful Habsburg rhetoric of the Frankfurt Reichstag of 1489 against rebellious Flanders, France and Hungary from twenty years previously was now becoming the hallowed tradition of German federal political leadership at monarchic and imperial level, because it had been repeated in the same forceful manner so many times that the territorial authorities in the Reich began to believe it. In the era 1480–1520 the general need for political reform in the German federal system was finally harnessed, not without considerable opposition, to the monarchic principle of territorial state rule by the stratagems of Frederick III and Maximilian I. AEIOV led to *Haus Österreich*, which developed into the *aetas maximilianeae*. In the words of Ernst Bock:[11]

Nothing more aptly demonstrates the statesmanlike achievement of Maximilian and the historic prescience of his overall grasp of affairs than the fact that his life's labours in imperial institutional reform not only withstood the immediate opposition of his rivals in European power politics but also the onslaught of the Reformation era without major damage or serious concessions. His imperial reforms were even able to hold up for three centuries the total decay of the Old Reich which had already become a clear possibility under his father, Frederick III, and which so nearly succeeded during the course of the Thirty Years' War.

During his lifetime Maximilian had truly and consciously striven to turn the dreams of his father into the world-wide dynastic realities and ambitions of his grandsons, Charles and Ferdinand. In practically no time at all, indeed, in just one generation, a grubby little central European dynasty had been forged into a supra-national great power in Austria, Germany, the Netherlands, Burgundy, North Italy, Iberia and overseas in the Spanish colonies, and in south-east Europe against the expanding Turks. There it stayed, despite modifications as a result of the wars of Marlborough, and of Napoleon, until the end of the First World War. That achievement was Maximilian's.

Let us conclude this analytical biography of Emperor Maximilian I by repeating what was stated at the end of chapter 11, after explaining how Maximilian had made provision for the *menu-peuple* in his last will and testament.

Biography is limited by the fact that universal movements intersect in the individual life; if we are to understand them we must seek for new foundations outside the individual. It is not possible for biography to become scientific. We must turn to new categories, shapes and forms of life which do not emerge from the individual life. The individual is only the crossing point for the cultural systems and organizations into which his existence is woven; how can they be understood through him?

Notes

(These notes refer to the text and also serve as a guide to further reading.)

1 Introduction

1 Sebastian Brant: *The Ship of Fools* (1494), trans. E.H. Zeydel, New York, 1962, pp.62–70, 124, 216, 261–3, 323–7.

2 *Ibid.*, pp.323–4 (from the Hundredth Ship of Fools). Brant was also pro-Maximilian; cf. P. Heitz (ed.): *Des Sebastian Brant Flugblätter*, Strassburg, 1915.

3 A. Schulz (ed.): 'Weisskunig Nach den Dictaten und eigenhändigen Aufzeichnungen Kaiser Maximilians I, zusammengestellt von Marx Treitzsauerwein von Ehrentreitz', *Jahrbuch der Kunsthistorischen Sammlungen des Allerhöchsten Kaiserhauses*, Vienna, 1888; A. Schulz (ed.): 'Fragmente einer lateinischen Autobiographie Kaiser Maximilians', in *ibid.* S. Laschitzer (ed.): 'Theuerdank, Facsimilie von 1517', in *ibid.* Q. von Leitner: *Freydal. Des Kaisers Maximilian I. Turniere und Mummereien*, Vienna, 1880–2. See now the work of Professor Dieter Wuttke at Bamberg University.

4 T. Ilgen (ed.): *Joseph Grünpeck: Die Geschichte Friedrichs III. und Maximilians I.*, Leipzig, 1891, and the Grünpeck manuscripts in the Austrian National Library, Vienna. S. von Birken (ed.): *Johann Jacob Fugger: Spiegel der Ehren des Hochlöblichen Kayser- und Königlichen Erzhauses Österreich*, Nürnberg, 1668.

5 Hippolithus a Lapide (B.P. von Chemnitz): *Dissertatio de ratione status in imperio nostro Romano-Germanico*, Stettin, 1642.

6 L.von Ranke: *Deutsche Geschichte im Zeitalter der Reformation* (popular edition), vol. 1, Leipzig, 1914.

7 H.Ulmann: *Kaiser Maximilian I. Auf urkundliche Grundlage dargestellt*, 2 vols, Stuttgart, 1884, 1891 (reprinted by H. Geyer Antiquariat, Vienna, 1967).

8 R. Buchner: *Maximilian I, Kaiser an der Zeitenwende*, 2nd edn, Göttingen, 1970, p.110. H. Wiesflecker: *Kaiser Maximilian I*, 1, Munich, 1971, pp.1–43.

9 V. von Kraus (ed.): *Maximilians I. vertraulicher Briefwechsel mit Sigismund Prüschenk*, Innsbruck, 1875.

10 H. Fichtenau: *Der junge Maximilian 1459–82*, Vienna, 1959.

11 Niederösterreichische Landesregierung (Kulturreferat) (ed.): *Ausstellung Friedrich III,* Wiener-Neustadt, 1966.

12 T. Musper (ed.): *Kaiser Maximilians I. Weisskunig*, 2 vols., Stuttgart, 1956. Buchner, *op.cit.*

13 A. Schröcker: 'Unio atque concordia: Reichspolitik Bertholds von Henneberg 1484–1504', Würzburg University thesis, 1970.
14 Land Tirol (Kulturreferat) (ed.): *Ausstellung Maximilian I*, Innsbruck, 1969: S. Appelbaum (ed.): *The Triumph of Maximilian I (1512)*. *137 Woodcuts by Hans Burgkmair and Others*, New York, 1964. See also *Maximilian's Triumphal Arch*, New York, 1972.
15 Buchner, *op.cit.*, p.55. Cf. L. Cuyler: *The Emperor Maximilian and Music*, Oxford, 1974.
16 H. Wiesflecker: *Kaiser Maximilian I*, vol. 1 (1459–1493/4), Munich, 1971; vol. 2 (1493–1500), 1975; vol. 3 (1500–8), 1977. The following have written very perceptively on Maximilian's politics in recent years: E. Bock, F.H.Schubert and H.Gollwitzer.
17 Of the many studies, see G.von Pöllnitz: *Jacob Fugger*, 2 vols, Tübingen, 1949, 1951; M.Jansen: 'Jacob Fugger der Reiche', *Historisches Jahrbuch der Görresgesellschaft*, 30, 1909, pp. 491–536.
18 Cf. *Hofkammerarchiv* (HKA), Vienna: Gedenkbücher; Herrschaftsakten; Sachbetreffe. *Haus-, Hof-und Staatsarchiv* (HHSA), Vienna: *Maximiliana*.
19 Cf. HHSA: Mainzer Erzkanzlerarchiv (MEKA), Reichstagsakten (RTA), Reichskammergericht (RKG), Reichshofrat (RHR), Urkunden, Varia.
20 E. Bock and H. Gollwitzer (eds): *Reichstagsakten. Mittlere Reihe*, vol. 3 (2 pts, 1488–90), Göttingen, 1972–3.
21 Cf. HHSA: Handschriftensammlung (HS). C. von Böhm: *Die Handschriften des Haus-, Hof und Staatsarchivs*, Vienna, 1873f. (with supplements). Cf. HKA: Gedenkbücher (GB). F. Walter: 'Die sogenannten Gedenkbücher des Wiener Hofkammerarchivs', *Archivalische Zeitschrift*, 42–3, 1934, pp. 137–58. O. Brunner: 'Das Archiv der niederösterreichischen Kammer und des Vizedoms in Österreich', *Jahrbuch für Landeskunde von Niederösterreich und Wien*, New Series 29, 1944–8', pp. 144–66.
22 A.F. Pribram, R. Geyer and F. Koran: *Materialen zur Geschichte der Preise und Löhne in Österreich* (one vol.), Vienna, 1938. H.Helczmanovski (ed.): *Beiträge zur Bevölkerungs-und Sozialgeschichte Österreichs*, Vienna, 1973. W. Abel: *Massenarmut und Hungerkrisen im vorindustriellen Deutschland*, Göttingen, 1972, and Hamburg, 1974.
23 A pioneering work is P.Goubert: *Louis XIV and twenty million Frenchmen*, Harmondsworth, 1970. See also G. Parker, *Philip II*, New York, 1978, Chs 1–5, 12.

2 Man and image

1 HHSA: HS-W 321, fols 178–178 verso.
The transcribed Latin text is worth repeating.

Miraculum. Morbus Gallicus per preces Imperatoris curatur. Maximiliano primo invictissimo Caesare commorante in Oppido Fiessen et in ipso Monasterio S. Magni, plures vndique Legati ac Comissarii confluebant: prandente vero eo in Abbatia, cuidam vini haustus offerebatur, post cuius sumptionem, inoeperunt vesicae in euis ore oriri, quae de genere morbi Gallici erant. Ipse igiter pyssimus Imperator pro eo multam anxius intentissime Deo et S. Alagno hiuius loci Patrono supplicavit, ut ipsum infectio desereret. Ecce in momento remissis in ore vesicis, nihil illuis morbi sensit amplius, qui aegrotus fuerat: Quare Deo et S. Magno dignas retulerunt grates. Acta haec sunt circa Annum Dni. 1497. Ex vita et miraculis S. Magni Abbatis.

1 Cf. O. Kostenzer: 'Medizin vor 1500', *Ausstellung Maximilian I. Katalog*, Innsbruck, 1969 (Beiträge), p. 60.

That Maximilian was interested in medical cures is brought out in HHSA: HS-B376, 'Memoriale oder Gedenkbuch Maximilians I', fols 41–3 verso, especially 41 v., item 6, 'Item ain würtzlin haist gratail wechst auf dem hohen gepirg ist gut für die pestillentz wann ain graust oder die pestallentz ankombt so schneid ain wenig von der wurtzen klain vnd trincks In ainem wein so swint alle kranckhait von aim'. Did Maximilian take a wonder drug in wine as a cure for the onset of syphilis and all other ailments? One may hope for his sake that he truly believed that he did indeed possess such a medicament. On the influence of the stars on illness, and of Siamese twins on the politics of a new age, plus Maximilian's inclusion in the pages of Grünpeck's *Prodigiorum interpretatio* of 1502, there is a fascinating essay by D. Wuttke: 'Wunderdeutung und Politik', in K. Elm *et al.: Landesgeschichte und Geistesgeschichte. Festschrift für Otto Herding*, Stuttgart, 1977, pp.217–44, which well captures the low superstitions and pseudo-medical personal fears of the high and mighty. See chapter 13.

2 Cf. O. Benesch and E.M. Auer, *Die Historia Friderici et Maximiliani*, Berlin, 1957, esp. pp.28ff., and illustrations with descriptive texts, pp.115ff.

3 *Ibid.*, illustration 6, p.117.

4 *Ibid.*, illustration 16, p.120.

5 *Ibid.*, illustrations 17, 18, 19, 23, pp.120–1. Re plate 1, the *Ausstellung Maximilian I* Catalogue contains this and other illustrations in the present volume together with a valuable commentary.

6 One of these was Dr Georg Tannstetter, Maximilian's physician and mathematician, who predicted the circumstances of the ruler's death.

7 See the article by Kostenzer in *Ausstellung Maximilian I, passim*.

8 *Ibid.*, pp.60–4 and further bibliography there, especially the essays of Schadelbauer and of Sbrik.

9 The portraits reproduced in *ibid.* provide a useful guide to his appearance. Cf. L. Baldass: 'Die Bildnisse Kaiser Maximilians I', *Jahrbuch der Kunstsammlungen des Allerhöchsten Kaiserhauses in Wien*, 31, 1913–14. L. Baldass: *Der Künstlerkreis Kaiser Maximilians I*, Vienna, 1923. J. Pope-Hennessy: *The Portrait in the Renaissance*, Princeton, 1979, pp.166–71, discusses the Habsburg love of portraiture by starting with Maximilian and Bianca Maria. German rulers tended to favour an older tradition of realism; hence the quarrelsome face of Bianca (see Plate 17), the bluff and hearty pose of Maximilian (see Plate 3), and the beaky stare of Archduke Sigismund (see Plate 13).

10 H.T. Musper: *Albrecht Dürer*, Stuttgart, 1965, p.118.

11 An impressive list of funerary endowments concludes with the famous tomb of Emperor Maximilian I at Innsbruck: see P.E. Schramm (ed.). *Denkmale der deutschen Könige und Kaiser*, 2, 1273–1519, Munich, 1978.

12 Translated from Bock, 'Doppelregierung', *op.cit.*, p.291. A stylish appreciation of Maximilian as a multi-faceted person was delivered at the anniversary celebrations in Linz during 1969 by Hans Sturmberger, now republished in his collected essays, *Land ob der Enns und Österreich*, Linz, 1979, pp. 127–53.

13 Benesch and Auer, *op.cit.*, illustration 20; p.121. For the formula 'Alles Erdreich ist Österreich Untertan', see the facsimile from Frederick's 1437 notebook in *Ausstellung Friedrich III. Katalog*, Wiener-Neustadt, 1966, illustration 48; for background, H. Wiesflecker: 'Friedrich III und Maximilian', in the same catalogue, pp. 48–63. H. Fichtenau: *Der Junge Maximilian (1459–82)*, Munich, 1959. A. Lhotsky: 'AEIOV, *Mitteilungen des Institut für österreichische Geschichtsforschung*, 60, 1952.

14 Cf. P. Diederichs: '*Kaiser Maximilian I als politischer Publizist*', University thesis, Jena, 1933; E. Weller; 'Die ersten gedruckten kaiserlichen Mandate', *Serapaeum*, 24, 1863.

15 Landesarchiv Innsbruck, Kopialbuch 1493, fol. 123.
16 By E. Bock: 'Die Doppelregierung Kaiser Friedrichs III. und König Maximilians in den Jahren 1486–93, Ein politisch-historisches Generationsproblem', *Aus Reichstagen des 15. and 16. Jahrhunderts. Festgabe der Historischen Kommission bei der Bayerischen Akademie der Wissenschaften*, Göttingen, 1958, pp.297, 339.
17 Cf. W. Erben: 'Ursprung und Entwicklung der deutschen Kriegsartikel', *Festschrift Theodor Ritter von Sickel*, Innsbruck, 1900, pp.1–57. H.M. Möller: *Das Regiment der Landsknechte*, Wiesbaden, 1976.
18 Benesch and Auer, *op.cit.*, illustrations 32, 33, p.124.
19 *Ibid.*, illustrations 35, 36, 37, pp.124–5.
20 *Ausstellung Maximilian I*, illustration 129; p.159.
21 Benesch and Auer, *op.cit.*, illustration 38, p.125.
22 Kostenzer, *op.cit.*, *passim.*
23 *Ausstellung Maximilian I.*, illustration 48, p.73.
24 *Ibid.*, illustration 20; p.39. Briefly recounted in C. Hare: *Maximilian the Dreamer*, London, 1913, pp.112–13. The interesting analysis by G.S. Williams: 'The Arthurian model in Emperor Maximilian's autobiographical writings, *Weisskunig and Theuerdank*', *Sixteenth Century Journal*, XI, 1980, pp.3–23, appeared too late for me to take into account. We overlap on a number of points, over which I could well have profited from her scholarship.
25 Heinz Engels in the facsimile edition of *Kaiser Maximilians Theuerdank*, Kommentar-band, Stuttgart, 1968, pp.29–40.
26 H. Rupprich: 'Das literarische Werk Kaiser Maximilians I', *Ausstellung Maximilian I*, pp.47–55, esp. p.49.
27 Cf. Johannes Cochlaeus: *Brevis Germanie Descriptio (1512)* (edited by Langosch), Darmstadt, 1976. G. Strauss: *Sixteenth Century Germany. Its Topography and Topographers*, Madison, 1959. But note the tantalising comments in L. Grote and D. Wuttke: 'Kaiser Maximilian in der Schedelschen Weltchronik', *Mitteilungen des Vereins für Geschichte der Stadt Nürnberg*, 62, 1975, pp. 60–83, already for the years 1492–3.
28 *Maximilian's Triumphal Arch*, New York (Dover Reprint), 1972. There is a substantial literature on many aspects of Maximilian's career of self-glorification and scholastic-humanistic flattery, ambivalence and dabbling. He is probably Europe's most narcissistic ruler: a veritable King Psapho. See also *The Triumph of Maximilian I*, New York (Dover Reprint), 1964.
29 HHSA: Böhm Nr. 1330 (HS-W 1095).
30 When Maximilian was eight, his mother, Eleonora, died after a particularly difficult childbirth. Her effigy was carved on her tombstone, erected two years later in 1469 *(Ausstellung Friedrich III*, illustration 36, p.356). Cf. Wiesflecker, *op.cit.*, 1, pp. 80–1. At that time her husband, Emperor Frederick III, ordered from the same stone-mason his own sculpted tombstone. Although he lived another twenty-four years, he believed in the wisdom of preparing himself for joining his wife in death in good time. Sculptor Niklas Gerhaert van Leyden did the work for 200 fl. See *Ausstellung Friedrich III*, illustration 37, p. 386.
31 Sister Kunigunde, married to Duke Albrecht in Munich, with whom Maximilian kept close and friendly contact. He liked his brother-in-law socially, and was a doting uncle to Kunigunde's children, as only a mother's brother traditionally can be in a pre-industrial society. Her portrait (Plate 11) was done in 1480 when Kunigunde was a beauty of 15, and Albrecht was already courting her, against her father's express wish.
32 Well reproduced in F. Dörnhöffer: 'Ein Cyklus von Federzeichnungen mit arstellungen von Kriegen und Jagden Maximilians I', *Jahrbuch der kunsthistori-schen Sammlungen des Allerhöchsten Kaiserhauses*, 18, 1897, pp. 1–55.

3 The politics of land-hunger

1 Wiesflecker, *op.cit.*, 1, pp. 354–5.
2 Chancellor Serntein to Paul von Liechtenstein, Duisburg, 3 April 1509; Kraus, *op.cit.*, pp. 120–4.
3 *Ibid.*, pp. 79–80, Maximilian to Sigismund Prüschenk, Kempten, 21 September 1491, 'Got weiss daz mir mein heroben vmbzotln von hertzen leid ist vndt doch so tar ich vor armut.'
4 Wiesflecker, *op.cit.*, 1, pp. 160–1.
5 *Ibid.*, p.148.
6 Translated from Maximilian to Emperor and Electors, Bruges, 1488, Kraus, *op.cit.*, pp. 62–3.
7 Many years later a certain Bernhart Tallant complained to Protonotar Serntein that although he and his wife had brought up one of King Maximilian's natural children as one of their family, and although they had served His Majesty for many years, risking life and property whilst Maximilian was in prison in Bruges, which had ruined the family, so now Maximilian neglected them and they had to sell everything in the house and go begging in an unseemly manner at the neighbours' doors (HHSA: *Maximiliana*, 43 (V), fol. 75).
8 HHSA: *Maximiliana*, Kart. 1, fol. 22. Personal handwriting of King Maximilian to Archduke Sigismund, Graz, 8 August 1490.

Hochgeborn. furst frewnliche. lieber veter Wier woltn gern ewr liebe Newe Maer wissen lassen so gend dy vnsrn so mit grasser vreiterey vmb Das kain nichtz gebyss ist ob es rat od. weys vm sy ist Doch wirt ewr liebe. stadion alle sachn berichtn. Datm zu gretz im suntag nach affare vginis Anno dnij 1490 pmp Maximilian Ro Kunig.

9 Walter von Stadion was Archduke Sigismund's personal envoy and retained in service after Maximilian took on the government of Tirol on 16 March 1490. Three years later Maximilian was to use Stadion in the Sforza marriage negotiations. Wiesflecker, *op.cit.*, 1, pp. 262–3, 365.
10 *Ibid.*, pp. 288–90.
11 *Ibid.*, p. 352.
12 Kraus, *op.cit., passim,* esp. pp. 97–8. HKA: Niederösterreichische Herrschaftsakten (NÖHA), A 6/A, Grafschaft Hardegg, fols 7–8, 19 verso, 21 verso (*Kaufbriefe* of 1495 and 1500 (copies), running to 350,000 fl. gross).
13 A particular problem were the Turkish invasions of Inner Austria in the later 1460s, early 1470s, early 1480s and from the 1490s onwards. Lampoons called Frederick III the Arch-sleeping-cap of the Holy Roman Empire. A vicious pamphlet declared that the senile old emperor spent his days at Linz collecting mouse-droppings and catching flies. By spring 1493, Frederick's bad leg had turned septic and the smell was so great that he resorted to hiding coins in his chambers in order to have the company of his servants, who only came in the hope of finding some money. Wiesflecker, *op.cit.*, 1, pp. 352, and the plates facing 353, 356.
14 HHSA: *Maximiliana*, Kart.1, fol. 36, Maximilian to Archduke Sigismund of Tirol, from Rottenmann in Styria, 13 June 1490, writing that he has visited the silver-mine there and found a large seam of ore, enough for four-and-a-half to six years' work. He praises the layout of the mine, 'dy genk sint dik vnd prait aber gar Hert' (the passages are fat and wide but quite firm).
15 'The greatest flaw in Maximilian's political talent lay in his attitude to money. He was not able to cope with it' (translated from Buchner: *op.cit.*, pp. 49–50).

4 Austria – the land

1 H.E. Feine: 'Territorialbildung der Habsburger im deutschen Südwesten', *Zeitschrift der Savignystiftung für Rechtsgeschichte*, 80, *Germanistische Abteilung*, 67, 1950, pp. 270–308. *Cf.* G.W. Sante (ed.): *Geschichte der deutschen Länder (Territorien Ploetz)*, 1, Würzburg, 1964. M. Mitterauer: 'Ständegliederung und Ländertypen', *Herrschaftsstruktur und Ständebildung*, 3, Munich, 1973, pp. 115–206.

2 For a survey of the Burgau as an estate record, HHSA: HS-W 321, folios 289–312. An excellent survey which breaks new ground is P. Blickle: *Landschaften im Alten Reich*, Munich, 1973, pp. 96–108 (for Habsburg Swabia), 159–254 (for Tirol) and 255–315 (for Vorarlberg).

3 H. Pirchegger: *Geschichte und Kulturleben Deutschösterreichs, 1526–1792*, Vienna, 1931, Maps.

4 Territorial Estates Ob der Enns to Maximilian, Linz, 1493, in Kraus, *op.cit.*, pp. 97–8.

5 Cf. A. Loehr: *Österreichische Geldgeschichte*, Vienna, 1946, pp. 29–35.

6 HKA: GB 14, fol, 41; GB 15, fol. 216. Much more work needs to be done on the fiscal archives to reveal the banking operations centred on the Vienna *Hubhaus*, especially in the 1490s under the guidance of Hans Geyer (1457–1525), who was ennobled in 1502 for his financial services to Maximilian. H. Kühnel: 'Die landesfürstlichen Baumeister der Wiener Hofburg, 1494–1569', *Anzeiger der phil.-hist. Klasse der Österreichischen Akademie der Wissenschaften*, 1959, Nr. 24, pp. 298–304.

7 F. Fischer: 'Die Sensenausfuhr aus Österreich', in I. Bog (ed.): *Der Aussenhandel Ostmitteleuropas, 1450–1650*, Cologne, 1971, pp. 286–319.

8 K. Grossmann (ed.): *Jakob Unrest. Österreichische Chronik*, Weimar, 1957, *passim*. W. Neumann: 'Die Türkeneinfälle nach Kärnten', *Festgabe H. Steinacker*, Munich, 1955.

9 F. Mayer: 'Materialien und kritische Bemerkungen zur Geschichte der ersten Bauernunruhen in Steiermark und den angrenzenden Ländern', *Beiträge zur Kunde steiermärkischer Geschichtsquellen*, 13, Graz, 1876; 14, 1877; and the same author in *Mittheilungen des historischen Vereins für Steiermark*, 23, 1875, pp. 107–34.

5 Austria – the population

1 H. Widmann: 'Die Einhebung der ersten Reichssteuer in Salzburg im Jahre 1497', *Mitteilungen der Gesellschaft für Salzburger Landeskunde, Festschrift aus Anlass des 50. Jährigen Bestandes der Gesellschaft*, 1910, pp. 91–106. R. Jung: 'Die Akten über die Erhebung des gemeinen Pfennigs von 1495 ff. im Stadtarchiv zu Frankfurt-am-Main', *Korrespondenzblatt des Gesamtvereins*, 8, 1909, pp. 328–35. P. Blickle: 'Gemeiner Pfennig und Obrigkeit', *Vierteljahrschrift für Sozial- und Wirtschaftsgeschichte*, 63, 1976, pp. 180–93.

2 K. Klein: 'Die Bevölkerung Österreichs (circa 1500–1750)', in Helczmanovski, *op.cit.*, pp. 47–112.

3 *Ibid.*, pp. 49, 105, 112.

4 *Ibid.*, p. 97. E. Kirsten (ed.): *Bevölkerungs-Ploetz*, Würzburg, 1955–6.

5 Klein, in Helczmanovski, *op. cit.*, p. 106.

6 E. Lichtenberger: 'Von der mittelalterlichen Bürgerstadt zur City', *ibid.*, p. 305.
7 E. Kunze: 'Wandlungen der Sozialstruktur', *ibid.*, p. 345.
8 *Ibid.*, pp. 301, 346–7, combining evidence from fifteenth-century Vienna with eighteenth-century Krems and Stein.
9 *Ibid.*, p. 301.

6 Standards of Life

1 An early exception is F. Eulenberg: 'Zur Bevölkerungs- und Vermögensstatistik des 15. Jahrhunderts', *Zeitschrift für Sozial- und Wirtschaftsgeschichte*, 3, 1895, pp.424–67.
  See also the cautionary remarks in F. Braudel: *The Mediterranean*, 1, London, 1971–2, pp. 418ff., on his model of the Mediterranean economy, *circa* 1600. The best German regional survey is R. Endres: 'Zur wirtschaftlichen und sozialen Lage in Franken vor dem dreissigjährigen Krieg', *Jahrbuch für fränkische Landesforschung*, 28, 1968.
2 HHSA: *Maximiliana*, Kart. 43 (36/V), fols 8–12. The Viennese complained furiously to Maximilian's Lower Austrian counsellors that the new trade routes via Antwerp and the Elbe and Oder had disrupted further the old spice and wine routes via Venice and the Danube, which threatened Viennese entrepôt trade north to Bohemia, Silesia and Poland. The Italian wars now made it even worse.
3 By far the best survey and documentation is A. Rosenkranz: *Der Bundschuh. Die Erhebungen des südwestdeutschen Bauernstandes in den Jahren 1493–1517*, 2 vols, Heidelberg, 1927.
4 *Ibid.*, 2, pp. 80–2, 95–7.
5 Particularly H. Öhler: 'Der Aufstand des Armen Conrad im Jahre 1514', *Württembergische Vierteljahrshefte für Landesgeschichte*, Neue Folge, 38, pp. 400–86. More generally, G. Franz: *Der Deutsche Bauernkrieg*, seventh edition, Bad Homburg, 1965, pp. 19–30. Feine, 'Territorialbildung'.
6 P. Blickle: *Die Revolution von 1525*, Munich, 1975, is the best monograph. In English, the most useful collection of documents is G. Strauss (ed): *Manifestations of Discontent in Germany on the Eve of the Reformation*, Bloomington, 1971. The recent international debate on origins, organisation and consequences of 1525 is made available by Bob Scribner and G. Benecke (eds): *The German Peasant War of 1525 – New Viewpoints*, London, 1979, which also includes extracts from Blickle's work.
7 Cf. J. Chesneux: *Secret Societies in China*, Ann Arbor, 1971, combined with G. Skinner: 'Marketing and Social Structure in Rural China', *Journal of Asian Studies*, 24, November 1964; February 1965; May 1965. The only really effective work done so far towards producing an *economic* history of the German Reformation era is in Clemens Bauer: *Gesammelte Schriften*, Feiburg-im-Breisgau, 1965. Such work centres on the response of territorial state treasuries to meet the cumulative effect, on things like interest rates and retail prices, of Reichstag monopoly fiscalism to pay for Maximilian's wars against France and Venice. These matters were disastrous to the monetary policies of nearly all the German small states in the 1510s, but it still has to be documented satisfactorily from the archives. One of the ways into the subject is to follow through the level of economic *Fehde*, *Schmähschrift* and *Einlieger* activity. See the documents and illustrations appended to G. Benecke: 'Northwest Germany, Lippe, and the Empire in Early Modern Times' (typescript), St Andrews University thesis, 3 vols, 1970. The fiscal archives will undoubtedly produce a basic reinterpretation of the early Reformation and its

artisan-peasant revolts, which would put the exciting work of the current school of urban social history into a wider perspective and give a more truly holistic analysis.

8 To preserve his monopoly position as the only rightful exploiter of Tirolean mining wealth by virtue of his regal rights, Maximilian ordered the destruction of miners' and woodmen's settlements on the southern borders with mainland Venice in 1496, followed by an embargo on all trade in raw materials with the North Italian plain. On 10 August his bailiffs were instructed to ascertain the location, poverty or otherwise of all squatters, plus the amount of foreign (i.e. Italian) investment they were receiving, and then to destroy their enterprises and expel them from the territory. 'Die örter so noch vorhanden, und durch sy vormaln gen Welschen Landen, wie vorstet verkaufft, oder verlazzen sein, nyder zu hawen, und aus dem Land zuvertreiben . . . [and in order to protect the supply of timber to his own mines] doch daz Sy hinfur in andern Walden, nach sunst nicht weitter greiffen, noch aus dem Land verkauffen on sonder unser bevelh, damit die Wald zu unserm Perckwerch auf künfftig zeit dienend gehayt werden.' Landesarchiv Innsbruck, Kopialbuch 1495–6, fols 347–8.

9 E. Egg and W. Pfaundler: *Kaiser Maximilian I. und Tirol*, Innsbruck, 1969.

10 A vivid insight here is F.H. Schubert: 'Blasius Hölzl und die soziale Situation in der Hofkammer Maximilians I', *Vierteljahrschrift für Sozial- und Wirtschaftsgeschichte*, 47, 1960, pp. 105–15.

11 Landesarchiv Innsbruck, Kopialbuch 15, 1492, fols 48–48 verso.

12 See Landesarchiv Innsbruck, Kopialbuch 17, 1494, fol. 57; 'hannsen Frechen verschreybung des Schäffl Salz halbn im Phannh ze Hall im Yntal'.

7 The City

1 W. Abel: *Massenarmut und Hungerkrisen im Vorindustriellen Deutschland*, Göttingen, 1972, and Hamburg, 1974. A useful survey of the monographic literature is provided by E. Maschke and J. Sydow (eds): *Gesellschaftliche Unterschichten*, Stuttgart, 1967. For the following discussion compare the debate concerning the relative purchasing power of building labourers' wages 1260 to 1954, which confirms our gloomy picture here. E.H. Phelps Brown and Sheila V. Hopkins: 'Seven Centuries of Building Wages', *Economica*, 1955, pp. 195–206; 'Seven Centuries of the Prices of Consumables compared with Builders' Wage-rates, *Economica*, 1956, pp. 296–314; 'Wage-rates and Prices: Evidence for Population Pressure in the Sixteenth Century', *Economica*, 1957, pp. 289–306; 'Builders' Wage-rates, Prices and Population: Some Further Evidence', *Economica*, 1959, pp. 18–38. Also note the warning of Ralph Davis: *The Rise of the Atlantic Economies*, London, 1973, p. XIV, but see also his chapters 2, 6 and 7. C. H. Freudenberger, reviewing Abel in *Central European History*, 2, 1969, pp. 170–6.

2 From an assessment of the tax records in the region around Zürich, for example, the population is thought to have almost doubled between 1428 and 1505. D.Sabean: 'Famille et tenure paysanne', *Annales*, 27, 1972, esp. pp. 904–5.

3 Translated from *Staatsarchiv Detmold*, L 9 Bd. 1, fol. 196. See G. Benecke: 'Labour relations and peasant society in northwest Germany c.1600', *History*, 58, 1973, pp. 355–6.

4 M.J. Elsas: *Umriss einer Geschichte der Preise und Löhne in Deutschland*, 2 vols, Leiden, 1936–49. A.F. Pribram, R. Geyer and F. Koran: *Materialien zur Geschichte der Preise und Löhne in Österreich*, 1 vol., Vienna, 1938. See the discussion of the Elsas Archive

by W. Abel: 'Preis-und Agrargeschichte', in *Wege und Forschungen der Agrargeschichte. Festschrift für Günther Franz*, Frankfurt-am-Main, 1967, pp. 67–79.

5 G. Strauss: *Nuremberg in the 16th century*, New York, 1966, pp. 200–1. Contrast C.L. Sachs: *Nürnbergs Reichsstädtische Arbeiterschaft (1503–11)*, Nuremberg, 1915, pp. 40–4, and Appendices.

6 Abel, *Massenarmut und Hungerkrisen* . . . , pp.22–4.

7 See the important modifications of Abel resulting from the case study of one south Baltic coastal town, H. Hauschild: *Studien zu Löhnen und Preisen in Rostock im Spätmittelaler*, Cologne, 1973.

8 For the following survey, Pribram, *op. cit., passim*. Hans Tscherte (d. 1552), one of the architects of the Vienna *Hofburg*, was commissioned by Maximilian in 1517 to run the Vienna *Bürgerspital*. He was a friend of Dürer, and an expert on mathematics and fortification, Kühnel, 'Landesfürstliche Baumeister', pp. 304–7.

9 F. Braudel: *The Mediterranean*, 1, p. 420.

10 Contrast Phelps Brown and Hopkins, *op.cit.* (1956), Appendix B, pp. 311–19 for the English urban situation. Compare H. Zatschek: 'Die Handwerker Wiens', *Jahrbuch des Vereins für Geschichte der Stadt Wien*, 8, 1949–50. Compare the *Annales* article of G. Verlinden *et al.*: 'Prices and Wage movements in Belgium', in P. Burke (ed.): *Economy and society in Early Modern Europe*, London, 1972, pp. 61–2, 71, 83, n. 45.

8 Rural life: thresholds of violence

1 This and the following evidence comes from A. Tille: *Die bäuerliche Wirtschaftsverfassung des Vintschgaues in der zweiten Hälfte des Mittelalters*, Innsbruck,1895, especially pp. 185–8.

2 Translated from HHSA: HS-B 753, Urbar Ortenburg, 1499, fol. 10.

3 P.J. Wichner: 'Ueber einige Urbare', *Beiträge zur Kunde steiermärkische Geschichtsquellen*, 13, 1876, pp. 94–5.

4 As in Emperor Maximilian's own prayer-book, 'Dear Lord, we are all your peasants' (Lieber Gott, wir sind alle Deine Bauern), in R.M. and G. Radbruch: *Der deutsche Bauernstand*, 2nd edn. Göttingen, 1961, p. 29a.

5 Translated from *Urbar* Ortenburg 1499, last entry (peasant No. 124).

6 Translated from *ibid.*, fol. 9 verso.

7 Translated from HHSA: HS-R214, 'Ein prawch wie man kauffen und zalln soll', Memorialsachen vmb Ao. 1510, Carthusia Gemnicensis, fol. 136.

8 F. Mayer: 'Die ersten Bauernunruhen in Steiermark', *Mittheilungen des Historischen Vereins für Steiermark*, 23, 1875, pp. 112–13.

9 *Ibid.*, pp.114–15; 'Lieben sun, habts enke arm leut schon da bitt ich enk vmb, vnd was si enk schuldig sein des nembts vnd huets ier vor steier, vnd nembts nit streboichsen da bit ich enk vmb'.

10 *Ibid.*, pp. 122–34.

11 'Diep und zaubrerin . . . und ander mallafitz nuer im peytl gestrafft werden', F. Mayer, F. Bischoff and J. von Zahn: 'Kleinere Mitteilungen zur Geschichte der Bauernunruhen in Steiermark, 1478–1515', *Beiträge zur Kunde Steiermärkische Geschichtsquellen*, 14, 1877, p. 121.

12 *Ibid.*, p. 122.

13 *Ibid.*, pp. 123–5.

14 Mayer, 'Ersten Bauernunruhen', *op. cit.*, pp. 130–2.

For further documentation on how the revolt was suppressed see F. Mayer: 'Materialien und kritische Bemerkungen zur Geschichte der ersten Bauernunruhen', *Beiträge zur Kunde Steiermärkische Geschichtsquellen,* 13, 1876, pp. 1–32. For fiscal and constitutional background, F. von Mensi: *Geschichte der direkten Steuern in Steiermark,* Graz, 1910, vol. 1, pp. 481ff.; vol. 2, pp. 10ff. General background, also for times of greater stability, is in H. Stradal: 'Stände und Steuern in Österreich', *XIIth International Congress of Historical Sciences,* Vienna, 1965, Louvain, 1966, especially pp. 148–9. Contrast neighbouring Tirol in T.R. von Sartori-Montecroce: *Geschichte des Landschaftlichen Steuerwesens in Tirol,* vol. 2, Innsbruck, 1902.

15 Mayer, 'Materialien', pp. 12, 22, 24, Maximilian was prepared only to come as far as Vienna. He had other problems on his mind, above all the French in North Italy, and the great dynastic alliance between the Habsburgs and the Hungarian monarchy. He was only prepared to work through military commissars and leaders of the territorial Estates.

16 Matthias Lang was treated with venom and prejudice by the Augsburg chroniclers, Clemens Sender and Wilhelm Rem, *Die Chroniken der deutschen Städte,* Leipzig, 1894–6, vol. 23 pp. 8–9, 83, 232–3; vol. 25, p. 114: especially Rem's entry for 1513, 'Er [Lang] was hie thumbprobst und bischoff zu Gurg und hett sunst auch vil pfrienden und ward hernach kardinal, er verzärt alle jar 50 bis 60 M. fl. und het lecht 10 M. fl. auffzuheben; er bracht gelt zuwegen, wie er macht.' (I am grateful to Philip Broadhead for these references.)

9 Mining and the creation of wealth

1 See ch.3,n.14. For example, Maximilian was also asked to appoint 'informed miners' to settle a dispute between miners, peasants and foresters at Schwaz in the centre of his Inn Valley mining industry, HHSA: *Maximiliana,* Kart. 46 (XV), fol. 177 (undated). For general background, see L. Scheuermann: *Die Fugger als Montanindustrielle in Tirol und Kärnten,* Innsbruck, 1959. M. von Wolfstrigl-Wolfskron: *Die Tiroler Erzbergbaue,* Innsbruck, 1903; S. Worms: *Schwazer Bergbau,* Vienna, 1904.

2 HHSA: HS-R 275, Soldregister Hallein, 1507. See K.-H. Ludwig: 'Der Salzburger Edelmetallbergbau des 16 Jahrhunderts als Spiegel der Moderne', in E. Zwink (ed.): *Salzburg Dokumentationen,* 19, Salzburg, 1977, pp. 111–34.

3 Soldregister Hallein, fols. 2–27 Cf. J. Vozar: 'Die sozialen Folgen des Bergbaues', in I. Bog (ed.): *Der Aussenhandel Ostmitteleuropas, 1450–1650,* Cologne, 1971, pp. 569–83, especially 574–7.

4 See ch.8, n.7.

5 Landesarchiv Innsbruck, Kopialbuch 14, ältere Reihe, 1491, fols 9–13, Innsbruck, 27 February.

6 *Ibid.,* fols 2, 29.

7 *Ibid.,* fol. 11.

8 From Landesarchiv Innsbruck, Pestarchiv Suppl. Nr. 897, cited in Max von Wolfstrigl-Wolfskron: *Die Tiroler Erzbergbaue, 1301–1665,* Innsbruck, 1903, p. 35. Wolfskron lists 593 mines worked in the late-medieval and early modern period.

9 *Ibid.,* pp. 52–6. One of the Perl heiresses, Dorothea, married Maximilian's protonotar and later chancellor, Cyprian von Serntein. Her letters to her husband from the summer of 1512 have been published. E. Rensing: 'Briefe einer deutschen Edelfrau des 16. Jahrhunderts', *Archiv für Kulturgeschichte,* 25, 1935, pp. 321–6.

10 S. Worms: *Schwazer Bergbau,* Vienna, 1904, document 17, pp. 162–4.

11 *Ibid.*, and Wolfskron, *op.cit.*, p. 343.
12 Worms, *op.cit.*, pp. 95–6, 167–71. Sigismund's earlier attempt on 26 March 1485, to find in favour of the bosses was thereby reversed. See pp. 164–7.
13 *Ibid.*, p. 168.
14 *Ibid.*, p. 170, 'khain *arbaiter* soll auch von khains khlagens wegen abgelegt werden, der anderst seiner schicht treulich ausswarth, man bedarf sein dann stunt nit. Wer huetleut aber derselben ainen ablcgten, die sollen gestrafft werdn.'
15 Landesarchiv Innsbruck, Kopialbuch 16, ältere Reihe, 1493, fols 122–3.
16 The three crucial documents are in *ibid.*, fols 106–8 (undated), fols 112–13 (undated), fols 122–3 (13 July), translated below.
17 Wolfskron, *op.cit.*, pp. 282–4, listing the smaller investors who included neighbouring burghers, mining-managers, parish priests, Maximilian's own courtiers and servants, local knights and nobles, customs and law officers.
18 Landesarchiv Innsbruck, Kopialbuch, ältere Reihe, 1493, fol. 112.
19 As early as August 1492 Maximilian's representatives in Inner Austria had sought to raise the equivalent of 24,000 fl. in extraordinary land tax in order to hire troops against marauding Turks. It is unclear how much was actually paid. Mensi, *op.cit.*, 3/iii, p. 63.
20 Landesarchiv Innsbruck, Kopialbuch, ältere Reihe, 1493, fols 123–4, order of Maximilian, setting up the array of battle on 15 July. The sordid business of using troops, who had been inspired by anti-Turk crusading zeal to put down their own fellow Christian Austrians, marks a sad ending to the grand propaganda of the just monarch defending the true faith as preached by the humanist chronicler, Schedel, in that very year of 1493. See L. Grote and D. Wuttke: 'Kaiser Maximilian in der Schedelschen Weltchronik', *Mitteilungen des Vereins für Geschichte der Stadt Nürnberg*, 62, 1975, illustrations 1, 2; pp. 73–4, 76–83. Contrast J. Kunisch: 'Das Nürnberger Reichsregiment und die Türkengefahr', *Historisches Jahrbuch*, 1973, p. 67.
21 *Ibid.*, fol. 122, 'sonnder ausserhalben der obrikait besamlung vnd pundtnuss, die doch bey leib vnd gut zu straffen, verboten sein.'
22 *Ibid.*, fol. 108, 'Itm, welhe der noch vil sind nicht in der puntnuss wern, vnd den ausganngn gescheftn lebn woltn, die behielt man.'
23 *Viz.*, *ibid*, fol, 108, 'auch den hauptleuten des Lannds vnd zu Trienndt beuolhn *in gehaim* auf 800 knecht zubestelln wann man Sy wissn lass. das man die eylenntz hab souver der kn. Mt. vnd Ew. vnns. Ratsleg gefielen dem furderlichn nachzukomen'; fol. 112, 'mit 800 geruster vnd guter knecht, so Jr haubtman 700 derselben allenthalben auf die stett vnd gericht slagen, vnd derselben stettn vnd gerichten sagen solt das man derzu notdurft der kn. Mt. auch Jrer Land vnd Leut bedurff in derselben stett vnd gericht sold vnd der kn. Mt. Liferung . . . zupringn'; fol. 113, 'Ob nun die gesellschaft oder puntnuss zu gross wurd, ist not daz Jr Hr Haubtman etlich weiter verordnet oder bestellet.'
24 *Ibid.*, fol. 123, 'damit man grundt an Rechten hab vnd nicht zu schimpf kum, was auch das Recht gibt, dem furderlichen voltziehung beschehe'. Contrast Schedel's fawning praise of Maximilian in elegant Latin as the greatest justiciar and protector of men from 1493, in Grote and Wuttke, *op.cit.*, p. 76.
25 This line of inquiry is now being developed for Salzburg. See K.H. Ludwig: 'Der Salzburger Edelmetallbergbau', in *Salzburg Dokumentationen*, Bd. 19, Salzburg, 1977, pp. 111–34, especially 124 f.
26 Melchior of Brixen, head of Maximilian's Innsbruck Council, and a leading shareholder at the Gossensass silver-mine.
27 An important silver-smelter in Schwaz.
28 Not included in this Kopialbuch.
29 Retired from ruling Tirol in 1490, and died in 1496.

30 Fuchs was a military counsellor and von Vells a treasury counsellor, as well as master of the saline at Hall near Innsbruck. Both were members of Maximilian's Innsbruck government.

31 Not included in this Kopialbuch.

10 The court of Maximilian and Bianca Maria

1 E. Egg and W.Pfaundler: *Kaiser Maximilian I. und Tirol*, Innsbruck, 1969, pp. 146–7.

2 A. Gatt: 'Der Innsbrucker Hof zur Zeit Kaiser Maximilians I. 1493–1519' (typescript), Innsbruck University thesis, 1943, Landesarchiv Innsbruck, COD 5499, Appendix VII.

3 *Ibid.*, pp. 149ff.

4 Cf. Landesarchiv Innsbruck, Kopialbuch, 1495–6, Lit. RS, Nr. 18–19.

5 Dr Baldrioni Baptista, an Italian physician from Trent, whom Maximilian retained for personal consultation. O. Kostenzer: 'Medizin um 1500', in *Ausstellung Maximilian I., Beiträge*, p. 62. It was this man whom Maximilian called for during his last illness in January 1519 (see chapter 2).

6 Translated from Victor von Kraus: *Maximilians Beziehungen zu Sigismund von Tirol*, Vienna, 1879, pp. 55–7.

7 Gatt, *op.cit.*, p. 144. Egg and Pfaundler, *op.cit.*, p. 156.

8 P. Krendl: 'Spanische Gesandteberichten über Maximilian I., den Hof und das Reich', *Mitteilungen des Instituts für Österreichische Geschichtsforschung*, 87, 1979, pp. 101–20, shows that the visiting Spaniards were also very unimpressed with the rapaciousness of Maximilian's courtiers.

9 Gatt's thesis is the best study here, but as Professor Stolz pointed out in his examination report, the Viennese archives also need to be taken into account. In 1943 that was clearly not possible. N. Castillo-Benito: 'Tradition und Wandel im fürstlichen Hofstaat Ferdinands von Österreich 1503–64', in J. Engel (ed.): *Mittel und Wege Früher Verfassungspolitik*, Stuttgart, 1979, pp. 440–2, shows how Maximilian's last *Hofstaatsverzeichnis* from Wels, January 1519, was adapted to provide closer liaison between the inner groups of advisers to Charles and Ferdinand in the 1520s.

10 HHSA: *Maximiliana*, Kart. 45 (alt 39–X–2), fols 41–3.

11 Cf. HHSA: *Maximiliana*, Kart. 45 (alt 39–X–2), fols 14–15. Summary account including military expenses just short of half a million ducats, including the entry 'pro aliis expenses uxoriis – 10^m [10,000 ducats]'. Maximilian had eleven surviving natural children and their upkeep along with that of their mothers had also to be borne in mind, see HHSA: HS-W. 1095 (Böhm Nr. 1330).

12 Gatt, *op.cit.*, *passim*, esp. p. 192. Victor von Kraus: 'Itinararium', *Archiv für österreichische Geschichte*, 87, 1899.

13 Translated from HHSA: *Maximiliana*, Kart. 43 (V/5), fol.12 (no date).Cf.Kart. 46 (XV), fols 37, 64–5. This lady is not among the twenty-seven Germans listed as present in Bianca's *Frauenzimmer* at a later (but unspecified) date. Gatt, *op.cit.*, pp. 42–3.

14 HHSA: *Maximiliana*, Kart. 43 (V/5), fols 50, 54.

15 Gatt, *op.cit.*, pp. 42–3.

16 The correspondence is reprinted in G. Rensing: 'Briefe einer deutschen Edelfrau des 16. Jahrhunderts an ihren Gatten', *Archiv für Kulturgeschichte*, 25, 1935, pp. 321–6.

17 HHSA: *Maximiliana*, Karts 45 and 46, analysed as follows. Cf. G. Heiss: 'Politik und Ratgeber der Königin Maria von Ungarn', *Mitteilungen des Instituts für österreichische Geschichtsforschung*, 82, 1972, p. 120.
18 HHSA: *Maximiliana*, Kart. 45 (alt 39, X), fols 14–15. In a note appended to Dr Gatt's thesis, Professor Stolz explains the word *stat* as *Kostenanschlag* (estimate of costs).
19 Translated from HHSA: *Maximiliana*, Kart. 45, fols 14–15.
20 Compare Maximilian's own rather wide concept of *Ehre* in dynastic-diplomatic spheres of interest. P. Sutter-Fichtner: 'The politics of honor: Renaissance chivalry and Habsburg dynasticism', *Bibliothèque d'Humanisme et Renaissance*, 29, 1967, pp. 567–80.
21 HHSA: *Maximiliana*, Kart. 45 (alt 39, X), fols 17–24.
22 HHSA: *Maximiliana*, Kart. 46 (XIII/2), fols 138–44.
23 *Ibid.*, fols 146–58, 'die personen, so taglich zu Ynnsprug Vnderhalten werden', and as follows in the text here.
24 'Jst kranck vnd wierdeth hin aus in der stat gespeyst', HHSA: *Maximiliana*, Kart. 46, fol. 142.
25 HHSA: *Maximiliana*, Kart. 45 (XIII/I), 'Kunigin Maria Stat', for processions: 69 horses for 23 women and 91 men, for everyday use: 35 horses for 37 women and 60 men – representing an 8 per cent reduction in staff but a 50 per cent cut in the total number of horses at the court's regular disposal.
26 HHSA: *Maimiliana*, Kart. 46 (XII/2), fols 165–8, 221–4.
27 HHSA: *Maximiliana*, Kart. 45 (XIII/1), fols 31–40 verso. Cf. Landesarchiv Innsbruck. Raitbücher, 1490–1519: Gatt, *op.cit.*, pp. 108–11, 127–33.
28 HHSA: *Maximiliana*, Kart. 46 (XIII/2) fols 245–6, 248 verso, 251.
29 HHSA: *Maximiliana*, Kart. 46 (XIII/2); Kart. 45 (XIII/1), fols 57 verso, 59.
30 Translated from *ibid.*, fols 245–6.
31 HHSA: *Maximiliana*, Kart. 45 (alt 39–X), fols 34–5. Cf. HKA: GB 5, 10.

11 Menu-Peuple

1 Landesarchiv Innsbruck, Kopialbuch, ältere Reihe, 15, 1492, fols 32v–33:

Margreth Wuestin. Bekennen vnd thun kund ofennlich mit dem brieue daz wir der erbern Margrethen weylend Jorgen Wuesten verlassen wittib vmb Jr lanng vnd geflissen diennste so sy gethan hat weylend der hochgeborn Elienorn geborn von Schotten Ertzhertzogin zu österreich Loblicher gedechtnuss in Jrer lieb Zymmer die gnad hiemit gethan haben. Also daz wir das nechst Schäffl mit saltz so in vnnserm Phannhaus zu Hall ledig wirdet Jr vor mennigclichn wochenlichn veruolgen lassen, oder aber souil gelt wie man von anndern gibt davon Raichn wellen ongeuerde. Vnd Emphelhen darauf vnnserm getreuen lieben Lienharden Vellser vnnsm Rate gegenwurtigen vnd ainem yeden vnnserm künftign Saltzmair zu Hall so das also zufällen kümbt, daz du bemelt Margrethen ain Schäffl saltz oder souil gelt dafur all wochen gebest, vnd das in dhain weg lassest. Das ist vnns. ernnstliche meynung wie vrkund ditz briefs. Geben zu Jnnsprugg an Mittich nach Sunntag Jnuocauit Anno uts[upra].

2 M. Köfler: 'Eleonore von Schottland. Versuch einer Biographie', Innsbruck University thesis, typescript, 1968.
3 *Ibid.*, p. 208.

4 *Ibid.*, p. 207, as cited in Jacob Mennel's Maximilian chronicle, 1518, 'Graf Sigmund . . . und Leonora, kunig Jacobs von Schotten dochter, kain kind . . . aber der uneelichen weyber, wan er gar ain grosser frawn man gewesen ist, find ich kain zal.'

5 Landesarchiv Innsbruck, Kopialbuch, ältere Reihe, 15. 1492, fol. 67, 'Seyen wir kurtzlich deshalben durch bemelten vnnsern gnedigen herren von österreich ersucht, also haben wir seinen Räten geantwurt, Sy kennen zum tail selber die kinder, nu seyen der vil, also mugen Sy die all vnd yede auffschreiben lassen'. A year later Maximilian was postponing payment, saying that he was too busy with the French war to deal with the matter. Victor von Kraus: *Maximilians I. Beziehungen zu Sigmund von Tirol, 1490–6*, Vienna, 1879, document 48, p. 51.

6 Köfler, *op.cit.*, pp. 149–66, especially p. 153; F. Engel: *Tabellen alter Münzen, Masse und Gewichte*, Rinteln, 1965, p. 8.

7 W. Rottleuthner: *Die alten Localmasse und Gewichte . . . in Tirol*, Innsbruck, 1883, p. 83; A.F. Pribram *et al.*: *Materialien zur Geschichte der Preise und Löhne in Österreich*, Vienna, 1938, pp. 102, 150.

8 Landesarchiv Innsbruck, Kopialbuch, ältere Reihe, 14, 1491, fol. 11.

9 Victor von Kraus: *Kaiser Maximilian I. Sein Leben und Wirken*, Vienna, 1877, pp. 137–8, including an itemised 'Küchenzettl', Bozen, 6 January, 1510.

10 *Ibid.*

11 Landesarchiv Innsbruck, Kopialbuch, ältere Reihe, 15, 1492, fols 18–19.

12 See C. Gilbert: 'When did a man in the Renaissance grow old?', *Studies in the Renaissance*, 14, pp. 7–32.

13 Landesarchiv Innsbruck, Kopialbuch, ältere Reihe, 16, 1493, fols 39–40, worth 10 gulden.

14 *Ibid.*, fol. 31.

15 *Ibid.*, fols 88–93, 'Gerichts vnd Landsordnung', Innsbruck, 3 March 1493, with prices as follows.

16 F. Verdenhalven: *Alte Masse, Münzen und Gewichte*, Neustadt/Aisch, 1968, p.40.

17 Gatt, *op.cit.*, pp. 108–11, 127–33, as follows in the text.

18 B. Seufert: *Drei Register, 1478–1519*, Innsbruck, 1934, p. 337. There are six versions of Maximilian's last will and testament. The one used here is in HHSA, Familien Urkunden Nr. 1117 (from the original in Landesarchiv Graz). It is printed in F.B. von Bucholtz: *Geschichte der Regierung Ferdinand des Ersten*, 1, Vienna, 1831, pp. 476–81. For comparative material, see generally E. Sudeck: *Bettlerdarstellungen vom Ende des XV. Jahrhunderts bis zum Rembrandt*, Strasbourg, 1930, pp. 5–11. A. Semler: *Geschichte des Heilig-Geist-Spitals in Überlingen*, 1957. W. Berger: *Das St.-Georgs-Hospital zu Hamburg*, Hamburg, 1972.

19 HKA: GB 7, 8, 10, *passim*.

20 Bucholtz, *op.cit.*, p. 479.

21 *Ibid.*, p. 480, 'Wir wollen vnd ordnen auch das in jedem Spital, an ainem gelegen Ort ein Pilt von vnser Persohn vnd vnserem Angericht Conterfehet gegossen werde . . . '

22 *Ibid.*, p. 481. Cf. p. 495. As Maximilian's closest associate and propagandist, Marx Treitzsauerwein, advanced to German Secretary under the new chancellor's regency government of the future Ferdinand I in Vienna, 1520.

23 Wilhelm Dilthey (1833–1911), 'Autobiography and Biography' (translated by H.P. Rickman): *Pattern and Meaning In History*, New York, 1962, pp. 92–3.

12 Practical Politics

1 Cf. François Rabelais: *The Histories of Gargantua and Pantagruel*, Harmondsworth, 1955. Also Mikhail Bakhtin: *Rabelais and his World*, Cambridge, Mass., 1968. Of course, Rabelais refers to the later wars of Francis I and Charles V.
2 Cf. O. von Zingerle: *Mittelalterliche Inventare aus Tirol und Vorarlberg*, Innsbruck, 1909.
3 Victor von Kraus: *Itinerarium Maximilian I*, Vienna, 1899, pp. 20–5. The work also appeared in the *Archiv für österreichische Geschichte*, 87. H. Moser: *Die Kanzlei Kaiser Maximilian I. Graphematik eines Schreibusus*, 2 vols, Innsbruck, 1977, in establishing the linguistic peculiarities of Maximilian's chancellery, reproduces a significant set of documents and references to everyday bureaucratic procedure.
4 Cf. K. Dziatzko and K. Haebler (eds): *Einblattdrucke des XV. Jahrhunderts*, Halle, 1914, pp. 237–63, 449–50. P. Dietrichs: *'Kaiser Maximilian I. als politischer Publizist'*, Jena University thesis, 1933.
5 Kraus, *Itinerarium*, p. 22. 'dann wir tannczen hie stetigs an ain pheiffer vnd auff ainer stelczen'.
6 *Ibid.*, pp. 26–7
7 *Ibid.*, p. 28
8 *Ibid.*, translated from p. 29.
9 *Ibid.*, pp. 30–3. See also Egg and Pfaundler, *op.cit.*, *passim*.
10 Victor von Kraus: *Kaiser Maximilian I. Sein Leben und Wirken*, Vienna, 1877, p. 137. Cf. K. Treusch von Buttlar: 'Das tägliche Leben an den deutschen Fürstenhöfen des 16. Jahrhunderts', *Zeitschrift für Kulturgeschichte*, 1897, pp. 33–41.
11 Kraus, *Itinerarium*, pp. 7n, 53–6.
12 Maximilian's complete itinerary has not been published. There are gaps for the childhood years, as well as 1506–7 and 1518. Some piecemeal itineraries are less reliable than others, due to Maximilian's habit of leaving his officials behind to finish business whilst he moved on. This applied especially to business generated at his Reichstags. Discrepancies have still not been fully eliminated, and some mistakes remain. Kraus, *Itinerarium*, is still the best, albeit incomplete account, and all others should be checked against it. For 1506–7 see H. Wiesflecker: *Kaiser Maximilian I, vol. 3, 1500–8*, Munich, 1977, esp. pp. 338ff. For the years of childhood there is H. Fichtenau: *Der Junge Maximilian 1459–82*, Munich, 1959, pp. 3–29. See also *Haus-, Hof- und Staatsarchiv*, Vienna, *Maximiliana*, Zettelkartei 1477–1505; Rep II 19/i, 1500–3; *Maximiliana*, Kart. 46, 1492–5, 1498; HS-W 321 (Böhm Nr. 639). For castle administration generally, and, under Maximilian, in some detail, see C. von Braitenburg: 'Wie das Hauptschloss Tirol im 16 und 17 Jahrhundert verwaltet und bewirtschaftet wurde', *Schlern*, 53, 1979, pp. 556–65.
13 Brought out with the notion of 'aetas maximilianeae' by F.H. Schubert: *Die deutschen Reichstage in der Staatslehre der Frühen Neuzeit*, Göttingen, 1966, and usefully developed in its late-medieval context by E. Schubert: *König und Reich*, Göttingen, 1979.
14 Wiesflecker, *op.cit.*, 1, pp. 194–8.
15 G. Benecke: *Society and Politics in Germany, 1500–1750*, London, 1974, Part IV; Appendices giving the *Reichsmatrikel*.
16 Selected from W. Andreas: 'Deutsche Reichstagsakten, Mittlere Reihe', *Festschrift. Die Historische Kommission bei der Bayerischen Akademie der Wissenschaften, 1858–1958*, Göttingen, 1958, pp.118–31; Ulmann, *op.cit.*, *passim*; Buchner, *op.cit.*, *passim*.
17 Opened by Maximilian late in April. He then left to organise Tirolean troops against Venice. The Reichstag granted nothing and soon dispersed. F.H. Schubert, *op.cit.*, pp. 190–1.
18 Maximilian failed to assemble the most important territorial delegations in his

attempt to obtain men and money for Swiss, French and Italian campaigns. Ulmann, *op.cit.*, 2, pp. 568–70. For the eventual papal-Venetian fiscal rapprochement that defeated Maximilian's attempts to force Italy during the War of the League of Cambrai, see the elegant study by F. Gilbert: *The Pope, his Banker and Venice*, Cambridge, Mass., 1980.

19 E. Ziehen: *Frankfurt, Reichsreform und Reichsgedanke 1486–1504*, Berlin, 1940.

20 By far the best monograph on the years 1488–90, which now documents for the first time the real turning point in Maximilian's career, in his reshaping of the Reich's home and foreign policy, marking above all the shift from rivalry with the French in the Netherlands and providing a lull before the development of Valois-Habsburg conflict in the Alps and North Italy, is that of Ernst Bock, which is scattered and almost lost as a series of introductions to *Deutsche Reichstagsakten unter Maximilian I.* vol. 3, two parts paginated together, 1488–90, Göttingen, 1972–3. Here it is well worth bringing this work together to indicate the unified whole that it really is:

I A The foreign political position of the Reich in the autumn of 1488 and the Reichstag called to Speyer on 6 January 1489 which did not materialise (August 1488–May 1489), pp. 45–96.

  B The development of the Austrian question in the Alps and Southwestern part of the Reich and the reconciliation of Emperor Frederick III with Duke George of Bavaria (August 1488–March 1489), pp. 281–307.

  C The Swabian League and its conflicts with the Wittelsbachs (July 1488–March 1489), pp. 371–401.

  D The attempts of Emperor Frederick III and King Maximilian to reach agreement between Duke George of Bavaria and the Swabian League up to the meeting at Dinkelsbühl (February–June 1489), pp. 633–55.

  E From the removal of the Reichstag from Speyer to Frankfurt until its opening. The beginnings of the Cologne customs' conflict and relations between the Reich and the Swiss Confederation after the death of Hans Waldman, mayor of Zürich (February–June 1489), pp. 841–66.

II F The Frankfurt Reichstag (late June–26, July 1489), pp. 987–1017.

III G Records dealing with the implementation of decisions taken at the Frankfurt Reichstag. Collection of the *ad hoc* Frankfurt money grant and the Reich war in the Netherlands (August 1489–May 1490), pp. 1231–55.

  H Synopsis of accounts of the war, pp. 1347–55.

Recent publication of the 1495 Reichstag records appeared too late for me to take into account.

21 *Ibid.*, documents 289, 300, 316a, 330, 332a, 362, 363–4, 365b, 368, 370, p. 1408 n. 291. Maximilian's Austrian territorial *Landtage* are also vital for his fiscal affairs. *Landtag* grants increasingly kept him from final bankruptcy. The Innsbruck *Ausschusslandtag* of 1518 brought in 400,000 fl.-one –third for court costs, and the rest to redeem alienated domain revenues. See H. Stradal: 'Stände und Steuern in Österreich', *XII International Congress of Historical Sciences, Vienna, 1965. Studies presented to the International Commission for the History of Representative and Parliamentary Institutions*, Louvain, 1966, pp. 133–62

22 This and the following account is taken from Bock's introductions and selected *Reichstagsakten*, supplemented by J. Janssen (ed.): *Frankfurts Reichscorrespondenz*, vol. ·2, pt. 2, 1486–1519, Freiburg/Breisgau, 1872, esp. pp. 517ff.; Ulmann, *op.cit.*, I, pp. 68–70, 30ff.; and the articles of F.H. Schubert, H. Golwitzer and E. Bock in *Aus Reichstagen des 15. und 16. Jahrhunderts. Festgabe der Historischen Kommission bei der Bayerischen Akademie der Wissenschaften*, Göttingen, 1958, pp.212–340.

23 Janssen, *op.cit.*, 2ii, p. 519.

24 Cf. Bock, *Reichstagsakten*, documents 273a–i.

25 *Ibid.*, pp. 1236–8.
26 I thus disagree with Bock's interpretations and tabulation, *ibid.*, pp. 1233–4.
27 *Ibid.*, documents 264a, *Presenzliste*, 20–26 June, 1489; 300a, *Reichstagsanschlag*, 23 July 1489.
28 Translated from Landesarchiv Innsbruck, Kopialbuch 1495–6, Lit. RS, Nr. 18–19 (Auslauf), 1496, fols 103–4.
29 Landesarchiv Innsbruck, Kopialbuch 16, ältere Reihe, 1493, fols 88–93.
30 1 Star 29½ litres (dry volume).
31 1 Pfund (Tirolean) 32 Lot 564 grammes; 1 Lot ½ oz. (Tirolean).
32 One measure was approximately 2½ litres (dry volume).
33 According to his *Kopialbücher*, Maximilian issued on average about fifteen safe conducts per year.
34 *Ibid.*, fol. 94.
35 1 *Fuder circa* 2000 litres (dry volume). Verdenhalven, *op.cit.*, pp. 23–4.
36 Kopialbuch, 16, 1493, fols 95–8.
37 *Ibid.*, fol. 101.
38 *Ibid.*, fols 102–5.
39 Landesarchiv Innsbruck, Kopialbuch 13, ältere Reihe, fols 86–7, approved (*gwellt*) business.
40 Kopialbuch 13a, fols 124 verso–125.
41 Kopialbuch 13, fols 87 verso–88 verso. Otto Stolz: *Politisch-Historische Landesbeschreibung von Süd-Tirol*, Innsbruck, 1937, pp. 521–8.

13 Necessity and Mentality

1 Brief notes culled from information in various chronicles, above all from Lower Saxony, Franconia and Thuringia, Upper Rhine and parts of Austria by Alwin Schulz: *Deutsches Leben im XIV und XV. Jahrhundert*, Vienna 1892, pp. 462–3. For Lake Constance, Alsace, parts of Württemberg and Switzerland there is B. Amberg: 'Beiträge zur Chronik der Witterung, 2, 1300–1500', *1891/2 Jahresbericht über die Hohere Lehranstalt zu Luzern*, Beiheft, Lucerne, 1892, pp. 1–55, esp. pp. 40–5.
2 Cf. Marcel Granet: *The Religion of the Chinese People*, New York, 1975, *passim*, esp. pp. 37–56.
3 Popular *Practica* or 'Prognostications' survive as incunables, some even printed on single sheets. Fairground parodies were also printed, which mirrored the more substantial scholastic versions available to the rich and powerful at court and in council chamber. See Dziatzko and Haebler, *op.cit.*, pp. 322–4. It was material and superstition such as this that northern humanists like Erasmus and Rabelais were to parody in the next generation.
4 HHSA: HS-W 321, fol. 269.
5 *Ibid.*, fols 269, 272.
6 Translated from *ibid.*, fols 254–66.

14 Domus Austriae: What was the House of Austria?

1 Cf. *Putzgers Historischer Atlas*, Bielefeld, 1907, maps 18–19b.
2 A. Lhotsky: 'Was heisst 'Haus Österreich'?', *Anzeiger der phil.-hist. Klasse der*

österreichischen Akademie der Wissenschaften, 1956, Nr. 11, pp. 155–74. See W. Höflechner: 'Zur Heiratspolitik der Habsburger bis zum Jahre 1526', in *Festschrift für H. Wiesflecker*, Graz, 1973, pp. 115–21.

3 Cf. Otto Brunner: *Land und Herrschaft*, fifth edition, Vienna, 1965.
4 Lhotsky, 'Haus Österreich', p. 159.
5 *Ibid.*, pp. 160, 171.
6 *Ibid.*, p. 155.
7 Cf Llotsky: 'AEIOV', *passim*, also Lhotsky, 'Haus Österreich', p. 165.
8 *Ibid.*, pp. 168–9. The language is magnificently, oratorically propagandistic and worth repeating with all its original frills.

Nostra archiducatus Austriae cum suis provinciis, ducatebus, principatebus, marchionatibus, comitatibus, dominiis, terris atque districtibus ubertate maxima omnium frugum, quibus humanum genus sustentari solet, auro, argento ac universorum metallorum genere, pulcherrimis sitibus, firmis ac fortissimis munitionibus, civitatum, oppidorum, arcium, castellorum et villarum opulentia et, quod optimum, numerosissima et gentium et populorum multitudine est referta, ut non immerito cuivis alteri regno – absit verbo invidia – adaequi parari possit.

9 Cf. R.J.W. Evans: 'The Austrian Habsburgs. The dynasty as a political institution', in A.G. Dickens (ed.): *The Courts of Europe*, London, 1977, pp. 121–46.
10 Lhotsky: 'Haus Österreich', p. 169. F.H. Schubert: *Die deutschen Reichstage*, Göttingen, 1966, pp. 190–1.
11 E. Bock: 'Doppelregierung', p. 297.

Index

Aachen, 138
absolutism, 23
agriculture, 54, 57, 67f
agricultural labour, 61
Albrecht I, Duke of Austria, 175
Albrecht, Duke of Bavaria, 9, 36,
 140f, 179
Alsace, 35, 41, 52, 129, 141, 160, 162,
 177
Ampezzo, 39
Amsterdam, 129
Anne de Beaujeu, 31
Anne of Brittany, 27
Antwerp, 33
archives, Austrian, 4f, 49;
 diplomatic, 124ff; *Judenbücher*, 71;
 Kopialbücher, 89ff, 154; *Praktika*,
 157, 164; Reichstag, 4f, 140;
 urban economy, 60ff, *Urbare*, 68ff
Arme Conrad, 52ff
Aragon, 1, 177
Auersperg, Hans von, 74
Augsburg, 7, 10, 17, 41, 50, 55, 59,
 72, 96, 119, 122, 129, 158;
 Bishopric, 41
Augustus Caesar, 28, 31
Austria, 33, 35f, 39f, 41f, 123, 127,
 129, 141f, 160f, 175ff, 178f; clergy,
 51; domestics, 50, 110; economy,
 50f, 148ff; employer-monks, 66;
 excise, 153f; geographical
 mobility, 50; guilds, 50f;
 households, 48; living standards,
 49ff, 105ff, 112ff; markets, 50,
148ff, 169, 173; miners' revolt,
 85ff, 89ff, 111; mining wealth, 37,
 79ff; nobles, 51, 103f, 128, 153,
 172; peasant revolts, 45, 51f, 73ff,
 88, 93; pensions, 50, 117; the
 poor, 50, 108, 112ff, 119f;
 population, 46ff, 112ff, 148ff;
 rebellion of 1515, 54, 74ff, 90ff;
 social mobility, 50, 148; Styrian
 Estates, 72; territorial assemblies,
 54, 77, 115, 123, 153; territorial
 Estates, 42ff, 74, 77; textiles, 50;
 Turks, 51f; urban living, 58ff,
 112ff, 119f, 148ff; *Vorlande*, 39, 79,
 104, 115,

Baden, 52
bakers, 67f, 148ff
Balkans, 45
Bamberg: Bishopric, 44
Baptista, Doctor, 11, 97
Basle, 9, 163, 175
Bavaria, 17, 24, 35, 42, 44, 141, 176
Beck, Leonard, 18
beer prices, 65, 148ff
Berthold, Count of Henneberg,
 Archbishop of Mainz, 2f, 126,
 140ff, 144f
Bianca Maria Sforza, Empress, 9,
 49, 55, 94ff, 99ff, 103; court, 105ff,
 108f; finances, 100ff, 105, 110,
 117; *Frauenzimmer*, 95, 98f, 102,
 107; letters, 95ff; melancholia,
 97f; travels, 98

200

201